"Shinn sees and hears people as they are. He creates characters whose limited powers of articulation can nevertheless illuminate the full depths of their souls."

—CHARLES ISHERWOOD, NEW YORK TIMES

"One can only marvel at Shinn's ability."   —MATT WOLF, VARIETY

"Shinn just cannot write a fake or untelling word."

—DONALD LYONS, NEW YORK POST

"A voice emerges from an American place. It's got humor, sadness and a fresh and touching rhythm that tell of the loneliness and secrets of life . . . *Four* is a poetic, haunting play."

—DONALD LYONS, NEW YORK POST

"*Four* is a smart, broken-hearted play. Ambiguities abound in Mr. Shinn's world of blurred sexual and ethnic identities. A faltering dance of attraction and repulsion."

—BEN BRANTLEY, NEW YORK TIMES

"As in *Rent*, but with far less bombast and much more depth, Shinn's characters are East Village artists sharing an apartment and, at the annual emotional stocktake that is Christmas, they're on various rungs of the success ladder. Happily and unhappily, they over-articulate their dreams and desires, yet the secret of Shinn's success is the way he exploits the dramatic gap between what is said and unsaid. Shinn's *Other People* is really about fantasy and love. Writing like this is rare."

—DAVID BENEDICT, LONDON'S INDEPENDENT

"*Where Do We Live* is an exceptionally fine new play that probes with clarity and compassion the lives of a handful of New Yorkers just before, and just after, the events of September 11, 2001 . . . Shinn captures, as no playwright yet has, the strange, terrible continuity of those days in New York—how, for most people, little really changed, even as we were being told that everything had."

—CHARLES ISHERWOOD, VARIETY

"*Where Do We Live* is a deeply haunting play about a city struggling against darkness. It's not simply because its events occur either side of 9/11 that this play hits us where we live now. More disturbing is one's awareness as the play unfolds that all its talk of doing good can't preempt a fractiousness and dissonance that are part of New York's inherent beat."

—MATT WOLF, *VARIETY*

"A haunting, subtly constructed play . . . *The Coming World* tackles big themes—the nature of truth and love—with a deceptively light touch . . . Shinn creates a sense of loss and lost opportunities that is deeply affecting."

—CHARLES SPENCER, *LONDON'S DAILY TELEGRAPH*

"*The Coming World* is frightening, sensual and moving . . . Shinn has a delicate touch, combining a well-observed picture of the characters' lower-middle-class background with a poignant awareness of their stress."

—RHODA KOENIG, *LONDON'S INDEPENDENT*

Where Do We Live

and other plays

Where Do We Live

and other plays

Christopher Shinn

Theatre Communications Group
New York
2005

Where Do We Live and Other Plays is published by Theatre Communications Group, Inc., 520 Eighth Avenue, 24th Floor, New York, NY 10018-4156.

This publication is made possible in part with public funds from the New York State Council on the Arts, a State Agency.

TCG books are exclusively distributed to the book trade by Consortium Book Sales and Distribution, 1045 Westgate Dr., St. Paul, MN 55114.

LIBRARY OF CONGRESS CATALOGING-IN-PUBLICATION DATA
Shinn, Christopher.
Where do we live and other plays / Christopher Shinn.—1st ed.
p.cm.
ISBN 13: 978-1-55936-256-6
ISBN 10: 1-55936-256-1
I. Title.
PR6069.H488W44   2005
812'.6—dc22
2005032819

Book design and composition by Lisa Govan
Cover design by Mark Melnick
Cover photograph by Joshua Sanchez

First Edition, December 2005

To my sister

Contents

Preface

Collected in this volume are my first five plays. *Four* was written in the winter of 1996, in the midst of a troubled first love.
I wrote *Other People* in 1998, while reeling over the end of this
relationship. A year later, angry at a mentor, I began *What Didn't
Happen,* which I wouldn't finish till late 2002. In the fall of 2000
I started *The Coming World,* but put it aside when my father
became ill and I fell in love again. The relationship was brief;
I wrote *Where Do We Live* in its aftermath. My father died in early
2002, and in the year following I reworked *The Coming World* into
its present form.

These plays were written to exact revenge and bring the dead
back to life. They failed.

Acknowledgments

Many people directly impacted the texts collected in this volume. I'd like to thank in particular Doug Aibel, John Belluso, Emily Bergl, Mark Brickman, Michael Bush, John Buzzetti, Tom Cairns, Jeff Cohen, Dominic Cooke, Suzanne Cryer, Heath Cullens, Curt Dempster, John Dias, Steven Drukman, Jason Scott Eagan, Daryl Edwards, Robert Egan, Daniel Evans, Paige Evans, Tim Farrell, Jesse Tyler Ferguson, Carol Fineman, James Frain, Charles Fuller, Adam Garcia, David Greenspan, John Guare, Ron Gwiazda, Jessica Hagedorn, Nicholas Allen Harp, Robert Hogan, Annalee Jefferies, Tony Kushner, Carmelo Larose, Todd London, Mike Lubin, Josh Lucas, Austin Lysy, Luke Macfarlane, Joe Mantello, Matt McGrath, Janet McTeer, Lynne Meadow, Evangeline Morphos, Burl Moseley, Angela Nevard, Keith Nobbs, Chris Noth, Kate Packenham, Dale Peck, David Petrarca, Jacob Pitts, Frank Pugliese, Connor Ratliff, Kent Rees, Ian Rickson, Armando Riesco, Tim Roseman, Doraly Rosen, Tim Sanford, Pablo Schreiber, Sarah Schulman, Jon Schumacher, Andrew Scott, Mandy Siegfried, Paul Sirett, Crystal Skillman, Steven Skybell, Victor Slezak, Chris Smith, Sonya Sobieski, Stuart Spencer, Aaron Stanford, Liz Stauber, Sarah Stern, Wendy Streeter, Moritz von Stuelpnagel, Joe Stipek, Pier Carlo Talenti, Lisa Timmel, Peter Vilbig, Francine Volpe, John Wellmann, Isiah Whitlock, Jr., Graham Whybrow, Michelle Williams, Michael Wilson, Richard Wilson and Aaron Yoo.

I'd also like to thank, for their considerable support, George Lane, Robbie Baitz, David Turner, Ben Kessler, Walter A. Davis, Judi Farkas, Jerry Patch, Bonnie Miller, Dr. Andrew Ponichtera, Dr. Guy Minoli, Dr. Israel Klein, Debra Walsh, Anne Wilson, the Ovid Foundation, the John Simon Guggenheim Memorial Foundation, the Peter S. Reed Foundation, the Robert Chesley Foundation and the NEA/TCG Theatre Residency Program.

Finally, I must thank my mother, Maryanne Shinn, and my late father, David Shinn, without whose encouragement and financial help I could not have written these plays.

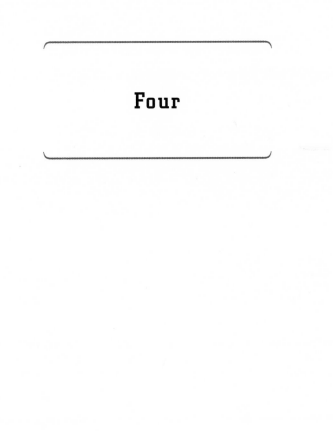

Four

Production History

Four was originally produced by the Royal Court Theatre (Ian Rickson, Artistic Director) in London on November 31, 1998. It was directed by Richard Wilson; the set design was by Keith Kahn, the lighting design was by Johanna Town, the sound design was by Paul Arditti and Rich Walsh, the costume design was by Hattie Barsby and the stage manager was Cath Binks. The cast was as follows:

JUNE	Connor Ratliff
JOE	Joseph Mydell
ABIGAYLE	Shauna Shim
DEXTER	Fraser Ayres

It was produced by The Worth Street Theater Company (Jeff Cohen, Artistic Director) at the Tribeca Playhouse in New York City on June 21, 2001. It was directed by Jeff Cohen; the set design was by Lauren Helpern, the lighting design was by Traci Klainer, the sound design was by Paul Adams, the costume design was by Veronica Worts and the production stage manager was Michal V. Mendelson. The cast was as follows:

JUNE	Keith Nobbs
JOE	Isiah Whitlock, Jr.
ABIGAYLE	Vinessa Antoine
DEXTER	Armando Riesco

It was subsequently produced by Manhattan Theatre Club in association with The Worth Street Theater Company in New York City on February 19, 2002. It was directed by Jeff Cohen; the set design was by Lauren Helpern, the lighting design was by Traci Klainer, the sound design was by Paul Adams, original music was by David Van Tieghem, the costume design was by Veronica Worts and the production stage manager was Jason Scott Eagan. The cast was as follows:

JUNE	Keith Nobbs
JOE	Isiah Whitlock, Jr.
ABIGAYLE	Pascale Armand
DEXTER	Armando Riesco

Characters

JUNE
JOE
ABIGAYLE
DEXTER
MOTHER (offstage)

Place

Hartford, Connecticut.

Time

The Fourth of July, 1996.

Note

Simple sets, quiet mood, lonely lights, no intermission.

Scene 1

Lights rise on June, sixteen, white, in jeans and a T-shirt, slightly overweight. He stands next to a pay phone. He lights a cigarette. It's about 5:30 P.M. at an abandoned section of a commercial strip in a suburban town outside Hartford. We hear the occasional car pass. The sky is moving into the bright blues and golds of early evening. The phone rings. June looks at it, waits a moment, then picks it up.

JUNE: Hello? Hey. Yeah. No. On time. Yeah. So. What's up . . . No, my parents. Yeah. Fourth of July party. People. Lots of people . . . Yeah. So. You wanna pick me up? I'm at where the Marshalls used to be. Where are you calling from? Oh . . . Jeans. T-shirt. No one is here, so . . . Okay, cool. Bye.

(He hangs up the phone, looks around. Blackout.)

Scene 2

Lights rise inside the Phillips house. Middle class. Living room. Abigayle, sixteen, black, wearing a pink nightgown, watches TV. She is on the telephone. A cordless.

5

ABIGAYLE: I don't like this show . . . I don't like this show. Bothers me. *(Takes a bite of cheese from a tray)* Because my father wanted it taped . . . At a conference in Boston . . . What time's your barbecue ending? How's the cooking? . . . Mom's already asleep. She's tired . . . She's always tired. I don't know what it is . . . Oh! I hate this show. No, some guy just got shot. I don't know why my father likes this show . . . I don't think that would be a good idea, Dexter. I just don't. I'm sorry . . . You know how I feel. About you. About what you do. You know how I feel. And I decided I can't. I can't be a part of that . . . So get rid of your weed then. Yeah, right . . . Stop. Now you gotta stop. I called you as a friend. Not to talk about all this . . . When I was seven, I was at the movies, and it was my turn to buy popcorn and my Dad had gone in to get us a seat so I was out there all alone. And it was my turn to get the popcorn and I didn't want to miss the previews because I loved the previews so I was kinda uptight about missing them, and just as I'm opening my mouth to order my popcorn this big hairy white man cuts in front of me and says, "Large popcorn and a large Coke." And I'm standing there, about up to his waist, he's wearing these dirty smelly jeans, I'm standing there with my three dollars in my hand, and I look at the cashier, who I know saw me because we made eye contact, but she didn't say, "Excuse me, it's not your turn" to the man. She just took the man's order. What do you think of that? . . . I brought it up to change the subject . . . She goes to bed because she's tired. I don't know. You ask her . . . I don't like this actor. This cheese is so good . . . Why do you ask that? . . . Yeah, you could say that. Not sad, really. But dissatisfied, yeah. You know. I deal. I have it together. I know what I want. It's just that I'm not always getting it . . . How are you gonna satisfy me? No I don't think so. Not like that . . . I dunno. I have these *thoughts* . . . Not about you. About the world. Everything . . . I wanna go somewhere, too. But not with you. Where's there to go, anyway? The park? . . . I'm gonna go. Because. Look, I'll talk to you later. Don't eat too much you get sick. Bye . . .

(She clicks off the phone. Blackout.)

Scene 3

Joe, forty, black, dressed in a sweater and slacks, a little overweight, enters the abandoned parking lot. June stands by the pay phone. He does not see Joe.

JOE: June?

(June turns to Joe.)

JUNE: Oh—hey.
JOE: Hi there.
JUNE: Hey.
JOE *(Looking around)*: My God, what a wasteland!
JUNE: Hmmm?
JOE: —My car's over here.
JUNE: Oh, okay.
JOE: You okay?
JUNE: Yeah, yeah—used to shop here.
JOE: Hmmm?
JUNE: It was a Marshalls—anyway.
JOE: Oh. Okay. Well—my car!
JUNE: Yeah. Let's go.

(They go to the car as lights fade on the parking lot. They strap themselves in. Silence as this happens. Joe begins to drive. A few seconds of awkward silence. Joe turns on the radio to a classic rock station. June unrolls the window a little.)

JOE: So. On the road.
JUNE: Yeah.
JOE: I love driving. Driving's got to be the most American thing there is. You having a good Fourth of July?
JUNE: Yeah. S'fine.
JOE: Fourth o' July. Yeeeup.
JUNE *(Shyly)*: Like apple pie.
JOE: Hunh?
JUNE: Driving. You said—it was the most American thing there is. Like apple pie.

7

JOE: Oh. Yeah. Gas. The smell of gas. Burning oil. Exhaust fumes puffing out the back. The wind. The world passing by at this speed. So *fast*. The idea of *going*. The act of *going*. Somewhere. To a place. Or no place—not knowing where you're going. Just *going*.

JUNE: I got my license last April.

JOE: You have a car?

JUNE: No, my parents do. But I don't really borrow it.

JOE: One car or two?

JUNE: One.

JOE: Mmmm. Maybe we'll see some fireworks.

JUNE: Where?

JOE: It's the Fourth of July. Fireworks everywhere.

JUNE: Like backyard kind?

JOE: You have those as a kid?

JUNE: Yeah, yeah, um, we had sparklers. And one red one. When I was five, I think. But it burned the lawn. It's illegal here.

JOE: Illegal. Hah.

JUNE: I think it is, isn't it?

JOE: Everybody does it. Cops don't do a thing. That's another American thing.

JUNE: What?

JOE: Breaking the law!

JUNE: Oh.

JOE: There's this show I love. You ever watch *Law Rules*?

JUNE: No. I don't really watch much TV.

JOE: Most of the time on that computer.

JUNE: Yeah, I guess.

JOE: *Law Rules*. Great show. It follows the criminals. Week to week. Instead of the cops, you know how most of them follow the cops? This one follows the criminals in a certain precinct. Brilliant idea.

JUNE: Yeah, that is a good idea.

JOE: We're breaking the law.

JUNE: We are?

JOE: Yeah. This state still has adultery laws.

JUNE: What do you mean?

JOE: If you're married. It's illegal to have an affair. Believe it or not.

JUNE *(Laughs)*: We're having an affair?

(Joe laughs.)

JOE: So do I look like my voice?

JUNE: Oh—yeah, I guess.

JOE: This how you imagined me?

JUNE: Yeah, I guess. I didn't really imagine anything.

JOE: You look a lot like I imagined you. You're a cutie.

JUNE: Whatever.

JOE: What, you are. So come on, fill me in. All I know's that you're seventeen—

JUNE: Yeah, sixteen—

JOE: Sixteen, gay, you like English, you wanna be an actor or a politician

JUNE: Maybe—

JOE: You uhhh, what else do I know . . . you lived here your whole life, you play tennis . . .

JUNE: Guess that's about all we got to.

JOE: All I can remember. What else?

JUNE: Well . . . I dunno, what do you want to know?

JOE: Favorite movies, I was thinking we'd go to a movie tonight, you know.

JUNE: Oh yeah?

JOE: I've always seen a movie on the Fourth of July. That's the most American thing you can do, go to the movies.

JUNE: Besides driving.

JOE: Driving *to* the movies! You're right, *that* is the quintessential American action, *driving* to the movies, *going, anticipating*—so uhh—what's your favorite?

JUNE: Umm . . . I don't really have any favorite movies.

JOE: How could you not have favorite movies?

JUNE: Just . . . I guess I haven't thought about it much. I'd have to think about it.

JOE: Okay, favorite book?

JUNE: God. That's hard.

JOE: Just any book. Any writer you like.

JUNE: Well—you're like an expert. I feel stupid.

JOE: Don't be *scared* of me. You're not intimidated by me, are you?

JUNE: No, not really.

JOE: You're very smart. I can tell, just from talking on the computer and the phone. You are well beyond your years.

JUNE: Well, I like Truman Capote.

JOE: Blecch.

JUNE: What?

JOE: Minor minor minor.

JUNE: What're your favorite books?

JOE: No no, tell me more of yours, I'm just joking, Truman Capote's fine, just fine, *Breakfast at Tiffany's* made a great movie.

JUNE: Well . . . Gore Vidal—

JOE: Do you read any *straight* writers?

JUNE: Ummm . . .

JOE: There's three books, June. In the history of this country three great books. They are *Moby-Dick, The Adventures of Huckleberry Finn,* and whatever Faulkner you like the most. I prefer *The Sound and the Fury.*

JUNE: Oh. I read a short story by Faulkner I think—

JOE: They're big, these guys. Yeah. Sprawling, ridiculous, hilarious, heartbreaking, pretentious, unrelenting *stories.* They tell *stories* and they put so much in there, cram so much in. They are proud books, all of them. You've *got* to be proud of yourself, you've got to *believe* in yourself. When you say you like Truman Capote, say: "I love Truman Capote!" Say it with force! With flair! Present yourself! Make people listen! Get out from behind that computer!

JUNE: Okay.

(Beat.)

JOE: You need some confidence. Or some cockiness. A little *America.* Hah.

(Pause.)

JUNE: I don't really like America.

JOE: What?

JUNE: America, you know. Has done a lot of bad things.

JOE: Who hasn't?

JUNE: It's just—and our politics. Today. Washington—

JOE: Can I stop you? You're not offended that I'm stopping you?

JUNE: What?

JOE: You may not like America, but deep down you love it. You have to, it's your country, you may not like it, I may not like it, but I LOVE it because it is AMERICA. Do you understand?

JUNE: No.

JOE: You don't understand.

JUNE: Don't understand why America always has to be the best, you know. Always talking about being the best in the world, best defense, best health care, best you know—like, why can't we just be happy not being the best in a couple places?

JOE: You don't wanna be the best?

JUNE: What do you mean?

JOE: In what you do. The best. Don't you wanna. Do the best you can?

JUNE: Well . . . by wanting to be the best—you know, America— is all—such a—such a—puritanical—

JOE: Okay, no more politics, you're just gonna make me angry.

JUNE: Sorry.

JOE: No! No it's fine. No no. Hmmm. Well *I* love America. Movies. Fast food. Cars. Freedom! Hah. I'll give you the most American Fourth of July you've ever had. America, real America.

JUNE: Heh.

JOE: The radio. The radio's got to be louder. And the windows. Have to be all the way down. And ya gotta go FAST— *(Rolls down his window and cranks up the radio. He speeds up)* See, it's all about EXCESS—being BIG, being LOUD! YOU WITH ME?

JUNE: I guess.

JOE: BE WITH ME! BE WITH ME! *(Joe honks the horn wildly)* Scream or something! Come on!

JUNE: Scream?

JOE: Yeah! Scream out the window! Come on!

JUNE: Ummm . . . I—can't.

JOE: Come on, you can't. Sure you can!

JUNE: I don't—really—that's not my style—

JOE: On the count of three—

JUNE: I just—

JOE: One, two, three!— *(Nothing from June)* I see. That's okay. We'll get you screaming later.

(Joe laughs. Blackout.)

Scene 4

The Phillips house. Clock reads 6 P.M. Abigayle gets up from the couch and turns off the VCR. She knocks on a door, opens it a crack, and speaks quietly:

ABIGAYLE: Mom? Mom? You all right? . . . Six o'clock. Dad didn't call yet. He's gonna call later . . . You want some cheese? . . . You want me to open the window? You cold? . . . Okay. Okay then . . .
    You need anything? . . . Okay.

(The phone rings.)

'Night, Mom.

(She shuts the door and goes to the couch. She picks up the phone and clicks it on.)

Hello, Phillips residence. Hi, Dexter. I thought I told you good-bye. You're never getting in my pants, why do you call? . . . That was a joke. You're so easily offended, dag. No, I was just checking in on my mom. Well she is. She is. She goes in and out of sleep. Yeah . . . Nothing. Sitting home. Doing work. No. I don't like the fireworks. No. 'Cuz you're under the bridge with all those people, all those drunk people, you know? And there's all this trash, all this litter everywhere. And it's noisy. Just all those people.
    How's your barbecue doing? Mmm-hmmm . . . I told you, he's in Boston. She's *asleep*, how many times I have to tell you? . . . No you are *not* coming over. You are *not* picking me up. I'm staying in. I'm gonna do work. I have things to do. And I have to be here when my dad calls. I told you, Boston. Conference. Literature. *Professor.* Dag, do you even listen to *anything* I say? . . . My voice does not sound like honey on graham crackers, shut up. You know, you have an obsession with food, that's all you ever talk about, your momma's cooking, your brother's barbecue, you're always comparing everything to food, calling me chocolate. —Just because I eat a piece of cheese and like it does not make *me* obsessed—

(We hear sounds of banging from the bedroom.)

Hold on.

(Abigayle puts down the phone and goes to the bedroom.)

Yeah, Mom? . . . Okay.

(Abigayle goes back to phone.)

Dexter, I have to go. I have to help my mother. I am NOT calling you back. I have work to do. Studying. Reading. Improving my brain. Yeah, my brain. You can't improve nothing. You going to watch the fireworks? Okay. Bye.

(Abigayle hangs up. More sounds of banging. Abigayle looks toward the bedroom. Blackout.)

Scene 5

A darkened movie theater. June and Joe sit. Joe has a bag of popcorn, a box of Twizzlers, and a Coke. June has nothing.

JUNE: So you've already seen this?
JOE: Thrice.
JUNE: I haven't seen it. I like him.
JOE: He is *hot*, isn't he?
JUNE: Uhh—yeah.
JOE: What?
JUNE: You talk loud.
JOE: No one's listening. No one *cares*—
JUNE: This isn't—I mean, this isn't the kind of movie . . . you know.
JOE: I know nothing.
JUNE: That . . . people like us—it's just—the people here are kinda—kinda—
JOE: Human.
JUNE: It's just—whatever, I guess you're right. I do like this actor though.
JOE: He's gay.

JUNE: He is?

JOE: Uh-huh.

JUNE: How do you know?

JOE: I was at a conference in L.A. a few months ago. Adapting classic literature into films. Which I am all *for*, by the way. Anyway, I met a few people who know these kinds of things.

JUNE: God. That's amazing.

JOE: He's a little boy. Such a little boy. The one all of us want, or want to be.

JUNE: He's thirty-three, I thought.

(Joe checks his watch.)

What time is it?

JOE: Almost there.

JUNE: Cool.

JOE: You sure you don't want anything?

JUNE: Yeah, I'm pretty full.

JOE: When'd you eat?

JUNE: Before I left.

JOE: What'd you have?

JUNE: Just—you know. Hot dog, whatever.

JOE: One hot dog?

JUNE: Yeah.

JOE: How are you full on one hot dog?

JUNE: I am, I'm okay.

JOE: You are lying to me.

(A beat.)

So tell me more.

JUNE: About what?

JOE: Your life, I want to know everything about you. You said you won some award or something.

JUNE: For an essay. It was nothing.

JOE: What was it about?

JUNE: The homeless.

JOE: For or against.

(June starts to answer.)

Hah! Tell me about your parents.

JUNE: My parents?

JOE: Yeah. I'm curious.

JUNE: Well, what do you wanna know?

JOE: Just tell me about them. How they met, what they do. Tell me about your name.

JUNE: My name?

JOE: Yeah. June. That's not exactly a man's name.

JUNE: I know. You should have seen me in elementary school.

JOE: Let me guess—June the uhh—June the Goon. June the . . . Fruit. Juney-Baby.

JUNE: Well . . .

JOE: I'm sorry, I was trying to be funny. So why'd they name you June? Were you conceived in June?

JUNE: Well I was supposed to be born in June.

JOE: Supposed?

JUNE: I was born in April. I was six weeks premature. I was supposed to be born in June, so they named me June.

JOE: Wow.

(Beat.)

So you just turned sixteen.

JUNE: Well, a couple months.

JOE: Did you have a party?

JUNE: Not really. Just my parents. Made me breakfast.

JOE: Well that's nice.

JUNE: Before church on Sunday. We had brunch.

JOE: What'd they get you?

JUNE: Umm . . . some shirts from Eddie Bauer. A few books.

JOE: What books?

JUNE: A book of monologues.

JOE: Like acting?

JUNE: Yeah. And a biography.

JOE: Who?

JUNE: Lowell Weicker?

JOE: *Maverick.*

JUNE: Yeah.

JOE: I hate him, think he's a pompous asshole. So you done a lot of acting?

JUNE: I've had a few roles. A few shows. Mostly chorus.

JOE: So why aren't you out to your parents?

(A silence.)

JUNE: I dunno.

JOE: You love them?

JUNE: Yeah. A lot. I love my parents. A lot.

JOE: We all do. So why don't you tell them?

JUNE: Because I can't.

JOE: Why not?

JUNE: I don't want to. I dunno.

JOE: You waiting till you have a boyfriend?

JUNE: I don't think I'll ever tell them.

JOE: Why?

JUNE: I dunno. 'Cuz I'm the only son. I know my mom wants grandkids. I just—I don't really feel right about it.

JOE: About being gay?

JUNE: I don't like that word.

JOE: What word?

JUNE: Gay.

JOE: Queer?

JUNE: Shhhh.

JOE: You know people here?

JUNE: I might. I dunno.

(A beat.)

It was my dad's idea to name me June. My mom wanted to name me Franklin.

JOE: Eeee. So what do they do?

JUNE: My dad works for the state. The Department of Transportation, he studies, like traffic patterns and stuff—like predicts what traffic patterns will be, helps re-time stoplights and stuff. And my mom's a dental assistant.

JOE: You have sparkling teeth then.

JUNE: Not really. I do love them. A lot. I just . . .

JOE: Does anyone know?

(A beat.)

JUNE: Well, you.

JOE: Me.

JUNE: And . . . yeah, I guess that's it.

JOE: Tell me when you got online.
JUNE: When?
JOE: Yeah.
JUNE: About three months ago.
JOE: Why?
JUNE: Just seemed—

(The lights dim. We hear the pre-movie no-smoking/no-talking spiel.)

JOE: Beautiful.
JUNE: What?
JOE: The lights go down like you're sinking into a great collective dream. Suddenly you're anonymous. You get that sexual charge. Charge of excitement, anticipation, danger. Hold this.

(Joe hands June his popcorn and whips out a cellular phone and dials. Lights rise on Abigayle, on the couch. She answers the phone.)

ABIGAYLE: Hello?
JOE: Hi, sweetie.
ABIGAYLE: Hi, Daddy.
JOE: Happy Fourth of July.
ABIGAYLE: Happy Fourth of July to you too.
JOE: Did you tape my show?
ABIGAYLE: Mmm-hmmm.
JOE: Thank you so much.
ABIGAYLE: Mom's asleep.
JOE: How's she doing?
ABIGAYLE: She's okay.
JOE: Okay then.
ABIGAYLE: How's Boston?
JOE: Quite a spot on the Fourth of July. A lot of pride here. A lot of *white pride.*
ABIGAYLE: Boston's such a white city.
JOE: That's why your daddy loves it. I stand out here! I confront these academics simply by the color of my skin.
ABIGAYLE: You making people mad?
JOE: I'm making people listen, so yeah, I guess I am making people mad. What are you doing tonight?

(June takes a bite of popcorn.)

ABIGAYLE: Just staying in.
JOE: You're not going out?
ABIGAYLE: Nah.
JOE: Well okay. I'll see you tomorrow then. Should I call later?
ABIGAYLE: No, don't call later, Mom's getting to sleep.
JOE: Okay, baby.
ABIGAYLE: Okay, Daddy.
JOE: I love you.
ABIGAYLE: I love you too.
JOE: Bye-bye.
ABIGAYLE: Bye.

(Joe hangs up. Abigayle hangs up.)

JOE: My daughter. Bound for greatness.
JUNE: Mmmm.
JOE: Popcorn.

(June hands Joe the popcorn. They watch the movie.
Abigayle stands up, looks into her mother's door. Comes back to the phone, picks it up and dials.)

ABIGAYLE: Hello, Dexter? What are you doing? . . . If you wanna pick me up for a little while, you can. I changed my mind.

(Beat.)

A woman can change her mind. But only for fifteen minutes.

(Beat.)

That does not give you plenty of time! You're so nasty! . . . Because I'm *bored*. No other reason. And I'm sick of these thoughts. In my head. I need to go away from them for a while. I don't expect you to understand what I'm talking about. Just come and pick me up.

(Blackout.)

Scene 6

In Dexter's car. Driving. Dexter is nineteen, half Puerto Rican, half white, wearing baggy jeans, a T-shirt, and a baseball cap. Abigayle sits next to him, looking out the window.

DEXTER: I don't know about all that, you know. All that food. It was getting to be too much. But I didn't know anything, I mean, my aunt, my aunt was there, and she was like all telling me how I'd grown and shit. So. You know.

ABIGAYLE: What in God's green earth are you talking about?

DEXTER: I don't know. So uhm—why'd you change your mind?

ABIGAYLE: Can't I just change my mind?

DEXTER: There's gotta be a reason, right? You change your mind, something happens, right?

ABIGAYLE: I just changed my mind. No reason.

DEXTER: Always a reason. I always went to church on Sunday with everybody and then I stopped going to church 'cuz I changed my mind.

ABIGAYLE: And why'd you do that?

(Beat. Dexter tries to think.)

So you can get off this subject now.

DEXTER: No, I know why, I'm just trying to figure out how to ar-tic-u-late it.

ABIGAYLE: Mmm-hmmm.

DEXTER: Damn. You gonna be all bitchy, I don't wanna be with you. I'll take you *home.*

ABIGAYLE: You'll take me however I am. And don't call me a bitch.

DEXTER: I didn't call you a bitch.

ABIGAYLE: Yes you did.

DEXTER: I said you were acting bitchy. I didn't call you a bitch. I never call a woman a bitch.

ABIGAYLE: You call your mother a bitch.

DEXTER: She's my mother!

ABIGAYLE: Mmmm-hmmmm.

(A beat.)

DEXTER: All right. Starting over. Commercial break. La-di-da. Where you wanna go?

ABIGAYLE: I dunno. Where is there to go?

DEXTER: The park.

ABIGAYLE: I don't like the park.

DEXTER: Then where? You don't wanna see the fireworks, you don't wanna go to the park. You don't wanna go nowhere.

ABIGAYLE: I don't like anywhere. I hate this town.

DEXTER: Why?

ABIGAYLE: There's nothing here but *town*. Even the city. It's not even a city. Nothing happens here.

DEXTER: Mark Twain lived here.

ABIGAYLE: Nine thousand years ago.

DEXTER: There's stuff. The Hartford Whalers.

ABIGAYLE: You like hockey?

DEXTER: No. So we'll just drive then. Drive around. That's fun.

ABIGAYLE: Let's drive to New York.

DEXTER: New York? That's two hours!

ABIGAYLE: I was just kidding. Dag.

DEXTER: Oh.

ABIGAYLE: It would be fun if you had a convertible. That would be fun.

(Beat.)

DEXTER: Hey uhhh—I was thinking of something.

ABIGAYLE: What?

DEXTER: Your story. About the movie.

ABIGAYLE: Yeah?

DEXTER: Made me remember something myself.

ABIGAYLE: What'd it make you remember?

DEXTER: Made me remember my first trip to McDonald's.

ABIGAYLE: Your first trip to *McDonald's*?

DEXTER: Yeah. Why you say it like that?

ABIGAYLE: Go, tell your story.

DEXTER *(In a vaguely performance-like tone)*: Well, I was remembering that I had wanted to go to McDonald's for a while, 'cuz my friend Chris Taylor had his *birthday* party when he was *six years old* at McDonald's, but I didn't become *friends* with him until *after* he turned *six*—

ABIGAYLE: Can you just talk normal?

DEXTER: What? What'd I do?

ABIGAYLE: Just talk normal.

DEXTER: I talk how I talk. How do I talk?

ABIGAYLE: I'm sorry. Keep going.

DEXTER: So, what I was saying was, *Chris* Taylor would not stop *talking* about how *great* McDonald's was, how he had *McNuggets* and all this shit, and *orange drink,* and *fries,* and a *sundae,* and how Ronald *McDonald* was there, and shit, so I was excited, right? And every time home from school the bus would go in front of McDonald's. Now I asked my mother to take me to McDonald's, but she said she didn't have any *money,* which was bullshit because she was always buying *crossword puzzle magazines* and *Vaseline* for her lips, so I knew she had money, there was just some *reason* she didn't want to go to McDonald's. So I went to McDonald's myself. I *walked* home from school, *to* the McDonald's, and I was *scared,* walking in there, never having been there before, having all that excitement and butterflies in my stomach like before when I play a game—

ABIGAYLE: —Don't start bragging about your basketball skills—

DEXTER: I didn't!

ABIGAYLE: Don't start!

DEXTER: Chill! All right, *so,* I get into the McDonald's—and I go up in the line, and this guy, big brother nine feet tall—

ABIGAYLE: You're not black, he's not a brother.

DEXTER: I grew up with black people!

ABIGAYLE: Keep going, tell the story.

DEXTER: I look up at the *menu,* way up high, I look up at the *menu* and I realize—shit, I can't read. I can't read nothing but, like, Dick and Jane, and shit, I don't know *shit* about what they got at McDonald's. All I remember is the *commercial.* The Big Mac *commercial* and the chicken *McNuggets* and the *orange drink* and the *sundae* and the *fries* 'cuz Chris Taylor was always talking about what he ate. So I stand there all scared and I say, "I'll have a Big Mac, a Chicken McNuggets, an orange drink, fries and a sundae." Ain't that fucking funny?!

ABIGAYLE: Where'd you get all that money?

DEXTER: Hunh?

ABIGAYLE: That's a lot of money.

DEXTER: I took it.

ABIGAYLE: From who?

DEXTER: I don't remember. I just took it.

ABIGAYLE: You just made up that story.

DEXTER: I did not!

ABIGAYLE: Yes you did. Where'd you get that money?

DEXTER: I don't remember! So! Anyway, the story ends . . . you know, I paid and I sat down and I ate all the food and I thought it was GREAT, the best—MMMMMMM—just the best fucking food *ever*, right? But I had basketball after that. Basketball at South Catholic. I went there and I started playing and then I started feeling like a big lump was in my belly or something, and I threw up all over the court, and the shit was, you could *see* the chunks of chicken and the fries and shit, it was *nasty*, and everyone made fun of me like, you just threw up you jerk, and my mom was like where the *hell* did you eat that shit? Yeah. Yeah. So—that's the end.

ABIGAYLE: Oh.

DEXTER: What?

ABIGAYLE: Nothing.

DEXTER: You not impressed by my story?

ABIGAYLE: Your story's good. It's a good story.

DEXTER: My dad's used to work at McDonald's, dat's where my mom met him and shit.

(A beat.)

I made up that last part. I didn't throw up. I just kept burping a lot.

(Abigayle smiles. Dexter shrugs cutely.)

So where you wanna go?

ABIGAYLE: Go to South Catholic.

DEXTER: Hunh?

ABIGAYLE: Go to South Catholic.

DEXTER: Why you wanna go there?

ABIGAYLE: Where do you want to go?

(Dexter has no answer. Blackout.)

Scene 7

Joe and June, in the car, at a parking lot. Joe is eating a Whopper. June is sipping a Coke.

JOE: The scene where the guy is standing there, and the light is coming in through the window, and you know he's gonna, the other guy's gonna go through the door, and the guy doesn't know it, and his pants are down, and the first thing that comes into his mind, and you can see it on his face, I mean, I'm projecting here, but you can see it on his face, the first thing that comes into his mind when the guy comes through the door with the gun is, Shit, my pants are down. And he's embarrassed. Embarrassed to have his pants down. That's his initial reaction. And *then* he gets scared, *then* he realizes he's gonna die. Just brilliant. So what'd you think?

JUNE *(Shrugs)*: I liked it. It was okay.

JOE: I'm gonna go run inside to the bathroom. You want anything?

JUNE: No.

JOE: You sure?

JUNE: Yeah.

(Joe goes. June looks in his Burger King bag. Takes a fry. Eats it. Takes another fry. Now a handful. He wipes his hands on his jeans. He takes a sip of the soda. He takes some Binaca from his pocket, sprays it in his mouth. He checks himself in the mirror. Runs his fingers through his hair. Looks out the window. Eats another handful of fries. Joe returns.)

JOE: All right.

(Joe starts the car.)

How are you doing?

JUNE: Okay.

JOE: You wanna keep going?

JUNE: What do you mean?

JOE: You okay? You wanna keep going? I have more planned, but I can take you home.

JUNE: No, I'll keep going.
JOE: All right, let's drive.

(Joe drives.)

What about you.
JUNE: What?
JOE: You have any ideas?
JUNE: About what?
JOE: About where to go. I don't want this to be all me. I figured
    we'd go see the fireworks at ten. Down by the bridge.
JUNE: Oh.
JOE: You don't sound enthusiastic.
JUNE: Well—no, I will, I just—
JOE: We got two hours till then.
JUNE: Yeah.
JOE: And we can do stuff after that. The night does not end with
    the fireworks.
JUNE: Well . . . I dunno, it's really up to you.
JOE: No, no, it's up to you. What do you want? What do you
    wanna do?
JUNE: Well . . . I mean, I don't know. Maybe if you told me your
    idea . . .
JOE: My idea. My idea . . . Well I'm trying to gauge you, June.
    Trying to see just where you wanna go, what you wanna do.
    I want this to be an enjoyable experience for you. You're not
    giving me very much.
JUNE: I'm having a good time.
JOE: Tell me where you wanna go.
JUNE: It's up to you, really.
JOE: Tell me where.
JUNE: Well . . . where do you wanna go?
JOE: I'm not gonna answer that question. We're just gonna drive
    in silence.

*(They drive in silence. A few moments pass. Joe reaches over and
puts his hand on June's leg. June doesn't move. More silence. Joe
keeps his hand on June's leg.)*

You said you had a friend.
JUNE: Huh?

JOE: You told me on the computer. The first night we met. That you had a gay friend. Who you'd fooled around with when you were little.

JUNE: Oh. Yeah.

JOE: What was his name?

JUNE: Todd.

JOE: Todd. That's right. Todd. What's he doing tonight?

JUNE: I dunno.

JOE: How come you don't speak to him anymore?

JUNE: Well I just . . . never really . . . once middle school came, you know . . . he started acting weird.

JOE: How's weird?

JUNE: He started, like . . . acting like a girl.

JOE: Like a faggot?

JUNE: Yeah, I guess.

JOE: Wearing flamboyant clothes?

JUNE: Well, no, just . . . well I guess, a little . . . like he'd roll up the bottoms of his pants and stuff.

JOE: Uh-huh.

JUNE: And uhh . . . he started hanging out with all girls.

JOE: All girls.

JUNE: Yeah.

JOE: He still go to your high school?

JUNE: Yeah.

(A beat.)

Yeah, and so, we just kinda stopped talking.

JOE: That's too bad.

JUNE: Not really, I mean . . . I dunno.

JOE: You still see him in school?

JUNE: Yeah, like, in the halls and stuff.

JOE: And?

JUNE: And what?

JOE: What do you say to each other?

JUNE: Nothing. I don't talk to him.

JOE: Why not?

JUNE: Just don't.

(Pause.)

Just don't.

JOE: So whaddaya think he's doing tonight?

JUNE: Probably out.

JOE: Out where?

JUNE: Well he . . . I know, you know, people talk and stuff . . . I know he goes to Chez.

JOE: Chez. The bar Chez.

JUNE: Yeah.

JOE: He likes older men?

JUNE: I dunno, I mean . . . he goes there—he has his tongue pierced.

JOE: *Really?* I thought only dykes did that.

JUNE: Why?

JOE: Going down on each other.

JUNE: Oh. Yeah, he got his tongue pierced, and his nose . . . and he dyed his hair black. He looks completely different now, he wears makeup, I see him put on makeup at his locker. Pancake.

JOE: Why?

JUNE: To cover his acne, I guess.

JOE: And he doesn't get the shit beat out of him?

JUNE: Well . . . I guess people just leave him alone . . . because he's too weird or something.

JOE: People leave you alone?

JUNE: Yeah, I guess.

JOE: Why is that?

JUNE: Well . . . I guess I don't really talk a lot.

JOE: Mmmm-hmmmm.

JUNE: Yeah. So . . .

JOE: So what's Todd doing tonight?

JUNE: Probably getting laid or something. He sleeps around. People—say he has it.

JOE: Has *it*. It?

JUNE: Yeah.

JOE: Mmmm-hmmm.

JUNE: So . . .

JOE: Think he's at Chez?

JUNE: Yeah, probably.

JOE: Wanna go see him?

JUNE: No.

JOE: We're only five minutes away.

JUNE: No, I don't wanna do that.

(Joe takes his hand away.)

JOE: Why are you so scared of him?

JUNE: I'm not—

JOE: You're not scared of meeting a complete stranger from the computer, but you're scared of someone who was your friend?

JUNE: I don't want him to know.

JOE: Why not?

JUNE: I just . . . I feel dumb.

JOE: Why?

JUNE: I dunno.

(Long silence.)

Once when we were thirteen . . . he was still pretty normal. I know, 'cuz I used to be on this swim team, and he used to dive, and . . . I mean, I really wasn't speaking to him or anything. And we had this really, this swim coach, our swim coach, and he was the diving coach, too . . . and I just . . . I had a funny feeling about him.

JOE: Fag?

JUNE: —Yeah. Or—just a funny feeling. But yeah.

JOE: What's his name, maybe I know him.

JUNE: Um, Ted . . . Vollanski or . . . Ted Vollman I think.

(Joe laughs, then stops.)

JOE: Don't know him.

JUNE: And . . . anyway . . . this one day I got home, I mean, I never saw anything, I just, the way Todd and Ted would, like, talk to each other, it made me mad. Like after practice, not in the locker room, but like right outside, like where you wait to get picked up, the pool parking lot . . . like they'd talk to each other . . . and I didn't get mad or anything, I just—I thought it was weird. And I'd just stand there. And I noticed one night—

JOE: Uh-oh.

JUNE: What?

JOE: No, no, keep going, I'm just anticipating.

JUNE: What?

JOE: The story. It's a beautiful story, keep going.

JUNE: Oh.

JOE: Keep going.

JUNE: Yeah so . . . one night my mom was really late to pick me up . . . And I saw Ted give Todd a ride home. Like in his car. Which coaches—I mean, you're not supposed to—I mean it just seemed weird to me. And I got home that night and I couldn't stop thinking about it. I mean, I just—I just was thinking about it so much, it was just making me really mad, like I didn't know what to do, and I just kept walking in circles around my room . . . and I decided to call him.

JOE: Todd.

JUNE: To see, like just to see if he was home. So I called, I had memorized the number, I mean, so I just went and called . . . and he picked up.

JOE: Todd.

JUNE: Yeah. And I thought I was just not gonna say anything, you know? But instead, I don't know why or anything, I just said like, "Is Todd there?" And he said, "Yeah. Who's this?" And I said . . . I just said . . . I said, "You're gay, aren't you?" Like meanly, like, "You're gay, aren't you." And he just . . . and there was just silence . . . he didn't hang up . . . and then he said, "Who is this?" And I said, "You're gay." And he didn't say anything. I just held the phone in my hand really tight. And there was nothing so I said it again. "Who is this?" And then—and then I hung up.

JOE: You hung up.

JUNE: I hung up. You know, and I never spoke to him after that. I don't know if he knew it was me or not, but . . . I mean . . . I just never—I hated him after that.

JOE: You hated him.

JUNE: Yeah, I just . . . I dunno.

(Silence.)

JOE: And you don't want him to know?

JUNE: I'm too . . . I see him in the cafeteria, I mean, we look at each other really quickly, I always have to look away . . .

(Silence.)

JOE: Where do you wanna go now, June?

JUNE: Where do I wanna go . . .

JOE: Just tell me. Just tell me. This is your night. You're a young man, I'm an old man.

(Silence. June touches Joe's hand. June laughs a little.)

JUNE: I used to have my birthday parties at the movie theater when I was little. At the Showcase Cinemas. We'd all just go to the movies. I always wanted to sit in the front row, one of the front rows, so it was just—so the whole picture filled, you know, filled my eyes, so I couldn't see anything else, anyone in front of me or the ceiling or the exit signs or anything . . . I remember all those movies, just . . . having my soda . . .

(Joe puts his hand on June's leg. June looks out the window. He takes Joe's hand and moves it to his crotch. He closes his eyes. Joe starts moving his hand back and forth. Blackout.)

Scene 8

South Catholic. Outside a brick entryway. Some bushes. Lights rise on Dexter, dribbling a basketball quite fancily. Abigayle watches.

DEXTER: Coach Donovan said I'm the best Division II player he's ever coached.

ABIGAYLE: Mmm-hmmm.

DEXTER: He wants to set me up with a transfer. To a Division I school.

ABIGAYLE: You gonna go?

DEXTER: Well my grades are *bad*, you know. Plus my record.

ABIGAYLE: Mmm-hmmm.

DEXTER: But some schools are interested. Coach Donovan's gonna be in contact with them. He said. He's talking to some coaches. I keep calling him up! I think I'm annoying him or something. I just wanna . . . *know*. I wanna *know*, you know?

ABIGAYLE: Which ones?

DEXTER: What?

ABIGAYLE: Which schools?

DEXTER: A couple. Watch this.

(He dribbles rapidly between his legs.)

ABIGAYLE: That's good. *(Beat)* Show-off.

(Dexter laughs.)

DEXTER: Wanna play catch?

ABIGAYLE: No.

DEXTER: Noooo. Okay then you can just watch me all night!

(He giggles, dribbles some more. Then he stops and looks at Abigayle.)

ABIGAYLE: What?

DEXTER: How come you never say nothing?

ABIGAYLE: I say plenty.

DEXTER: You're not saying nothing. Don't wanna go nowhere, don't wanna . . . say nothing. Just tell me why you said yes to me.

ABIGAYLE: You were dribbling, we were having a good time, why'd you have to bring this up again?

DEXTER *(Smoothly)*: Just tell me. Why you said yes.

ABIGAYLE: Because I felt like it.

DEXTER: You and your answers, man. Okay, answer me this. You think I'm pretty?

ABIGAYLE: Do I think you're pretty?

DEXTER: Yeah. I know I'm a *white boy*, you ain't into that—

ABIGAYLE: Half white, half spic, don't sell yourself short.

DEXTER: Well I know you ain't *into* that, either one, so, why'd you say yes?

ABIGAYLE: I never said that, that I'm not into white boys, I never said that.

DEXTER: Well that's the feeling I get, is it true?

ABIGAYLE: No. Sometimes. But no. It's not true.

DEXTER: So tell me then. You think I'm handsome? You think I'm pretty? Come on, tell me.

(He poses for her, smiles. She smiles.)

ABIGAYLE: I don't like your questions. I don't want to answer them.
DEXTER: Well . . . what if I told you I think you're pretty.

(Pause.)

ABIGAYLE: I'd accept the compliment.
DEXTER: And . . .
ABIGAYLE: And that's it. Show-off.
DEXTER: Well what if I told you I think you're beautiful . . . chocolate?
ABIGAYLE: You just ruined it by calling me chocolate. I cannot accept a compliment where I'm compared to something you can buy for sixty cents at Dairy Mart.
DEXTER: All right, all right, what if I just told you I think you're beautiful. No chocolate.
ABIGAYLE: I know your intentions. You know that, right? You know you're not fooling me, don't you?
DEXTER: Damn! I don't have no intentions! You watch too much *Ricki*.
ABIGAYLE: I don't watch *Ricki*. Usually. I think sometimes you're . . .
DEXTER: I'm what? I'm what?
ABIGAYLE: Dag, you're so *eager*. Now I'm not gonna say it.
DEXTER: Watch this.

(He twirls the ball on his finger.)

ABIGAYLE: I think sometimes you look nice.
DEXTER: When's that?

(Dexter's beeper beeps.)

Fuck.

(He checks his beeper, shakes his head, puts it away.)

Man. I told him, I was *off* tonight.
ABIGAYLE: You gotta make a call?

DEXTER: Fuck that, I'm with you. So. You was saying.

ABIGAYLE: I wasn't saying anything.

DEXTER: You was saying I look nice sometimes.

ABIGAYLE: Yeah.

DEXTER: What do you mean, sometimes. When do I look nice?

ABIGAYLE: When you're smiling like a little boy.

DEXTER: You think I'm like a little boy?

ABIGAYLE: Sometimes.

DEXTER: You think I *look* like a little boy?

ABIGAYLE: Sometimes.

(He starts dribbling again.)

DEXTER: You don't even know that sometimes it's hard to talk to you. You don't even know that. 'Cuz you so smart, and so out there being smart, not hiding it or nothing . . . makes me scared. Like you gonna correct me or think I'm stupid. You think I'm stupid like a little boy, don'tcha?

ABIGAYLE: No.

DEXTER: You think I'm like playing with Legos and sticking my finger up my nose—

ABIGAYLE: That's not what I meant.

DEXTER: You think I'm not good enough for you. That I can't understand you. These thoughts. These thoughts in your head. Well I have thoughts too.

(He stops dribbling.)

Why don't you tell me some of your thoughts?

(She says nothing.)

Why won't you tell me anything?

(She says nothing.)

Before this night is out, you're gonna tell me your thoughts!

(He bounces the ball off the wall, again and again.)

I wish you wanted to see the fireworks. I don't know why you don't like 'em. Is it 'cuz of your mother?

32

ABIGAYLE: Is what because of my mother?

DEXTER: 'Cuz your mother's, you know. Does that make you all—scared of things?

ABIGAYLE: Scared of what?

DEXTER: Whatever you scared of. You act like you ain't but you gotta be scared of something.

ABIGAYLE: I'm scared of nothing.

DEXTER: That's something.

(He giggles. A quiet moment. Then Dexter starts walking around.)

I love the fireworks. In the sky like that. That's unreal. That don't happen every day. Everybody standing there, all these people, under the bridge, on the water, standing there, or sitting on their blankets, looking up at the sky, everyone looking up at the sky like that, all quiet as it goes up and then cheering when it explodes and shit. Man, I love that. That don't happen every day, you get all the people into the city like that, all of us who living out of the city go back in, and you got all the people, all looking up at the sky, and I know you say that there be, like, drunk people and kids running around being assholes, and niggers with guns and Latin Kings with knives and white boys with baseball bats and shit, but once the shit starts, you know, *everybody* stops. *Everybody* looks up at the sky. And is like . . . you know? Everybody's looking up there.

(Silence. He starts dribbling.)

Anyway, you don't wanna go, that's cool, maybe we can see the sky get all bright from here, like the clouds lighting up or something, that's cool too . . . you just wanna be alone all the time, I had a grandmother like that, that's cool, only she didn't get that way till she got old . . . I loved coming to high school here. I loved it. Everybody loved me. I walked down the hall and everybody loved me. Only thing I didn't like was confession. They made us go to confession. I had to kneel there, it was the only time I felt stupid, all the other times felt great. Everyone knew who I was, I played *basketball*, I was the leading *scorer*, they wrote about me in the *newspaper*. Confession was the only bad thing. I hated confession, I hated doing that. You believe in God? *(Abigayle shrugs)* I believe in God. I don't know why you wouldn't. My dad didn't believe in God. Look at that bitch. He's fat and got no teeth.

ABIGAYLE: Don't talk about your dad that way.

DEXTER: Don't tell me how to talk about my dad.

(Beat.)

I don't pray or nothing, I don't kneel down at my bed and *pray*, but a lot of things have happened to me, you know, in my life, a lot of moments, you know, and I'm always thinking, God, I mean I don't look up at the sky or nothing, but I'm always thinking, God, God, God, man, God, brother, help me out, God, man, what you doin', God, man, look at me, you know, I mean, I don't go to church or nothing—

(We hear a small firecracker go off. Dexter stops dribbling. Abigayle is next to him.)

Some crazy kids getting an early start.

(They look at each other. She kisses him.)

Yo, why you do that?

(She kisses him again.)

What you kiss me for?

ABIGAYLE: Are you okay?

(Dexter nods. They kiss. He drops the ball, puts his hand up her back.)

DEXTER: Oh you warm. You so warm. Oh.

(They kiss.)

ABIGAYLE: Let's go.

DEXTER: Where?

ABIGAYLE: Your house.

DEXTER: My house? Why not yours?

ABIGAYLE: I wanna go. Come on.
DEXTER: Mmm, kiss me again.

(They kiss.)

ABIGAYLE: I wanna go.
DEXTER: You so warm.
ABIGAYLE: Dexter.
DEXTER: Okay.

*(Lights fade on Dexter and Abigayle.
Lights rise on the interior of a Motel 6 room. June sits on
the bed. We hear Joe from offstage, the bathroom. The water is
running.)*

JOE *(Offstage)*: Anything good on TV?
JUNE: I'm not watching.
JOE *(Offstage)*: No, I mean, is there anything good on TV?
JUNE: I dunno. I don't really watch TV.

*(Joe enters from the bathroom, wiping his hands on his pants. He
sits on the opposite end of the bed from June.)*

JOE: I love motels.
JUNE: Why?
JOE: I just do. Just love 'em. They're always there. Always open. A
    room. A bed. A TV. A phone. A shower. All the things you
    need. Just the essentials. The essential tools of living. In a
    completely anonymous setting. You can reinvent yourself.
    Or *become* yourself.

(He opens the nightstand, takes out the Bible.)

And this book. The greatest book ever.
JUNE: The Bible?
JOE: Yeah.
JUNE: The Bible's the greatest book ever?
JOE: I think so. No book has inspired or enraged so many people.
    That makes it the best book.
JUNE: I wouldn't think you're religious.
JOE: I'm not. As *literature*. As *myth*.

JUNE: I hate going to church.

JOE: You hate church?

JUNE: I hate it.

JOE: Why do you go then?

JUNE: My parents go. We've always gone.

JOE: Turn on the TV.

JUNE: Hmm?

JOE: See what's on. Turn it on.

(Joe flips through the Bible. June turns on the TV, flips through the channels.)

I bet motels are one of the few places people feel comfortable reading the Bible. Church there's all that pressure, standing and kneeling and singing on key and dressing up and confessing sins and all that—too much, the words get lost. And how can you read a Bible in your house? You got the phone ringing, kids running around, television on—the words can't find a place. Anything on?

JUNE: Not much.

JOE: Turn it off.

(June does.)

JUNE: Ummm . . . I'm just . . . gonna take a shower.

JOE: Why are you gonna take a shower?

JUNE: I—want to.

JOE: You're nervous.

JUNE: No.

JOE: I'll put you at ease.

JUNE: No, I just feel . . . I'm not clean. I'm a little sweaty.

JOE: Okay, up to you.

JUNE: I'll just . . . I'll be quick.

(June gets up, goes to the shower. Offstage, we hear it turn on. June leaves the bathroom door open a crack. As Joe speaks, he opens a small black duffel bag. He removes two towels, some condoms, and a tube of lubricant and puts them on the nightstand. He speaks loudly. We can barely hear June's responses.)

JOE: I do volunteer work. I see a lot of kids in trouble these days. Sad kids. We didn't seem to be that sad when I was growing up. We learned to keep a lot inside. We didn't expect too much. In some ways, I think that was a good thing, you know? Anyway, I do this volunteer work a couple days a week, it's at the university, and the other day I was with this man, he was very poor, he was on food stamps and welfare, he was white, and he just—well he'd just had it. He was a little older than me, and he'd graduated from high school but had never gone to college, and he'd had a family—can you hear me in there?

JUNE: Yeah.

JOE: He'd had a family, and he'd lost his family, he'd left them, and then he married another woman, and he left her too, and then he stopped trying to be married, decided he didn't want to be married, wanted to be on his own, wanted to do what he wanted to do. The work I do—it's a counseling center— it's a health center—I see a lot of kids. It's a surprise to see an older person. Especially a man. Anyhow—and I was talking to this man. And he's there to get his blood tested, he lives on the Berlin Turnpike, I forget which motel, one of them, and we're talking, and as we're talking, I'm starting to realize . . . *(Joe takes off his sweater, revealing an undershirt)* I'm starting to remember this man. From a bar. A gay bar. I am convinced it is he, because the man I knew, this is during the early '80s, and I was going through a rough point at that time—good thing about the disease is that it's made most people start thinking about sex instead of just having it, you know what I'm saying—made people think about the other *person*, what they might have *inside* them, hidden away, invisible, which can only be a good thing *I* think, *I* think in many ways this disease is the best thing that could have happened to gay men because in a certain sense it's made us *human*—but I could go on forever about that, I'm getting away from the story. Can you hear me? Are you interested? I'll stop. I'll stop talking.

JUNE: No, you can keep going.

JOE: Well I realized that this was the first man I'd ever slept with. Because I remember he had a scar on the bottom of his left ear that looked like, well to me, then, in that dim light, looked like a snake I remember thinking— *(The shower goes off. Joe adjusts the volume of his voice. He checks to make sure the shades are closed and the door is locked during the follow-*

37

ing) —I didn't bring it up with him, of course, and I looked different so I was sure he wouldn't recognize me—and what I found interesting in a purely *theoretical* way was—well I started thinking about the myths of first love—first sex— how for gay boys today getting one's first AIDS test is equivalent to the straight boy losing his virginity—because—

(June comes out of the bathroom, wearing his T-shirt and jeans. He is not at all wet.)

What's wrong?
JUNE: Nothing.
JOE: You're all dressed. Did you shower?

(June looks over to the nightstand.)

Are you okay?
JUNE: Yeah—yeah—I'm fine. I just . . .
JOE: Just?
JUNE: I just . . .

(June's head is down.)

JOE: This was a mistake. Wasn't it? Let's not do this.
JUNE: No, I mean—
JOE: You don't want to do this. You don't have to.
JUNE: No, I just—I don't know, I—
JOE: I'll take you home.
JUNE: I don't wanna go home.
JOE: . . . What do you want?

(June puts his head into Joe's chest. He starts to stroke Joe's leg. His eyes are shut.)

June?
JUNE: I'm sorry. I do. I do. *(A whisper)* I'm horny.
JOE: You're what?
JUNE: I'm horny.

(June climbs onto the bed. He takes off his shirt. Joe looks at him.)

JOE: What do you want, June?

(June turns over, faces the pillow.)

I think you want to leave, June.

(June slides off his jeans. Joe watches him. Joe climbs onto the bed and begins to touch June.)

June? June? You're beautiful, June. You're a beautiful boy. You are beautiful, June. You're a beautiful boy. Let me get this.

(Joe shuts off the lamp. The room is dark, and we cannot see them.
Lights rise on Dexter and Abigayle on a bed. Abigayle sits opposite Dexter. We hear shouting, noise outside.)

DEXTER: See, I told you. I'm sure your house woulda been quiet.
ABIGAYLE: I want to be here.
DEXTER: Jus' all that racket. All this racket around here. Fourth of July. Why don't they just go and see the fireworks already.
ABIGAYLE: They have an hour and a half.
DEXTER: Yeah, I guess.

(Silence.)

See, it is a mixed neighborhood.
ABIGAYLE: What do you mean?
DEXTER: That I grew up in. Black people. And Koreans and shit. I grew up here.
ABIGAYLE: Mmm-hmmm.

(A beat.)

DEXTER: You know it's funny, I talk like I'm black, you talk like you a white girl.
ABIGAYLE: I don't talk like a white girl.
DEXTER: What are you talking about, you don't. Your mother white?
ABIGAYLE: No. She's black.

DEXTER: Man, you say it like that.
ABIGAYLE: Like what.
DEXTER: I dunno. Like—with anger or something.
ABIGAYLE: You have a nice room.
DEXTER: It's small but cozy, Miss Change-the-Subject.
ABIGAYLE: All these posters.
DEXTER *(Flippantly)*: I wish I was black.
ABIGAYLE: What?
DEXTER: Sometimes I wish I was black.

(Silence. Abigayle turns to Dexter and stares at him.)

What?

(She keeps staring.)

What?

(She stands, walks around to where Dexter sits on the bed. She starts kissing him. He kisses back. She pulls off his shirt.)

Whoa! I thought you said—
ABIGAYLE: Shhhhh.

(She keeps kissing. She fumbles for his belt.)

DEXTER: Wait a second, stop for a second—

(She keeps going. As she kisses him, she pulls down his pants.)

What are you doing? I thought you—
ABIGAYLE: Shhhhh.

(She climbs onto the bed, on top of him. We hear kids laughing from outside Dexter's window. The sound of paper-snaps.)

DEXTER: Abigayle—Abigayle?—Abigayle?—
ABIGAYLE: What?
DEXTER: You a virgin?
ABIGAYLE: No.
DEXTER: No?

ABIGAYLE: No.

DEXTER: Abigayle I don't have any rubbers—

ABIGAYLE: Shhhhhh—

DEXTER: I don't know if—I don't got nothing—

(She reaches over and shuts out his light. In the darkness, sounds of sex, from both sides of the stage. Family bickering heard from outside Dexter's room. Children laughing outside. In the darkness we hear a grunt of pain from June and Joe's motel room. Blackout.)

Scene 9

Lights rise on Dexter and Abigayle in a car. Silence. They drive. Lights rise on Joe and June in a car.

DEXTER: How come you ain't saying nothing?

ABIGAYLE: You're not talking, either.

(Silence.)

DEXTER: You shoulda taken the leftover barbecue. It's good.

ABIGAYLE: I don't eat meat.

DEXTER: Why not?

ABIGAYLE: I don't like it.

(Silence.)

JOE: You haven't said anything.

JUNE: Hmmm?

JOE: You haven't said anything about it. *(A beat)* Was it okay?

JUNE: No, yeah, it was . . . I just . . .

JOE: It was okay?

JUNE *(Smiling)*: Yes. I'm sorry that I couldn't—

JOE *(Smiling)*: Shhh, shhh, that's okay, June.

(Silence.)

DEXTER: You see that movie *Bridge Under Water* yet?

ABIGAYLE: What?

DEXTER: *Bridge Under Water?* With the flood—

ABIGAYLE: No.

DEXTER: Looks good. *(A beat)* Maybe you want to see it tomorrow?

ABIGAYLE: I have work.

DEXTER: Where do you work?

ABIGAYLE: Things around the house. Help my mother. And my father's coming home.

DEXTER: Oh.

(Silence.)

JOE: Where can we go now? *(A beat)* Maybe I should take you home.

JUNE: If you wanna go . . .

JOE: No, not unless you do.

(June shrugs. Silence.)

DEXTER: Your mother ever let people come over the house?

ABIGAYLE: She doesn't like it.

DEXTER: Makes her nervous?

ABIGAYLE: I think it makes her sad.

DEXTER: How?

ABIGAYLE: She doesn't like to be reminded.

DEXTER: Of what?

ABIGAYLE: Other people.

DEXTER: I don't understand.

ABIGAYLE: You don't have to.

(Silence.)

DEXTER: Damn. Fine.

(Silence.)

JOE: Half an hour till the fireworks. *(A beat)* You don't want to see the fireworks, do you?

JUNE: I will . . .

JOE: You don't want to.

(Silence.)

DEXTER: Your house coming up?
ABIGAYLE: Keep going down this road.
DEXTER: How much longer?
ABIGAYLE: About five minutes.

(Silence.)

DEXTER: So why don't you tell me one of the thoughts in your mind? One of the thoughts you wanted to get away from?
ABIGAYLE: You want me to just say it?
DEXTER: Yeah.
ABIGAYLE: That's not a conversation.
DEXTER: Why not?
ABIGAYLE: It's just not.

(Dexter makes a turn.)

Where are you going?
DEXTER: I wanna take you to a place.
ABIGAYLE: Where?
DEXTER: A place. I'm not telling. You'll see when we get there.
ABIGAYLE: I want to go home, take me home.
DEXTER: You'll go home.

(Lights off on Dexter and Abigayle.)

JOE: All right.
JUNE: What?
JOE: Time to make a decision.
JUNE: It's up to you, really.
JOE: Okay. We'll go to Chez.
JUNE: No!
JOE: All right, an answer! Emphatic at that!
JUNE: I just don't wanna go there.
JOE: You'll go there and you'll be someone, June. You won't just be dashes of light on a computer screen anymore. Won't be some dream figure, some fantasy creation, a sixteen year old with a swimmer's build and a hairless chest who's looking for—
JUNE: I never said that, I never said that's what I was.
JOE: I'm sorry. I get carried away. I'm sorry.

(Silence. Then:)

What do you want? Answer that and you'll know where to go.
JUNE: I told you, I don't know—
JOE: No. From this *life*? What do you want from this *life*?

(Pause.)

JUNE: What will this life give me. You're forgetting about that. It's not like I can just choose. It's not like I can just choose to be skinny, like that, decide I want to be skinny, or, or handsome, or whatever, you know, a famous actor, or whatever. It's not like you can choose those things.
JOE: Let's say you can. What do you want? Is that what you want? To be skinny? A famous actor?
JUNE: I don't know.
JOE: Let's start easy. You want to be happy.
JUNE: Yeah.
JOE: What would make you happy?
JUNE: I don't know.
JOE: If your parents loved you, would that make you happy?
JUNE: My parents do love me.
JOE: Yes, but they don't know you.
JUNE: I want a drink.
JOE: What?
JUNE: I want a drink. I want to drink.
JOE: Now?
JUNE: Yeah.
JOE: I'm not gonna buy you alcohol.
JUNE: I can get it myself.
JOE: Not with me driving, you can't.
JUNE: I just want a drink. It's the Fourth of July.
JOE: Let me tell you what you want.
JUNE: Tell me what?
JOE: What you want. What will make you happy. You want a boyfriend. You want to have sex. You want to be in love. You want someone sleeping next to you. You want someone to stroke your head. You cry yourself to sleep, don't you? You spend four hours a night on your computer, looking to meet someone—
JUNE: You don't know what I want—

JOE: You want someone to make you real, to *touch you*—
JUNE: You don't know what I want.
JOE: I'm being honest, I care about you.
JUNE: Maybe I should go. Maybe I should go.
JOE: Oh! Come on, June!—
JUNE: Let me out.
JOE: I'm not going to let you out in the middle of nowhere!

(They drive in silence. Joe begins to cry. June looks at him, then looks away. Blackout.)

Scene 10

Lights rise on the exterior of a very small church. Dexter sits on the stoop. Abigayle stands.

DEXTER: I bet we can see the fireworks from here. If you want.

(Pause.)

You have any brothers?
ABIGAYLE: You just won't leave me alone, will you?
DEXTER: You're here. You can walk away from me if you don't want to be here, okay? It's called legs, you got 'em.

(Pause. Again:)

You have any brothers or sisters?
ABIGAYLE: Why do you want to know?
DEXTER: I want to know you.
ABIGAYLE: What do you want to know?
DEXTER *(Impatiently)*: Do you have any brothers or sisters?
ABIGAYLE: No.

(Pause.)

DEXTER: You ever go to church?
ABIGAYLE: Before my mother got sick.
DEXTER: When did she get sick?

ABIGAYLE: When I was little. When I was four.

DEXTER: What's wrong with her?

ABIGAYLE: She's just weak. She just got weak.

DEXTER: You go to doctors?

ABIGAYLE: They don't know what it is.

DEXTER: So she's just, like . . . weak?

ABIGAYLE: Yeah.

DEXTER: Your father cool? *(Abigayle shrugs)* What's he like?

ABIGAYLE: He's a good man. He works hard. He loves me. Not much to say. He travels a lot.

DEXTER: Where's he go?

ABIGAYLE: I don't want to talk about him, okay?

DEXTER: Okay. Okay.

(Beat.)

I only like churches at night. When no one's in 'em. I stopped going. To church. But I like 'em when no one is in 'em.

ABIGAYLE: Why?

DEXTER: I don't know. Like they seem more real or something. You know? When I was little I'd sneak into the chapel at South Catholic during lunch. Before going and playing basketball at recess. I'd go into the chapel and just sit there for a little while. I had problems, you know. My mom and dad, they didn't get along. They was always fighting. I smoked my first joint when I was seven. You know that? *(Pause)* We used to go to this church. Me and my mom. After my dad left. My mom decided we should go to church. This was the one she picked. She said 'cuz it was the ugliest church there was and since she was ugly it was where she belonged. *(Laughs)* I liked this church. I liked the basement. It was all quiet and dark. I had sex in this church, lost my virginity. In the basement. To this girl, Ladrica. I was thirteen. She's dead now.

(Dexter's beeper beeps.)

Shit.

(He checks the beeper.)

S'nothing.

(Silence.)

I wanna show you something.

(Dexter takes out his wallet, takes out a picture and hands it to Abigayle.)

ABIGAYLE: What's this?
DEXTER: Me, my mom, and my dad. When I was eight. After a basketball game. My dad used to teach me. Basketball.
ABIGAYLE: Oh.

(She moves to give the picture back to him.)

DEXTER: No.
ABIGAYLE: No what?
DEXTER: Keep it.
ABIGAYLE: Why should I keep it?

(Dexter shrugs, then leans his head into Abigayle's chest and hugs her. A beat. Then she begins to stroke his head. He falls to his knees, eyes closed, still gripping her.)

It's almost ten. You're gonna miss the fireworks if you don't take me home.
DEXTER: I don't wanna go to the fireworks.
ABIGAYLE: I have to go, Dexter. Come on. *(Dexter doesn't move)* I have to go. My mother needs me.
DEXTER: Mmmm.
ABIGAYLE: Come on.

(She lifts him up. He stands, opens his eyes.)

DEXTER: Okay.
ABIGAYLE *(Holding out the picture to him)*: I don't want this.
DEXTER: It's for you.
ABIGAYLE: I don't want it.

(He looks at her a moment, then walks off. She puts the picture in her pocket. Blackout.)

Scene 11

The parking lot with the pay phone. June and Joe sit in Joe's car.

JUNE: Thanks.

(June starts to get out.)

JOE: Hold on.
JUNE: What?
JOE: I got you something.

(Joe takes a paper bag from the backseat.)

JUNE: What'd you get?
JOE: A little something.

(June looks in the bag.)

Don't look now.
JUNE: Okay.

(June closes the bag.)

JOE: You sure you don't want me to drive you home?
JUNE: Yeah.
JOE: Okay. Well . . . good luck.
JUNE: Thanks.
JOE: Email me if you want.
JUNE: Okay.
JOE: Bye, June.
JUNE: Bye.

(Joe drives off. June looks around. He opens the bag. Takes out a box of condoms. Puts them in his pocket. Then he takes out a stick wrapped in red paper and a pack of matches. He puts them down. He goes to the phone, sits down on the ground.
Lights rise on Abigayle's house. She enters the living room, immediately knocks on her mother's door.)

Four

ABIGAYLE: Mom? You okay? You want something? . . . The fireworks. But I decided not to. It was too crowded . . . Of course I love you. I love you, Mom. Don't cry . . .

(She takes a step in. The fireworks begin. Abigayle doesn't notice. We see the sky light up, but are too far away to hear the sound of their explosions.)

No, no, I'm not coming in—

(She stops. She notices the fireworks outside the window.)

You want a hug, Ma? What do you want? You want some water? You want to get up and look at the fireworks outside the window? What do you want? . . . I love you too. I love you too. Good night.

(Abigayle shuts the door, goes to the window, watches the fireworks.
June stands up, looks up at the sky.
Abigayle grabs the phone, returns to the window. Holds the phone. We hear banging from the bedroom. Abigayle stays where she is.
June digs in his pocket.
The banging is louder. Abigayle starts to cry. She goes to the door.)

You okay, Mom? . . . He's coming back tomorrow. He called. He's coming back early tomorrow. You wanna watch the fireworks? He just said that he was coming back tomorrow. You were asleep. Of course he said he loves you. Yes . . . Okay. I'm gonna go to bed now. Okay. Good night. I love you. Mom. Mom.

(Abigayle goes back to the couch. She holds the phone in her hand. She stops crying.
June picks up the pay phone, puts in the quarter, dials.)

JUNE: Hello? Hi, it's me. Yeah, I'll be back in a little while. I'm watching them right now. With some friends. Yeah. Yeah. So. Okay. See you guys later. Bye.

49

(He hangs up.
More banging from the bedroom. Abigayle gets up from the
couch, with phone, then exits.
Lights rise on Dexter, alone, looking up at the sky.
June lights a match, puts the flame to the sparkler. It spits
pale light. He watches it. The sky explodes in silent color. June
looks up at the sky, then back at the sparkler, then exits.
Dexter keeps his eyes fixed on the silent sky. It spins and swells
with color. His beeper beeps. He checks it, then exits.
The fireworks continue their garish, gorgeous assault.)

END OF PLAY

Other People

Production History

Other People was first performed at the Royal Court Theatre (Ian Rickson, Artistic Director) in London, on March 17, 2000. It was directed by Dominic Cooke; the set design was by Robert Innes Hopkins, the lighting design was by Johanna Town, the sound design was by Paul Arditti, the costume design was by Suzanne Duffy and the stage manager was Cath Binks. The cast was as follows:

STEPHEN	Daniel Evans
PETRA	Doraly Rosen
MARK	James Frain
TAN	Neil Newbon
MAN	Nigel Whitmey
DARREN/WAITER	Richard Cant

It was subsequently performed at Playwrights Horizons' New Theater Wing (Tim Sanford, Artistic Director; Leslie Marcus, Managing Director; William Russo, General Manager) in New York City on October 22, 2000. It was directed by Tim Farrell; the scenic design was by Kyle Chepulis, the lighting design was by Andrew Hill, the sound design was by Ken Travis, the costume design was by Mimi O'Donnell and the stage manager was Lee J. Kahrs. The cast was as follows:

STEPHEN	Neal Huff
PETRA	Kate Blumberg
MARK	Pete Starrett
TAN	Ausin Lysy
MAN	Victor Slezak
DARREN	Philip Tabor

Characters

STEPHEN, mid-twenties
PETRA, mid-twenties
MARK, mid-twenties
TAN, late teens
MAN, thirties/forties
DARREN, mid-twenties

*Note: Depending on the actor's versatility,
Darren and Man can be played by the same person.*

Place

New York City's East Village.

Time

Act One, a few days before Christmas, 1997.
Act Two, Christmas Eve, 1997.
Act Three, New Year's Eve, 1997.

Note

In the Royal Court production, we took our only interval after
Act Two, Scene 3. It worked well.

Act One

Scene 1

Hip restaurant, distant techno.

PETRA: People tell me this is really good, so.

STEPHEN: Yeah?

PETRA: No, you look a little—I was wondering if you.

STEPHEN: No, I'm, I guess I'm a little nervous.

PETRA: Yeah, you're nervous?

STEPHEN: We talked on the phone, you know, and he sounded—he sounded—how did he sound?—he said—I don't even remember practically, I was so—nervous. We had a kind of—it was a distant conversation, he said how excited he was to leave the, you know, the clinic, and how much it meant for us to take him in, you know. He talked a little about the movie, which, Christ, the phone has been ringing off the *hook* for him, these movie people calling every half an hour—anyway, whatever, I'm just, let's not talk about it, I'll just get more nervous. Why isn't he here yet? Let's not talk about it.

PETRA: Okay. They say the food is really good, really clean food. I can eat here.

STEPHEN: It's just this music you know.

PETRA: This music, yes.

STEPHEN: You know?

PETRA: Well it can't be helping your nerves.

STEPHEN: And this crowd is a little precious, look, over there—don't look, she's looking here—there, now, that's my editor, right there, in the, whatever, that incredibly boring Donna Karan—see?—the black?—

PETRA: I see—

STEPHEN: —who assigned me four new *blurbs* to do this week because so-and-so had a family emergency, so I have to write these movie reviews now and I was supposed to not have another assignment till after—oh wait: is this, do you hear this?—is this a techno version of "O Holy Night"? Oh, blecch!

PETRA: Christmas.

STEPHEN: Christmas. And these waiters, hello, heil Hitler, master race blondies, I bet they all run into each other at the same auditions.

PETRA: You're very nervous, Stephen.

STEPHEN: I know, and I told myself I wouldn't—hearing his voice—you know—I just wish he'd get here because—there's this *anxiety* I mean—part of me, eight months later part of me really has *forgotten* even what he looks like—and to think he will go from this incredible abstract force in my memory to this *physical*, undeniable *presence*—and that—and that I don't really *know* him now—on the phone when we—I think I'll have a drink.

PETRA: You're allowed to have a drink.

STEPHEN: Blather blather.

PETRA: Can I ask you a question?

STEPHEN: Of course.

PETRA: Are you still in love with him?

STEPHEN: No. *No.* I mean, I recognize, you know, we were never really in *love*, we were in, in *need*, or something, something passed *between us*, and it was *genuine*, but it was not—not by a long shot not—and I know that. No. But Mark and I have never really talked about—and perhaps we should have before I agreed to let him stay with us—but he sounded so—what was I going to say to him? He needs, he needs support now, after, you know, what *happened*. We'll talk about it. We'll talk about it. It'll be okay. It'll be *okay*, it will, it just—things are—*different*. Now. I mean, you know? I'm barely used to you being back here, two days, and now . . .

PETRA: I understand.

STEPHEN: Yeah . . . You are back. Which is wow. Go on, go, say something in Japanese for me.

PETRA: No.

Scene 2

Mark has joined the two.

STEPHEN: Because, no, listen: when you guys were away, endless misery for the first six months, incessant, but this one night, like less than two months ago, I had this epiphany, this total—can we even get some bread while we're—Mark, do you want any bread? I'll get the waiter.

(As Stephen looks around, signals:)

PETRA *(To Mark)*: I can't eat bread, the carbohydrates—they did studies—

STEPHEN: Anyway so, this guy. The date. Cafe, nice, blah blah, we swap stories, walk around the East Village, blab about ex-boyfriends, look at some clothes, decide, what the hell, let's go see a show! So we go to the half-price booth, we go to this musical, musical's over, so we go—Darren—*Darren's* his name—so the show lets out, we go for a drink. Now this will sound banal, mundane, but—we're in the bar—and I start to tell Darren about this *grant* I'm applying for for this *play* I've written—and by the way I'm nervous because I should be hearing if I got this grant or not before the new year, so keep your eye out in the mail—anyway—I tell him how I had just gotten so frustrated with my *job* and how I'd stopped even going on *auditions* because the stuff I was sent out for was so *wretched* and so how I decided to write a *play*—you know, and when you guys left I went back into therapy—and I'm just beginning to really *figure out* my patterns, you know, just, *pathological* sex and and this really degraded self-loathing "love" instinct I mean not-love but—but—I'm lonely, you know? You guys are—I'm kind of hating my life still and—I'm really *hot* for this guy actually, I mean he's

57

totally—he has this weirdo pseudo-British accent sort of, he's a musician, he's got this really sexy, like, *detachment* going on, this really careless *swagger* and *ambivalence*—

PETRA: A million years, he tells a story.

STEPHEN: Okay, okay: so I tell him about the grant and the play and he says he wants to read it. "I'd really like to read it, Stephen. Sounds totally cool." But I feel—I feel *weird*. I feel *something's off here.* Because—and I realize—I turn around briefly because I realize something about his *gaze*—he's not quite looking at me, he's sort of just looking *above* me, above my shoulder, and he's been fixed there the whole—and so I look behind me and I see that—and my heart—*breaks*—I see that he's watching the TV—above the bar. As he's talking to me. The—so I say, "Derek? Derek?" And he says, "Hold on."

PETRA: Darren or Derek his name is?

STEPHEN: He, whatever—"Hold on." And it's not—the show is like *Entertainment Tonight* but not, it's like a *lighter* version of *Entertainment Tonight*, they're interviewing some *blond* woman, some *sitcom*, and I turn back around and I start to say something else you know and he says, "One more sec." *One more sec.* And. And so. I mean that's it.

PETRA: So the story ends you went to bed with him.

STEPHEN: No! No he asked me to go home with him and I just said—"Not tonight but I'll call," or whatever. Because, you know, because I *saw* at that moment—I understood—I thought: *How many of the people I've slept with have actually looked at me?* And I decided no, I decided, I will not go to bed with *anyone* for the rest of my *life* whom I do not perceive has at the very least an *interest in me as a human being.* You know, as a separate person. Because—you know? There I am, sitting before him, a real—TV—me—and he picks—because *no.* Because that will not be my life. Anymore. Where's the bread? The service here, seriously. It's a postmodern restaurant, like, the waiters are just actors acting the role of waiters but really aren't waiters and if you were hip enough to understand it you'd enjoy yourself. You're not going home for Christmas, are you Petra?

PETRA: No, oh no, my parents think I'm still in Japan and I'm not about to—so if they call, you know, don't—

STEPHEN: Yeah, I'm not going home either, first time too, this year I am standing *up* for myself. Because it would be self-loathing to go back there. My play I'm working on, it's actually about, it's about these certain events, this thing that happened in my hometown, this really, this *beautiful* and *devastating* thing actually—but—I'll tell you about it but I'm talking a lot. What about you Mark? What are you doing for Christmas?

MARK: I'll be here.

(Pause.)

STEPHEN: Well. Well then we are going, we are going to have a fabulous Christmas I've decided.

PETRA: I'm glad you decided that, ha.

STEPHEN: We will!

PETRA: I know, I know, I'm just teasing.

(Waiter drops a basket of bread on the table.)

Well.

STEPHEN: Bravo. *(Reaches for the bread)*

MARK: Can we say grace first? *(Stephen and Petra look at Mark)* I'd like to say grace.

STEPHEN: I think it'd be a first for this place. We're in Dante's Fifth Ring and you want to say grace.

(Mark bows his head.)

MARK: God, bless you for this food before us, and bless those less fortunate, those in pain, those in hunger, those in need of your beauty and your bounty. Amen.

PETRA AND STEPHEN: Amen.

(A beeper goes off. Mark checks, shuts it off. He takes a piece of bread. Stephen follows. Petra sips water.)

Scene 3

Apartment. Stage right living room, homemade wall center, stage left Stephen's bedroom. Far right wall is small kitchen unit, hall off leading to Petra's bedroom. Upstage of kitchen unit is door leading to tiny bathroom and shower. Living room: a couch, a bookshelf, coffee table, small entertainment system. Stephen's bedroom: loft bed, small desk, boxes. Living room windows look out on street, Stephen's bedroom windows look out on brick. Lights rise on Stephen on his loft bed, Mark on the couch on the phone. Petra emerges from her room, bundled up in a long coat.

MARK: —Well yeah. I can come in, well. Um. You should.

(Petra exits the apartment. Stephen looks up from his bed.)

Well like I said I'll have to. Oh? Well I suppose this is all. Great, especially for. Well I can come in I can. Anytime. Okay. That's fine. But like I said. Till I see it. Okay. Yeah. Till I. Well that's great that people are. But like I said. Okay. Okay that's fine. Okay. Bye.

(He hangs up the phone. He opens up a book. Stephen climbs off his loft bed, grabs his coat from the closet, enters the living room.)

STEPHEN: Hey.
MARK: Oh. Hi.
STEPHEN: Hey thanks again for dinner.
MARK: Oh. You're welcome but, I have all this money.
STEPHEN: Yeah. I was gonna—oh, whatcha reading?
MARK: The Bible.
STEPHEN *(Laughs)*: Ha. *(Stops)* Oh—the Bible, really?
MARK: The Good Book.
STEPHEN: The Good News Bible.
MARK: The King James version.
STEPHEN: Right. Right. Um. Well I was going to go down to the deli and get myself a Snapple or—how are you feeling, you want anything?
MARK: I'm fine.
STEPHEN: Snapple has this new peach juice which is—anyway, I'm just, I'm just going to *say* this however foreign to my nature it is to speak *directly, honestly,* you know, but, that's one of the things I've been working on, so. So. I just: I want to know you're okay. I guess. You've been really quiet, and . . .
MARK: I'm fine. Really. I know I'm. I know this is. Different. Unlikely even.
STEPHEN: Well yeah! Very—it's definitely a—*new you* here, ha.

MARK: With the help of the Lord, yes. A new. Me.

(*Pause.*)

STEPHEN: I'm just, I'm a little uneasy, it's been so long you know and I feel a little—*lost* with you—and of course, our history, you know, and—your coming back here without our discussing—what's really *happened* in the—in the time you've been—gone—*you*—you not being something we've discussed and why—when you could stay anywhere why—I mean I knew it was a rough time so I didn't want to push but—now—just to know—what's going through your head.

MARK: Right. Well. I think you'll find I tend to be more—silent and not. Interested. In the past. Because. It causes me pain to think about it. My life is about. The new me. In so many ways. In this way (*Holds up the Bible*) especially.

STEPHEN: Right. Right, well. And that's great, that's what you needed to—recover. And I understand, I guess I'm just being selfish, you know Petra's the same way: she was in Japan for over half a year, you know, stripping, and she's finally given it up, you know, she saved a lot of money and she's come back so now she has money to write and to—do what she wants without having to—you know, and which *is* great— and she's the same, not wanting to—*talk*, to *define* herself based on—so. So. It's hard for *me* but I understand.

MARK: The past is—bad news. It's only good news now. For me. And thank God. Thank God.

STEPHEN: Right, sure. It's just so—different. But—well—hell you know—maybe we're all—getting it together, which is great. Like our apartment is about *health* you know, *healthy* living—we're all—being *proactive*—not to sound, not to sound New Agey but . . .

MARK: You don't sound New Agey.

STEPHEN: Right, well, we're making *improvements*.

MARK: Absolutely. God bless us. It's not easy. This world.

STEPHEN: Yeah! Yeah, and I guess, and it doesn't have to be now, I guess though I just hope we will you know eventually have a chance to *talk*, really *talk*, about the past year and—you know? just to—and—well maybe I thought—I'd feel better if I—if we—hugged, I mean we haven't because—I do love you, not, not in the past way but in this new way, you know?

MARK: Change is traumatic. It will take getting used to. The past me, Stephen. That's someone else. Have faith in. This me. Have faith in me now and know all will. Will be all right.

STEPHEN: Right.

MARK: I'll give you a hug.

STEPHEN: Good.

(Mark stands, hugs Stephen briefly, breaks the hug.)

MARK: You're my only friend. Only true, real friend in this world. I was too terrified to go at it alone, to jump back into the. Real world. Without you. God bless you. I say prayers of thanks that I am here with you.

STEPHEN: Right, right, well great.

(The phone rings.)

MARK: Oh, give me some peace! Let the voice-mail get it.

STEPHEN: Who are these, are these the movie people?

MARK: Yes. Oh, Stephen. I have the option—because most of what was used ended up being mine—of putting my name on the film. Which I haven't—seen. This is. A dilemma.

STEPHEN: Oh.

MARK: They're sending me the cut. It doesn't really matter. The Lord will guide me.

STEPHEN: Right. Um—well I have to get going on these *blurbs* I— I hope I didn't—upset you or—I just get neurotic, still, I hate it.

MARK: Then give it up. Release yourself to the Holy Spirit. What's "neurotic"? What is that? Hand it to God, he'll know what to do with it. It won't be easy. But you can do it.

STEPHEN: Yeah. Yeah. God, it's a Marianne Williamson moment! Right—well—you're probably right. I'm just—so proud of you. And Petra. And glad you'll be getting to know each other, I always kept you two apart, I kept my life so compart-mentalized before, you know. Well I'll let you get back to your reading. God, when I was a kid, I was into this totally weird Wiccan stuff. —Anyway. You want anything from the deli?

MARK: I don't need anything.

STEPHEN: Okay. *(Goes to the door)* Um. And just anytime you need anything. *Anything.* I am here for you.

MARK: Thank you.

STEPHEN: Anything at all. Just knock on my door. Anytime no matter what. I want you to be well.

MARK: I will be. And God bless you.

STEPHEN: Right. Okay. Just—wanted to say that. So. Off to get my Snapple!

(Stephen goes. Mark opens the Bible.)

Scene 4

Petra, in a red gown, sits at a small table with a Man. Music. Drinks.

PETRA: Oh now, this is fantasy.

MAN: Petra, I swear to God. During office hours. Countless girls. Sliding their leg against mine or hiking up their—literally coming onto me like I can't tell you. It was this basic business class I was teaching. Yeah.

PETRA: No, I don't believe you, no: countless?

MAN: Are you in college?

PETRA: No.

MAN: Graduate.

PETRA: Yes.

MAN: Where did you go to school?

PETRA: Twenty questions we're playing here.

MAN: Okay. What was your major?

PETRA: Clearly, I mean, you're smiling like something's going on in that brain of yours, so what are you getting at?

MAN: Well, you're smart, you're perceptive, maybe I've a little theory I'm working on. Acting?

PETRA: Oh God please, say anything but that.

MAN: Well then. No. Okay. But you did this to pay for school, you danced?

PETRA: I had a scholarship, a very substantial scholarship, but not nearly enough to live on, and I knew that this was the only thing I could—

MAN: Creative writing.

PETRA: Who have you been talking to? Which girl? Joanna?

MAN: Joanna, no. Joanna gives hand jobs.

PETRA: I don't.

MAN: Whoa! I didn't ask you if you did, I wasn't asking you to, I was telling you, no, I don't care to talk to Joanna. I like you. I want to hear you talk about your interesting life. I say that without irony. I mean it: you, you are interesting to me.

PETRA: Listen I had a poetry professor at NYU—

MAN: Ahh, NYU girl.

PETRA: No, listen: National Book Award this man won, and constantly, *constantly* asked me out to have "beer" with him, a "beer." I said I don't drink. Said why don't we go "work out" together. You believe this? Oh, no, I don't work out I say. Office hours: tells me my poems give him *erections*. Tells me he graded my poems, hands me the paper says, see this, this is my come on your poems, guess I gotta give you an A-plus. I am—I am eighteen years old, I am from Queens, my father doesn't barely know how to *write* or *read* and here is Mr. National Book Award, and my father was a decent man, he was—he was the kind of man who calls radio call-in shows and says I'm a white man and I can tell you that whites are still racist against blacks. So I know this is wrong, this man is *wrong*. But I am stunned and can barely move—I am smiling—I have no idea what to *say*. So he makes a joke, whatever, and I say, okay, and I gotta go, and I get an A-plus in the class. And I'm eighteen years old. So you're telling me girls are pulling up their *skirts* and—no. And if this is so, this is depressing.

MAN: See, the class I taught was a night class and maybe those girls tend to be more desperate. But hey, I always said no. I did. So if you stripped to get through school, and you went over to Japan and made a lot of money, what uh, why are you doing it now? What's the reason now?

PETRA: Well, what do *you* think? Why don't *you* tell me. Ha.

MAN: No, no, I know I've been talking a lot. But I really want to know from *you*.

(Pause.)

PETRA: Listen, I'm sorry, I'm just a little uncomfortable here, I think maybe you should talk with one of the other girls.

MAN: No, please. Here.

(He puts down a fifty-dollar bill on the table.)

Please.

(She stops for a moment. Then goes.)

Scene 5

The apartment, dark. Mark sits on his couch-bed, under covers, the phone pressed to his ear. Door opens, Petra enters tired. Mark hangs up the phone, door slams shut.

MARK *(Quietly)*: Hey.
PETRA: Oh, I didn't wake you up, did I?
MARK: No. I baked some cookies, couldn't sleep. Want one?
PETRA: Oh, I don't eat carbohydrates or sugar.
MARK: I'm sorry.
PETRA: Me too, ha. But sugar, I think it makes you depressed, it's not widely known. And carbohydrates turn to sugar—so I'm doing an experiment of cutting it out.
MARK: Good for you, Petra.
PETRA: But, I have this job interview in the morning so I should go to sleep. Stephen asleep?
MARK: Before you go to sleep, I made you this. *(Hands her a card)*
PETRA: Oh, you made this yourself?
MARK: I just wanted to let you know how much I appreciate your allowing me to stay here. How blessed I feel.
PETRA: Oh, how sweet. Oh, thank you.
MARK: So. Good night.
PETRA: Well, good night to you too. I hope it's warm enough in here.
MARK: It is. —Hey.

(Mark stands and walks over to Petra, gives her a big hug.)

PETRA: Oh.

(A few more seconds, then the hug breaks.)

MARK: Thank you.

PETRA: You're so sweet. Thank you again for the card. It's beautiful.

(Mark goes back to the couch.)

Good night.

MARK: Good night. And hey. Good for you, Petra.

PETRA *(Stops, turns)*: What?

MARK: Good for you for quitting stripping.

Scene 6

East Village street. Mark sits with pad, sketching. Tan, late teens, dressed in old jeans, a long-sleeve T-shirt and a wool hat, sees Mark, watches.

TAN: Hey, got a smoke?

(Mark turns to him.)

MARK: Sorry, I don't smoke.

TAN: No? Wow. 'Cuz you look like you do.

MARK: Sorry.

(Mark turns back to sketching.)

TAN: So why not me? *(No response. Tan moves closer, laughs)* I mean, hey, people in a coffeehouse, three o'clock, artists, musicians, whatever, man. Sitting smoking blah blah blah you know? Why draw that? I mean how interesting are *they*? That's shit, you know? That's like—a bowl of fruit—or my asshole—would be a better subject.

(Mark smiles politely, continues to sketch. Tan lights a cigarette. Mark looks at him.)

It's my last one. Whatever. You want one?

MARK: I told you.

TAN: Yeah, I know what you told me.

(Pause.)

'Kay then. Hey you wanna make a bet?

MARK: A bet.

TAN: I bet you ten bucks I can guess what brand of underwear you got on.

MARK: Ha, I don't uh.

TAN: Bet it's Calvin Klein.

(Beat.)

MARK: You're wrong.

TAN: I guess I owe you ten bucks. I don't got it though. Hey if you can't guess what kind I'm wearing we'll be even. Wanna find out?

MARK: No.

(Beat. Tan lifts up his shirt, reveals underwear sticking up out of his jeans.)

TAN: Fruit of the Loom!

Scene 7

Late lunch. Midtown restaurant.

PETRA: You know: *What was your major? Oh have I read anything of yours? Oh my daughter just graduated from law school and she wrote a legal thriller, kind of a John Grisham except a female version.*

STEPHEN: Brilliant.

PETRA: Then he asks me what I write. So I think—so I decide to tell him, who knows, I think, don't judge, okay?, maybe he really cares—you know, I give him the spiel. And he nods and says: *So why does this job interest you, Patricia?*

STEPHEN: Mmm-hmmm.

PETRA: So barely an hour ago this is, I still feel two feet tall. So I say, Look—I'm very blunt—I *say*, "I'm looking to work in a positive, stable environment, where I feel supported, where my work is appreciated, where there's a sense of structure."

And I say, and I say, "Because this sense of structure has been missing from my life." And he says: *Do you know PowerPoint? Do you know Excel? Do you know Quark?* No. No. No. And then! Then: *I actually majored in literature for about a year as an undergraduate, do you believe that?* And he's laughing; and I'm *not* laughing. I say Yes. Yes, I do believe that. Because I will not let him know I feel *humiliated.* Because I will have *dignity* even if—and he says: *Well* and they'll be in touch and on and on and then I'm on the street.

STEPHEN: Well I'm just—it's enough to make you want to go back to stripping.

PETRA: Well I won't do that.

(Beat.)

I mean, I dressed appropriately, right?

STEPHEN: Yes! God, I am so far behind in these blurb reviews, I have to get back.

PETRA: Right.

STEPHEN: I mean I have a few more minutes but. Who are these people? Oh—my boss wants to see me at four, who knows what that's about.

PETRA: Well, I try to count my blessings but—I can't believe you're eating that burger.

STEPHEN: I know, it's disgusting, isn't it. I wonder what Mark's doing right now.

PETRA: He's a sweetheart, Stephen.

STEPHEN: Yeah—but this Bible stuff. Whoa, you know.

PETRA: It bothers you?

STEPHEN: No, it's okay I mean—but—I just feel like we haven't . . . yeah, I mean, of *course* it bothers me—"The Lord will provide"? But. But I've never been addicted to crack, so. So what do I know. I mean, is he even sleeping with men anymore? I dunno, I just feel like I don't—those missing—oh I dunno, I'm just nervous really about this grant which I should be hearing about but—I wish we had more time, I feel so rushed, it's so hard to connect like this, you know, but—well what are you doing tonight?

PETRA: Oh, I'm seeing some old girlfriends really late—Christmassy thing. After this I'm gonna go to the library before it closes.

STEPHEN: Well we'll catch up. Hey have you seen *Men in Black*?

PETRA: No.

STEPHEN: No. Oh well. I sort of like Will Smith. *(Picking up check)* Christ, I have to stop this, my bank account is *fucked.*

PETRA: Yeah, Will Smith's very charming. They love him in Japan.

STEPHEN: Yeah, yeah, he's good.

Scene 8

The apartment. Tan sits on the couch, reads a magazine. Mark sits at the table with his pad.

TAN: "How to Get and Keep a Man in Your Bed." People live like this?

MARK: I don't know.

TAN: "Bulimia's Grip." "AIDS and Women: The Unreported Risks." "Leonardo DiCaprio Loves His Mom." Fuck, I'm cuter than Leonardo DiCaprio, he has *no* muscle. *Cosmopolitan* bullshit. I partied with him once, what a *dork.* So a chick lives here, I hope. *(Tan grabs remote, turns on TV: MTV)* Man this song *bites.* Fucking *poseurs.* Man this world is just full of fucking *poseurs.*

MARK: Could you turn that off.

TAN: What.

MARK: I just. I like to control what I. Expose myself to.

TAN: You mean you don't like MTV.

MARK: Well. Sort of.

TAN: 'Kay.

(He shuts it off. A beat.)

So look I'm waiting for you to take your dick out and it's been like half an hour and I'm getting a little nervous. *(Mark laughs)* I'm not a hustler.

MARK: I should hope you're not. I didn't expect that you were.

TAN: There's only one thing I do for money. I have a specialty. Thing I do I'm famous for is I jerk off on the street. Bare-assed, you know, bare *feet,* not a thing on, just me and my shit. In public, anywhere—it costs a lot because of the risk involved.

When a guy tries to pick me up that's what I say, I say I do one thing and it costs three hundred bucks but you've never seen anyone do anything like it and you never will again.

MARK: Sounds dangerous.

TAN: Do you mind if I just jerk off for myself? You can just watch. *(Smiles)* No charge.

MARK: If you want to do that, you should leave.

TAN: So why would you draw people in a coffeehouse, artists and shit? That's boring. What are you?

MARK: What am I? I am a filmmaker.

TAN: Oh yeah? You make movies?

MARK: I made one.

TAN: Huh. I know famous people. I told you I partied with Leonardo DiCaprio, dude is *soft.* So um if you like to control what you expose yourself to why'd you invite me over?

MARK: Look. You can leave, I mean. You're free to do whatever you want. I'm not here to. Do anything. To. I just thought. I thought I was being kind. I thought I would show you some kindness.

TAN: Yeah, what's that line, "I have always depended on the kindness of strangers," or whatever. Cool movie. Ha. Right. Okay. I got. What do I got. *(Takes a plastic baggie of pills out of his pocket, lays it on table)* These are not cheap either because these are good, just so you know. I got three Valium—I crush 'em up and snort 'em, you absorb it quicker that way . . . a few quaaludes. I have these things, basically they're like prescription strength Motrin, they're not opiate-based so basically they're just for if you have a very bad headache. Got some black tar from a friend out west . . . So.

MARK: I am a recovering drug addict.

TAN: Oh. Wow. Recovering, does that mean . . .

MARK: It means I've been sober for five months.

TAN: So are you a fag or what?

(The door opens. Christmas tree. Stephen enters behind tree. Tan puts the drugs away.)

STEPHEN: I got a treee-eee! I got a treee-eee!

(Stephen sees.)

Oh. Hi.

MARK: That's a beautiful tree.

STEPHEN: Well, I have to take the wires off, we'll see then. Of course it's too big and there's no space but I figured if we're going to have a beautiful Christmas we need a beautiful tree. Hi, I'm Stephen.

TAN: Hey. Yeah, there's nothing fucking worse than X-mas in New York.

MARK: Stephen, this is Tan.

STEPHEN: Tan? Tan's a—where did you get that name, it's great.

TAN *(Standing)*: Yeah man, Mark invited me over to take a shower, I thought he was *weird* or something but he's, like, the pope, so. City's driving me crazy, man! The *music*—BLAH BLAH BLAH BLAH BLAH BLAH, BLAH BLAH ALL THE WAY— ha!—yeah—you know—and people aren't happy. Couple days they'll be like joining *gyms* and buying the *patch* and shit.

STEPHEN: Right. Well, only a few more days of that I guess, so you'll survive. Anyway—I'll just dig up the ornaments and maybe, all of us, we can decorate the tree. I bought some Christmas music too—cheapo cassettes from the Duane Reade—and uhh alcohol-free egg nog. *(Pulls the tapes and the egg nog from the bag and puts them on the kitchen counter)* The ornaments and the lights and stuff are somewhere in my room, so.

(Stephen goes into his room. Throughout the following, we see him looking around his cluttered room for decorations.)

TAN: He cool?

MARK: Sorry?

TAN: What's he do?

MARK: He writes . . . movie reviews for an online magazine.

TAN: Cool. You two uhh? . . .

MARK: No.

TAN: Cool. Hey you know, look, I'm just—I'm not a squatter, okay, I have my own place, I support myself.

MARK: Yes?

TAN: I left home you know because my parents—and school—and me being—all that shit. But I don't want you to think I'm some, like, street-kid poseur 'cuz I'm *not*, some fucking—

MARK: Okay.

71

TAN: Yeah. So. *(Beat)* I wanna kiss you, man. You're sweet. You're weird.

MARK: You can't kiss me.

TAN: Why not?

(Stephen enters with a box.)

STEPHEN: Here we go. Hey, was there anything in the mail for me today?

MARK: Just the *Nation.*

STEPHEN: Right. Well. Let's take a look!

(Stephen undoes the wires; the tree spreads out.)

TAN: Hey, I think I'll take that shower now.

MARK: All right.

(Tan goes into the bathroom. Stephen looks at the tree. The shower turns on.)

STEPHEN *(Turning to Mark)*: Hey.

MARK: Hi.

(Stephen puts ornaments onto the couch.)

I feel as though you're upset with me.

STEPHEN: No—no. This is your home. My home is . . .

MARK: I thought a shower. He was so. Obviously hungry and I was reminded of. I guess he reminded me of—myself and. Clearly this is someone who's been shown no love, and—it seemed like the Christian thing to do.

STEPHEN: I'm just surprised all your Bible talk didn't scare him off.

MARK: What does that mean?

STEPHEN: Nothing—I don't mean—anything.

MARK: And I thought well maybe I should show some discretion but. But why show discretion because. Because of how we're taught to treat. People. Because how we treat them sometimes—makes them what they are.

STEPHEN: Absolutely.

MARK: Good.

(Pause.)

STEPHEN: So this is the part where you ask about my day.

MARK: I'm sorry. How was your day?

(Stephen starts to put a few decorations on the tree.)

STEPHEN: They did not like, listen to this, they did not like my *blurbs*, my blurbs were *rejected*, two of the four because, they said, they used words like *brisk* and *self-assured* as being qualities my blurbs did not *have*, you know, meaning, these are not *arch* enough—straight-faced, I'm sitting in the office, I'm nervous actually nervous, and, and have you noticed this trend among women, this trend where they do not *like* homosexual men, I mean I know that's a dangerous generality but she said, "These are too *soft*, these lack *punch*," I mean, she might as well have said I don't have the *balls* to write a blurb of *Men in Black*. So. So now I have to rewrite the blurbs and it's like, look, I don't want to go back to temping, which was which was *soul-murder*, which was pure degradation every hour on the hour, and I certainly do not want to "bartend" again and it's getting to the point where it's like— I mean I'm not gonna *move* where would I *move* Los Angeles? and it's—but what, can I do to make money that will not take all my energy and slowly and utterly *kill* me because I have been there before, you know, Huck Finn, "I've been there before," and, you know, he's off floating on a raft and happy and won't be civilized and of course he won't go back, he's a bright guy, but then, you know, Mark Twain wrote the book, not Huck Finn— *(Apartment buzzer)* Well. Saved by the buzzer just as I was getting incoherent. But I am, I'm enraged, and am I *wrong*, you know, am I *indulgent*, well I say *No* because that's what they want me to think so I'll shut up and be a good little— *(Pushing intercom button)* Hello?

PETRA *(Offstage)*: Hi I need help down here.

STEPHEN: Help?

PETRA *(Offstage)*: Come down.

STEPHEN: Okay. *(Lets go of buzzer, looks at Mark)* I hope everything's okay.

(Stephen goes. Tan emerges from bathroom, not wet, shower running. He's wrapped in a towel.)

TAN: Where'd whatshisname go?

MARK: Downstairs for a moment. Is something wrong?

TAN: Well the water pressure was bitching which shocked me so I should have known something was wrong. Um. It just wouldn't get hot. You know. Or even warm. It's ice. *(Mark looks away)* Everything okay?

MARK: Yeah.

TAN: Okay. Hey, can I borrow some underwear?

MARK: Sure.

(Mark goes to a bag, gets underwear, hands them to Tan.)

TAN: Calvin Klein. Cool. So why'd you invite me here, for real.

MARK: I've told you. *(Beat)* I baked a pie this morning. Would you like a piece?

TAN: Pie?

MARK: Apple pie.

TAN: Whatever.

(Tan goes back into the bathroom. Shower cuts off. Door opens. A tree.)

STEPHEN: Surprise!

(Stephen and Petra enter, with the tree, which is smaller than the first.)

PETRA: I had no idea. Ridiculous, can you believe it?

STEPHEN: It's a great New York story.

PETRA: Two trees we have.

STEPHEN: I told Petra this'd be our affirmative action tree—we'll put Kwanzaa and Hanukkah ornaments on it.

PETRA: Don't forget Solstice, people are getting into this whole Solstice thing.

(Stephen puts the tree in an opposite corner, sets it against the wall.)

I wanted to cheer myself up because of this interview, so I bought it.

MARK: Petra, do you want a piece of pie?

PETRA: Pie?

MARK: Apple p—that's right, the—

PETRA *(Laughs):* —no carbs.

MARK: How about it, Stephen. Let's have some pie.

STEPHEN: Well—all right.

PETRA: Oh, the best part I didn't tell you, the best part was how the guy kept telling me how skinny I was, at the interview, during, and finally he goes and comes back with a bagel. He says, *You're going to eat this,* and then I had to explain the whole no-carb thing to him.

STEPHEN: This no-carb thing sounds like a cult.

(Tan comes out of the bathroom fully dressed.)

TAN: Hey.

STEPHEN: Hey, Tan. We have two trees to decorate now. You wanna help?

TAN: I actually have a thing to go to, so, you know how it is.

MARK: You're leaving?

STEPHEN: Tan, this is Petra. Petra, Tan.

PETRA: Hello.

TAN: Hey. Yeah, so. Hey, thanks for the underwear.

MARK: You're welcome.

TAN: Yeah . . . Fuck, I'm looking for a jacket, I'm realizing I don't have one! Stupid!

STEPHEN: Oh, you should have a coat.

TAN: Whatever, global warming, El Niño, I'm okay.

STEPHEN: I'm sure I have a coat you can take.

TAN: I don't know, will it match my sensibility? Ha.

STEPHEN: Well . . .

PETRA: I have a man's hat you're welcome to take.

TAN: Got a hat. *(Takes it from his pocket, throws it on)*

STEPHEN *(Grabbing a long, gray overcoat from the closet):* Here, I don't wear this.

TAN: Really? *(Takes it, puts it on)* Cool, I look like a dirty old man, like a flasher or somebody. *(He "flashes" and laughs)* Okay, merry X-mas, joy on earth, peace to the world, all that shit. *("Bye")* Bah!

STEPHEN: Bye.

MARK: Bye, Tan.

(Tan goes. A moment.)

PETRA: So . . . who was that?

STEPHEN: Friend of Mark's. He was struck by the Christmas spirit and offered a streetboy a place to shower. He seems like a nice kid.

MARK: He is.

STEPHEN: That's sad.

MARK: He said the water didn't get hot.

STEPHEN: The shower? Really?

(Stephen goes into the bathroom. Shower cuts on. Mark exits.)

PETRA: How was your day, Mark?

MARK *(Offstage)*: I did a sketch today. How was your day?

PETRA: I suppose it could have been worse.

MARK *(Offstage)*: That's a good attitude to have.

(Stephen returns.)

STEPHEN: Hot water's fine.

(Mark returns with a piece of pie on a plate and a fork.)

MARK: Huh.

STEPHEN: Maybe he didn't know how to turn it on or something.

MARK *(Laughs)*: Well, I'm sure that wasn't it, it's a knob.

STEPHEN: Well—okay. Well maybe you're right. Maybe he didn't want to take a shower, how's that. So—tonight we decorate? Petra?

PETRA: Oh, remember tonight I'm going out with some old girlfriends? And I have to find some time to read tonight, I'm behind in my reading.

STEPHEN: Okay. Well we'll find a time we can all do it. Mark, maybe we'll go to a movie. I was telling Mark they rejected my blurbs today.

PETRA: Oh, really?

STEPHEN: Yeah, I don't want to talk about it.

PETRA: Well, I am going to take a little nap I think.

STEPHEN: Okay.

(Petra goes.)

So. Movie.

MARK: Actually, you know. This will sound—odd, but. I don't go to movies anymore.

STEPHEN: Oh.

MARK: It's just. I like to control what I. Expose myself to.

STEPHEN: Well not every movie is directed by Quentin Tarantino.

MARK: I know that. Here.

(Mark hands Stephen the plate of pie with fork and goes off.)

(Offstage) Yeah I think I'll just read and take a shower and get to bed early tonight.

(Stephen goes to couch and sits.)

STEPHEN: Okay. Well. Well maybe it's the perfect time to finish my Christmas shopping. I just figured out what I'm going to get you.

(Mark returns with a bottle of water.)

Well maybe tonight after I shop we'll just hang out and talk, we can talk—

(Stephen takes a bite of pie. Mark goes to the couch, sits.)

MARK: I'll be asleep when you get back most likely.

STEPHEN *(Chewing)*: Oh, right. Where's your piece?

MARK: I'm not having one.

STEPHEN: —Oh.

(Mark smiles. So does Stephen. Mark takes a sip of water. Stephen swallows his bite of pie.)

Scene 9

Strip club. Petra with the same Man as before.

PETRA: Before he died, then, you actually knew him.

MAN: I used to go to this diner all the time he worked at, you know, by where I work, the show was going up, we were all real excited for him—he was just our waiter, at the time.

PETRA: Wow.

MAN: Do you like it? You've seen it?

PETRA: I have.

MAN: You said you lived in the East Village, so I—

PETRA: No, I understand.

MAN: I mean, you're not—perhaps I'm being dumb, or presumptuous, I mean, what do I know? . . .

PETRA: You're not being dumb.

MAN: But you don't like the show, or? The critics, they liked it, people, people seem to—standing ovation the night I saw it—Pulitzer Prize. So I'm interested in why, if—isn't that—East Village—but—why don't you talk.

PETRA: Look—thirteen-year-old kids, fat girls, gay boys, they love it, so. I don't, truly, I don't think about it. No. If I did think about it I would get angry because. Because it's another example of. It's—*condescending*.

MAN: How is that?

PETRA: Because. Because I work hard and. I work to try to be an *artist*—which, it's an embarrassment to even use that word—

MAN: Why?

PETRA: Listen—I read. I work hard. And what the show says to me is—is am I indecent, or, or am "selling out" or am I *inauthentic* because I want, I want money or, or an apartment which is even just *decent*? I mean when do any of those characters *read*? What are they *doing* with all their time, I don't—and we *celebrate* these people, and don't get me wrong, everyone is *valuable*, but, but *what* are we celebrating?

MAN: Life. The artistic life. Refusal to compromise. Right?

PETRA: Wanna know who lives in the East Village? A lot of the actors in the show that's who. Those characters, it's like Peter Pan Neverland, refusal to grow up, join the real—I know it's a *musical* but it avoids asking any real, I mean, *genuine* questions and instead makes—makes a mockery of, my roommate said this and I agree—makes a *spectacle* of AIDS, gays, lesbians, blacks—it—*commodifies* actual—and tell me these people who are in it and who directed it have no idea how they're mocking themselves and their—their own *choices*—oh whatever.

MAN: No, no, please, this is!—You're . . . how can I say this . . . threatened by them. By these characters.

PETRA: Well. What I was going to say was. I'm not used to having to think too hard when I'm here.

MAN: Change the subject then. I want to hear one of your poems.

PETRA: Oh come on.

MAN: Why are you embarrassed? My goodness, the fact that you write poems—is fascinating to me! Would you tell me one?

PETRA: I, they're written down, so.

MAN: See, you are just—who you are—comes through and is—fascinating! So. So I know this isn't—I'm not stupid—*(Takes out his wallet)* I'm under no— *(Puts money on the table)* There. For a poem. For one poem.

PETRA: I'll talk to you but. No.

MAN: Okay. Okay. We talk. Here: I just saw this movie? *Boogie Nights*? What did you think of it?

PETRA: All those movies, *Trainspotting*, *Boogie Nights*, I—I can't.

MAN: Can't? . . . You don't . . . obviously don't.

PETRA: It's immoral because—I live in *this world* and—they—they romanticize—and *ignore*—what—they leave out of this *experience*, this, being *alive*—and I think: Is this what I must include? To be *valued*? Rewarded? *Depravity*? To be seen must I write what is more or less—more or less *pornography*, something that *titillates* with violence and sex? Or else—*My Best Friend's Wedding* and *The Celestine Prophecy*? Do you see?

MAN: I come here you know.

PETRA: You—?

MAN: You say: I live in this world. And I am interested in your opinions. I ask you about these plays and movies, which *I* see, which *you* see . . .

PETRA *(I don't understand what you meant by "I come here")*: You come here?

MAN: Here. How can I . . . ?

PETRA: Oh—it just gets me so angry. Drugs—drugs are not—violence, real violence, life, *life*—the poor, criminals, it is not—we romanticize it—it is like—a drug—like—the trauma, the trauma of actually seeing this world is such that we create fantasies, we reward those who create *fantasies* because God forbid we look at—reality—at *ourselves*—there are people in this country, *other people* who are fascinating and, and *troubled*—and yet—where are they?—and New York and Los Angeles constantly dump this—shit this shit

79

into this country, and people will—eat it because they're *hungry*—these *crumbs*—and I don't—I'm not judging those who watch or, or *read* this stuff—I watch it too sometimes—but I blame those who—look—I am trying to *transcend*—but there are pressures which prevent me—many *pressures* and—I mean you say, You say: I come here. I say: I work here.

MAN: I come here for fantasy. Is what I was going to say. And what is so wrong with fantasy? If that's what we need to live. Because. Don't we all have fantasies?

PETRA: But there's a moral . . . in terms of *art* . . . *(She stops)* I'm sorry.

MAN: Here's the deal. I want you to show me your life. Because it is so distant from my life. This is why I go to movies, and plays. And come here. And so I know, I am aware that perhaps you will find this—distasteful. Or immoral even. But you would get to see my life. Which you, you could not fathom. Where I work. The conversations I have. I am asking for—some time—dinner, dates, you will take me to coffee where you have coffee, I will take you to dinner where I have dinner. I don't—I'm a gentle man—and I am a—frightened man—and curious—and I don't—I know without money I am nothing to you. I am a very rich person, and I have herpes so I don't really have sex anymore.

(Pause.)

PETRA: Let me ask you this. Why if you are interested in getting to know somebody, in intimacy, why would you come here? To a pornographic place?

MAN: You're right. But I'll pay you not to come here. To accompany me as though—

PETRA: But why—in the first place—you're—you have money—you're—nice—and attractive—

MAN: Oh, come now. You tell me, how else might I have met you. In a club? Come up to you in some club in Tribeca, "Hey, how are you?"

PETRA: But—I'm not talking about just *me*—

MAN: I am. I find *you* fascinating. I don't find my secretary fascinating, I'm sorry.

(Pause.)

PETRA: I work here, this is my job, I don't go home as this person, I—

MAN: Here. *(Takes out a hundred dollar bill and writes on it)* Now you can call me and. Call me and just. Talk to me about your life. And then. We can get together and have dinner and coffee a couple of times and I will pay you for your time. *(Rising)* Take care, Petra.

(He goes. She takes the hundred dollars.)

Act Two

Scene 1

Christmas Eve day. An apartment. Darren is sitting on a couch, flipping through some channels. Stephen is pouring and steeping tea. A lava lamp on a nightstand, red globs in yellow water. Darren has a slight, ambiguous, Britishy-sounding accent.

DARREN: I'm glad you called. I didn't know why you didn't call.

STEPHEN: Oh, yeah. No I really liked you, I just, I was so overwhelmed and I've *been* so overwhelmed but lately I've just been feeling such a need to *connect*, things have been so—it's probably just the holidays, but. You know, God, these teacups are gorgeous! I mean that's kind of a weird thing to say, but. Do you, sugar, or? Darren?

DARREN: Oh, yeah, just—this show. Yeah, an embarrassing amount of sugar. Yeah, that set was a thousand dollars, the cups and the plates and stuff.

STEPHEN: *What?*

DARREN: Oh, that's right, you don't know—I sold a screenplay.

STEPHEN: Oh, you did?

DARREN: Yeah, *and* made a deal to coproduce the soundtrack. Three hundred thousand dollars against seven hundred.

STEPHEN: Oh my God! Well that's extraordinary! Well—my God!

DARREN: Yeah, like four spoonfuls.

STEPHEN: Okay. Well what's the screenplay about?

DARREN: Oh, you know, romantic comedy, East Villagers meeting cute, you know, stockbroker guy runs into squatter girl at ATM, blah blah blah the end.

STEPHEN: Well congratulations!

DARREN: Are you still working on that play?

STEPHEN: Yeah, I am.

DARREN: What's it about again?

STEPHEN: This incredible thing that happened in my hometown, this amazingly beautiful—

DARREN: Where are you from again?

STEPHEN: Darien, Connecticut? Kind of, kind of upper-middle-class suburb, about an hour away.

(Stephen comes to the couch with the tea.)

DARREN: So what are you doing for Christmas Eve tonight?

STEPHEN: Oh, um . . .

DARREN: I have to make the rounds at these endless horrible parties. Then I have to go out to la-la land on the twenty-sixth, so it's kind of a truncated holiday.

STEPHEN: Right. Yeah, I'm not going home to my family, first time actually, that would just be self-loathing, and I have two friends in town so—

DARREN: Do you like my lava lamp? I can't make up my mind about it.

STEPHEN: Oh—I don't like them in general. I always, I always thought they kind of looked like, I don't know, an abortion or something.

DARREN: Really?

STEPHEN: Yeah.

DARREN: That's kind of witty.

STEPHEN: Oh?

DARREN: There's *nothing* on.

STEPHEN: So how's Maria?

DARREN: Maria?

STEPHEN: What was her name? Marla?

DARREN: Magda, my friend Magda. Hey. I have something you'll like. *(Puts in a tape)* Watch this. *(Sits back on the couch)*

STEPHEN: God it's so *nice* to have a day off. Oh. Oh God.

DARREN: This is that homemade porno—

STEPHEN: Oh.

DARREN: They *totally* wanted it released, I mean gimmie a break—I have a friend who gets all these, he got the, remember the Rob Lowe tape?, but that's pretty boring. This is *hot*. Look at how big Tommy Lee's dick is. That's a fucking beautiful cock, you have to admit.

STEPHEN: Wow, it's really them. Pamela Anderson. Wow. *(Darren puts his hand in his pants, starts moving it around)* Oh. Oh God you know. Maybe. I feel—I hope I didn't imply by just—calling up and coming over—that I wanted to— *(Darren unzips his fly, reaches in that way)* You know, I think I'm gonna go.

DARREN: Aw, come on.

STEPHEN: Yeah, I don't . . . I don't know. Yeah, I think I'm gonna go.

DARREN: Hey, I'll stop the tape. No big deal.

STEPHEN: You know it's—I didn't, I just didn't expect you know—I hope I'm not—I just, I just—

DARREN: Do you have an erection?

STEPHEN: What?

DARREN: I'm asking if you have a hard-on. We'll just beat off.

STEPHEN: Well, I mean—

DARREN: If you're not gonna answer me—

(Darren reaches for Stephen's crotch. Stephen spills his tea.)

STEPHEN: Oh—

DARREN: Ow! —You didn't have to spill the tea, Stephen—fuck! Ouch.

STEPHEN: I didn't mean to—my unconscious talking I guess.

DARREN: Well why don't you leave before your unconscious breaks my VCR or my lava lamp.

STEPHEN: Good idea. Hah. Well my therapist will love hearing about this.

DARREN: Okay.

STEPHEN: My jacket.

(Stephen gets his jacket, puts it on. Darren goes into the bathroom. Water running.)

You know, I was just, just hoping to talk, you know, about, just. Sorry. Okay. Well, hey, have a good Christmas.

DARREN (*Offstage*): You, too.

(*Stephen hesitates. Touches his crotch, rubs. He looks off to the bathroom, looks quickly to the TV.*)

Hello?

STEPHEN: Yeah, no, I'm going—I just—I'll call you when—I mean I like you I feel—it's not that I don't want to, to—I just—

DARREN (*Offstage*): Okay, gotcha. Take care!

STEPHEN: You, too!

(*Stephen goes.*)

Scene 2

A restaurant, fancy, conservative. Classical piano plays from far off.

MAN: So what are you doing after dinner. How are you spending your Christmas Eve?

PETRA: Well, my two roommates are . . . we're exchanging gifts. And it's been a nightmare.

MAN: What's going on?

PETRA: Basically, my roommate Stephen's ex-lover, his name is Mark, had this big deal in Hollywood, started filming this movie, started doing a lot of drugs, then towards the end of it I guess basically had a nervous breakdown—so he went into rehab and became—found God more or less. And he's become friends with this street kid who's obviously unhealthy and on drugs and—he's ignoring Stephen, so. And this is very hard for Stephen to understand. So basically.

MAN: Wow.

PETRA: What.

MAN: Fascinating. *People. Their lives.* My God.

PETRA: What are *you* doing tonight?

MAN: Nothing. Watch TV. Tomorrow I'm gonna drive to Connecticut and see my folks. (*Beat*) What do you think of this restaurant?

PETRA: It's lovely. I'm so excited for my monkfish.

MAN: The monkfish, I've had it before. It's good.

PETRA: I can't wait.

MAN: Can I ask you a question?

PETRA: Yes.

MAN: And by the way, you look beautiful tonight. Stunning.

PETRA: Thank you.

MAN: Do your roommates tell you you're beautiful?

PETRA: No.

MAN: Well they should.

PETRA: You're sweet.

MAN: Why do you strip. *(Beat)* Why do you keep—when obviously you don't have to.

PETRA: Oh, is that obvious?

MAN: Is it material? Do you get good material?

PETRA: God, no.

MAN: So it's really just. The money.

PETRA: Well . . .

MAN: New York City's so expensive.

PETRA: Well, yes, but it's. Where. I feel I have to be.

MAN: It's a big country.

PETRA: But—here—the arts—that industry is . . . here. And I grew up here, to leave . . .

MAN: I see these guys at the club. You put yourself through a lot of misery.

PETRA: There's a lot—really—that I enjoy about dancing. A lot that I find fulfilling but. You know, office work is no less demeaning. And yes, I do believe I learn, or see, have access to particular men, there's a rare intimacy about the setting.

MAN: But it must make you crazy.

PETRA: Crazy.

MAN: You can tell me if I'm wrong.

PETRA: I . . . enjoy it. Dancing I. It makes me feel good.

MAN: Good how?

PETRA: It makes me feel special.

(Pause.)

MAN: I write poems sometimes, you know. *(Beat)* Does that surprise you?

PETRA: No.

MAN: You want to be a writer, but I—well—I just dabble, nothing serious, just for me. See generally I run away. I go to a spa. I see a movie. Take a trip. That's what I do. But you. You walk headfirst into it—your pain—every day. You have to, else you wouldn't be a writer.

PETRA: No.

MAN: No?

PETRA: No, because pain—and consciousness—both are difficult but—I should hope there's a difference between the two. I think I am *conscious*. But pain—I don't want my pain any more than you want yours.

MAN: See, that's what I—I mean, what *makes* you an artist? What happened to make you—I know how I got into investment banking, it's a pretty simple story. But you. This *person* you are, this *life*, what made you—how did it happen?

PETRA: Okay. Okay. I'm a freshman in college. A dorm, like a prison, falling apart, roaches, like rats in a lab we are, okay? My roommate is—Dominican or something—and one night she makes this big greasy pot of fish, in this very greasy yellow sauce, and she leaves it simmering on the stove. She goes out to meet her boyfriend. I go into the kitchen. I open the pot. Me. And it looks like sewage. A huge—ridiculous this pot is. And I take out a spoon and think: I'll try this. And I do. I take another bite. Another. And I know, I am a rational being, I know she's cooked this for her boyfriend, they'll be back soon—the whole pot. All of it. And I run into the bathroom and I sit there I'm numb I put my hand into my mouth, okay? And I'm covered there in—fish—covered— I look—a ghoul—green, literally—and I'm thinking: *What?* Because I know enough to know this is not normal or healthy in any way and I want to know: *Why?* Why would I have done this? Why do I feel this way? What in the world—literally, what in the world—in which I find myself living, what at this point in history, what could make a person feel this unbearable sadness and think these terrible thoughts? These thoughts: *I will never be loved. I cannot live in this world.* You see? Because—because my roommate is going to come home and say, Where is the fish, and the only answer is, Petra ate it. Petra ate the fish. And how can I go on? How can I go on without—and I know—that there are people who do not ask this question—because to know—is too much. Because society does not *afford* them the opportunity to know, and. Because they are in a constant state of *desire* and desire, *want*, inhibits consciousness. To become conscious you must stifle yourself, resist your impulses. Not that I had this language then. But I knew; I decided. I decided next time I would not eat the fish. No matter what. No matter what pain that caused me I would put the fork down and place the lid on the pot and.

(Pause.)

MAN: What's your name?
PETRA: My name is Petra.
MAN: What's your real name?
PETRA: My name is Petra.

(Pause.)

MAN: Two years ago I bought my wife a necklace. For Christmas. Okay. She opened it up—she didn't like it. And I said, Well, it's okay, take it back. But I felt . . . angry. I felt . . . sick. And then she stopped sleeping with me. Why? I didn't know. And then I was on a trip. I met a woman in a bar. And I had told myself many times that I would never, but I was angry at my wife. I. Hated her. Despised—and so, and so I had sex with this woman from the bar. So what you're saying is . . .
PETRA: Do you see? My story illustrates my awakening to consciousness; yours does not. This is the difference—what I was trying to say the other night—this is the difference between art and pornography as well. Art can be ugly and painful and full of disgusting things; but unlike pornography it *is conscious* of this.
MAN: Conscious or not, it's still horrible. Horrible. Look at Woody Allen—the ways people behave—despite what they know—I mean when did he decide, you know, to? I'm not an intellectual man. I don't have words. Thank you, Petra. Thank you for—you.

(Pause.)

Are you still in pain?
PETRA: —No.
MAN: I can't say I believe you, Petra.

PETRA: No. No. I have beauty in my life. I have art, I have friends—
MAN: That's not what I asked.

(They look at each other.)

I can't wait for the food. This is the best food.

(He sips from a glass of wine.)

Scene 3

Apartment, that night. Stephen arrives, entering with a bag. Mark's on the phone. He quickly hangs up.

STEPHEN: Hey sweets!
MARK: Hi.
STEPHEN: Merry Christmas Eve. How are you?
MARK: I'm fine. How are you?
STEPHEN: Ugh, shopping is *done!*
MARK: Good day?
STEPHEN: Great day! You?
MARK: Okay.
STEPHEN: How's Tan?
MARK: He hasn't come by.
STEPHEN: Oh? I hope he's all right.
MARK: Me, too.
STEPHEN: So are you all ready for Christmas Eve?
MARK: Yes.
STEPHEN: Are you going to church?
MARK: Tomorrow morning.
STEPHEN: Oh, maybe I can go with you.
MARK: I don't think that's appropriate.
STEPHEN: Oh?
MARK: My faith is very special to me. I take it very seriously.
STEPHEN: Well—I'm not going to sit there making pedophile jokes about the priest.
MARK: I'm sorry. You understand.

STEPHEN: Well. Okay, whatever you need. I bumped into Petra at the deli, she'll be here in a couple of minutes.

(Stephen goes into his room, takes stuff out of the bags.)

So were you on the phone with Hollywood?

MARK: When?

STEPHEN: When I came in. You were on the phone.

MARK: No, I was thinking of calling someone.

STEPHEN: Oh. Hey, did you get the mail?

MARK: Yeah, you didn't get anything.

STEPHEN: Fuck.

MARK: I got something.

STEPHEN: Yeah?

MARK: They sent me the cut of the movie.

(Stephen reenters the living room. Sees a large envelope atop the VCR.)

STEPHEN: The—your movie?

MARK: I need to make a decision by—it's going to be at Sundance so they need to know. If I want. My name on it. I haven't— watched it yet.

STEPHEN: Wow . . . well, I'm sure that's going to be difficult for you.

MARK: What do you care about Tan?

(Beat.)

STEPHEN: Excuse me?

MARK: When you came in: "How's Tan?"

STEPHEN: Are we all right here?

MARK: I mean just let me live my life don't. Judge me all the time.

STEPHEN: Okay . . . is there . . . something you'd like to talk about?

MARK: How's Tan, Who were you on the phone with, I mean. Just—no—exactly—there is nothing about all this I'd like to talk to you about as long as you're *judging* me—

STEPHEN: All right, wait a second—

MARK: Your rage is so transparent and it's just toxic, you know, it's poisoning this whole—

STEPHEN: Rage?

MARK: Yes, rage, at me, yes. I'm sorry we're not having sex, I'm sorry this is so upsetting to you.

STEPHEN: *Mark?*

MARK: "How's Tan?"

STEPHEN: Okay, okay I'm not going to yell and, and also it's Christmas Eve, but what I will say, what I will say is that you're, you're really—hurting my feelings here. Okay? So just—so just be a human being here for a second and let's go back to—

MARK: *What?*

STEPHEN: What? What?

MARK: What, I don't know how to be a human being now?

STEPHEN: That's not what I said.

MARK: What did you say then?

STEPHEN: Okay, let's take deep breaths—

MARK: Can you SHUT UP for a second? You're always fucking TALKING.

STEPHEN: Shut—Mark—what—I ask how you are, I ask about your life—you know if anyone should be angry here—Jesus Fucking Christ!—

MARK: Oh, thank you.

STEPHEN: Oh, *oh*, excuse me for taking the fucking Lord's name in vain, I'm sorry I'm not SPIRITUAL like you taking you know fucking becoming intimate with a fucking STREET KID hustler drug dealer whatever and you can't, you can't even fucking find ten MINUTES to talk to me—

MARK: Stop yelling!—

STEPHEN: Stop—no!—you don't, you don't ask to even read what I'm working on, you sit here all day, *my* house, you invite this *kid*—

MARK: So you're jealous, because you think, you have some *idea*—

STEPHEN: Well I'm sorry if I'm a little fucking cynical I mean where's, how are you being a good Christian all this religious BULLSHIT, I mean, go fucking pass out food to smelly ugly homeless men, don't give me this Christian shit about—being—

MARK: Stop yelling!

STEPHEN: —no, go deliver food to people dying of AIDS, go, fuck you—

MARK: STOP YELLING!

(Pause. Mark is beginning to cry.)

STEPHEN: Oh—come on—don't—don't—why are you—don't
cry—

MARK: You know I was—I was—away for a long time I wasn't in
the world and—I'm *adjusting* you know and it's not—I'm
doing the best I—it's hard and you could show some—compassion—

STEPHEN: Come on, don't cry—

MARK: —because—I just wanted—a safe space and—you fucking accuse me of—all this judging, all this—let he who is
without sin cast the first—you know?—I never said I was—
perfect and I'm sorry if I'm not who—you wanted—me—to
be—anymore—

STEPHEN: No, that's not—come on, don't cry. That's not it. I'm
sorry, I shouldn't have—yelled I. *(Mark breaks down. Stephen
puts his arm around him)* I just—if you're in pain I want to—
it's—shhhh, come on, Shhh. It's okay. Shhh.

MARK: I have to go to the bathroom.

*(Mark gets up, goes to the bathroom. Door opens. Petra. Stephen
picks up the phone, pushes a button.)*

PETRA: Hey!
STEPHEN: Hi.
PETRA: Who are you talking to?
STEPHEN: Shhhh.

(Stephen listens. Then gasps.)

PETRA: What?

(Stephen hangs up.)

Is Mark home?

(Toilet flushes. Mark enters, not crying.)

Hey sweetie!
MARK: Hey, Pet.

(Mark goes over to Petra, gives her a big hug and a kiss.)

PETRA: Okay boys. Are you ready for something?

STEPHEN: Uh-oh.

PETRA: Look what I *bought* myself for *Christmas*—can you guess?

STEPHEN: What is it?

PETRA: Okay, get ready . . .

(She opens her bag and removes—a bagel. She laughs hysterically. Stephen and Mark laugh with her.)

Scene 4

Apartment. Trees are decorated. Some presents and wrapping paper scattered. Laughter. Christmas music playing softly. Petra has her arm around Mark. Stephen sits across from them. Occasionally Petra runs her hand through Mark's hair. The large envelope is still atop the TV.

PETRA: No, I have another one. Even worse.

STEPHEN: Okay, wait, neither of you knows this one. I am at an audition for a play, this is back like three years ago, and it was a serious play, you know, really heady stuff, and I'm standing outside the room waiting, and we were to wait in this hallway while the auditions were going on, and I'm standing outside the room waiting, whatever, and I hear the actor giving his reading, of the sides. And I got a little startled and nervous because it was a very good reading, really unique and unorthodox but honest and risky, and suddenly my reading seemed so conventional. So he leaves, and he's this striking blond man, glowing eyes, very, that kind of ethereal beauty—and I say hey and he says hey and he goes down the stairs, and I'm waiting. I can hear the casting directors talking—the door to the room is made of this really cheap wood, it's like, cork or something, right? So I hear this older man's voice, middle-aged, and I hear him say, "My God, I could fuck that boy a thousand ways to Sunday. My *God*." You know. And this woman laughs and says, "He is *ohhhh*," and I hear the man say, "And he is *stacked* beneath those clothes, I can tell." And I hear someone else laugh. And, and then I hear footsteps, the door opens for me, and I go in, and there they are: poker-faced. And I say hi, and I meet the reader, some effeminate twenty-three year old, the third person I heard laughing. And I do my reading, very good, blah blah blah, good job, nice to see you, Stephen. But all I'm thinking, I'm leaving and I'm thinking, and I couldn't stay to listen to what they said obviously, there's another actor there now, but I'm walking down the stairs onto horrible West 42nd Street and it's cold and the only thought in my mind is: Did he want to fuck me a thousand ways to Sunday? Nothing about my audition, my reading, my talent, my choices, no, all I could think was: Did he wonder what I looked like under my clothes? And I felt soft and miserable. And went to the gym. For about a week. But. Like. I mean— it was all I cared about, would that fat fifty year old jerk off to my headshot that night?

PETRA: Because what can you do in that situation? You want the role! It's a good play so how do you not become, in some way, the person they want you to be? You have to be a Zen master not to want him to masturbate onto your headshot!

MARK: How we treat people—sometimes makes them what they are.

STEPHEN: God—you know? Who are these people? How do they sleep at night? Shame on them! Oh.

PETRA: People, my God. What about you, sweetie? You have any horror stories? My God, this is such a catharsis for me, it's such a *release* hearing all this stuff.

MARK: Um. Well. Yeah, I.

PETRA: Oh yeah? Good.

MARK: When I was um. Making my film, about two weeks before my, whatever, my, you know . . . okay: I'm just gonna try to— tell this. Okay. Deep breath, wow. Okay. So. We all went out after the shoot and basically started off by getting drunk before we moved on, you know, to everything else. And. I sat there with my actors and. This one, Adam, said to the group, said. *Mark fucks like a Calvin Klein ad.* Out of. The blue and. Adam had a small role, and the actors didn't know him too well but he was my friend so. He'd come out with us. We'd been talking about how many people we'd. Slept with. Was the topic of conversation and. I'd found myself *inflating.* Because I was embarrassed at how, comparatively, how *few.* Anyway. The actors look at him and. I say. What can I say?

That was a long time ago. Not even a year, Adam says. And the actors start *laughing.* Well. *What do you mean by that?* And Adam says. *I mean he has this vacant stare which never changes.* And I. Smile. And I say. *Adam you never open your eyes during sex so how would you know.* And. (*Mark starts to cry a little. Petra grabs his hand)* It was just then that I. I realized I. Well. So I laughed. We all laughed and. That night another actor came to my room at the hotel we. In West Hollywood, a nice, the Mondrian, we were there for two nights while we were filming in L.A. And this actor came in and. Went in and turned on the shower and said. We're gonna take a shower and fuck and I have some Percocets for later my mom she went just went to the dentist and. And. I did because. (*He stops the story. And stops crying. And laughs. And then silence)* Because, you know. Because I thought . . . (*He waves his hand, as if to signal that he won't go on)*

STEPHEN (*Grabbing a small, wrapped, flat gift)*: Here, here, last one.

PETRA: Ooooh.

STEPHEN: For you, Mark.

MARK: You got me another gift? Wow.

STEPHEN: Well, it's a little self-serving because it's for both of us, but—

(*Stephen hands Mark a small envelope. Mark opens it, takes out two tickets.)*

MARK: Oh, wow.

STEPHEN: It's supposed to be really good, it was a hit in London or whatever, so, and it's in previews now, and I thought. We used to have so much fun going to plays together, that used to be our thing, so. I thought it would be nice. And we could go eat after at Leshko's like we did when we had no money. And the only difference would be that we didn't have to usher to get in, or get TKTS or whatever.

MARK: Great.

STEPHEN: Yeah, so. Hey. Three minutes to Christmas! Eleven fifty-seven . . . now!

MARK: Thank you. It's on New Year's Eve.

STEPHEN: Yes. There's this, someone was telling me about some culture which believes in spending New Year's Eve in a ritualized, like, in this way where everything you do you do in hopes that your year will follow in that fashion. So if you want a year of clarity, you spend the evening cleaning your home—you make it symbolic and—so I just thought going to a play, karma-wise, might be a really nice, low-key way

(The buzzer buzzes.)

Huh?

PETRA: Who in God's name?

STEPHEN *(Answers with intercom)*: Hello?

TAN *(Offstage/through intercom)*: Hey uhh—Mark? *(Stephen looks to Mark)* Mark, come down! It's Tan!

(Mark stands.)

MARK: I suppose I should . . . go see him for a minute . . . I guess.

STEPHEN: Oh, okay.

(Mark grabs his coat and his sketchpad.)

PETRA: I hope he's all right.

MARK: I'll be back.

(Mark goes to the door, gets his coat. Petra starts collecting wrapping paper. Stephen goes to Mark.)

STEPHEN: Hey, are you going to be all right?

MARK: Yeah.

STEPHEN: I'm sorry about earlier.

MARK: It's okay.

STEPHEN: Anything you need, you know.

MARK: I know.

STEPHEN: If you're out just call—if you want to talk when you get back—just knock on my door.

MARK: Thanks a lot. Bye.

STEPHEN: See you later.

(Mark exits, door slams.)

PETRA: That kid is bad news, I hope he knows what he's doing.

STEPHEN: Well listen to this. We got into a little tiff before you got home—and he—you won't believe this and I grabbed the phone because he had been on it when I came home, and I just hit the re-dial, and wouldn't you know—no, guess. Guess who he's talking to.

PETRA: Ethan Hawke, how the hell do I know.

STEPHEN: Phone sex.

PETRA: Oh.

STEPHEN: He's. A fucking mess is what he is. He said he's—whatever. Merry fucking Christmas, Mark. I mean, what can I do?

PETRA: Well . . . you can—

STEPHEN: It's not fair. He can't be honest with me? I love him. I love him and I've done nothing except try to help him. This Bible shit.

PETRA: Maybe that's what he needs, Stephen.

STEPHEN: These stupid recovery programs!

PETRA: Why are they stupid?

STEPHEN: Because they turn people into—all that *shit* about: "That was some other person who was addicted, that was not me" and "God give me the strength." So he can't talk to me but he can call phone sex, FUCK him!

PETRA: He's a recovering drug addict. He must be—

STEPHEN: What, is this another I'm Okay You're Okay no, no, I am *fine* and *he*, is fucked-up, so, so I'm being judgmental, well, so *fine*, I think I'm allowed I think that's IN FACT I think it's *important*.

PETRA: Okay, calm down. I think you should try to understand that—

STEPHEN: And, and he buys me a BIBLE for Christmas! A Bible! Whooo!

PETRA: It's just his way of telling you who he is now. He's sharing—

STEPHEN: —yeah—

PETRA: Try to be selfless, take a step back and you'll see—

STEPHEN: Selfless? What, am I a therapist? No, I—I let him— I love him—I LOVE HIM—and he's—who the fuck knows what he's doing—he could be—you know?—

PETRA: I'm not on his side, I'm just trying—

STEPHEN: Oh no, well what's with, with all this, this hands all over him always hugging him, what the hell is that?

PETRA: I don't understand.

STEPHEN: I mean, there you are, I mean, what about me? Who's holding my hand? Who's hugging me? And where's my two-million-dollar three-picture deal?

PETRA: I think you have to ask yourself why you're so upset, Stephen.

STEPHEN: Because I am, and I'm allowed to be fucking upset, so, so fuck you, too!

(Stephen picks up some wrapping paper, puts it into the garbage, goes to his room, shuts the door. Climbs into bed. Petra looks around. She takes a small gift and unwraps it. It's her bagel. She sits on the couch and takes a bite of it.)

Scene 5

A luxurious bathroom. A huge, white circular bathtub, gray mottled walls. Gleaming chrome fixtures. Mirrors. A bathroom at the Royalton Hotel.

TAN: It's cool, isn't it.

MARK: It's really beautiful. So peaceful. Clean.

TAN: I swear to God. He books the room an extra night and leaves, lets me have it. Like once a month. Isn't that weird?

MARK: And all he leaves are dirty underwear?

TAN: He leaves them under the bed. And they're smeared—you know, come, shit, piss. You know. But—I tell him I jerk off onto them and then I mail them back to him. He leaves the envelope, already stamped and shit. But I don't jerk off onto them, and he can't tell the difference.

MARK: Sick.

TAN: So I just come and take a bath. Sometimes I order porno. They have that Simon Rex jerk off tape, *Young, Hard & Solo 2*.

MARK: Do they.

TAN: And I order a Black Angus. Mmmmmm.

MARK: Wow.

TAN: We can eat whatever. Just charge it to the bill. Guy's loaded. I met him by jerking off for him. And he always leaves a couple hundreds hid somewhere. In the room, you know. He draws little pictures on the bills. Little smiley faces.

MARK: Wow.

TAN: Beat off for him in Times Square, on 41st Street. Three A.M.

MARK: No cops?

TAN: You'd be surprised. How easy it is to do things and no one notices. I've had cops walk ten feet away and not even see.

(Beat.)

So we gonna take a bath together or what?
MARK: Tan.
TAN: I love how you say my name. Gives me a boner.
MARK: Yeah?
TAN: See for yourself. Bathtub! Wheee!

(Tan leaps into the empty bathtub. Only his head and shoulders are visible.)

MARK: There's such a light about you, you know. Underneath everything, you have this joy . . .
TAN: You could fit your whole bathroom in this tub.
MARK: I'm—just not—sure what's happening here, Tan.
TAN: Neither am I! *(Tosses his shoes out of the tub)* Wheeee! *(Mark laughs)* They give you free bubble bath. *(His belt comes ripping off; Mark stares away, at the mirror)*
MARK: Well, I guess I wonder why. I wonder why you're here and why. Why you don't. Go somewhere for help. You're. So young and. You know? It's wrong for me to. Well just in terms of me I shouldn't—my heart is starting to—hurt and. But. You should get help, and if I can.

(Tan laughs. Pants over the edge of the tub. Socks. Underwear. Tan giggles. Mark laughs.)

Okay. *(Tan takes off his shirt)* Well. Do you. Do you have anything to say about what I'm. Saying or?

(Tan stands, back to us, naked. Reaches, dims the light. Mark looks in the mirror, then closes his eyes.)

Look I. *(Opens his eyes, keeps them vaguely averted)* I got you a Christmas gift, and then I'm going to leave, okay? But I wanted to give you . . .

(Mark puts his sketchpad on the bathtub.)

100

TAN: Don't go.

(Tan opens the pad.)

Wow, it's your drawings. Oh wow. Is that me?
MARK: Yes.
TAN *(Flipping through)*: Oh wow.
MARK: Yes.
TAN: Wow.
MARK: You can jerk off if you want to.
TAN: What?
MARK: Okay. And then I'll leave. Okay?
TAN: Okay.
MARK: Lay down. In the tub.

(Tan does. We can't see him. Mark watches in the mirror.)

TAN: Can you see?

(Mark nods.)

I like you watching.
MARK: Open your legs a little.
TAN: Makes me feel good.

(Mark watches.)

Scene 6

Apartment. Stephen's asleep in his bed. Petra's at the kitchen table, reading. Mark enters.

PETRA: Hi.
MARK: Hi. Can I talk to you?
PETRA: Sure.
MARK: Is Stephen asleep?
PETRA: I think so.
MARK: Come here.

(Mark sits on the couch, wraps himself in a blanket. Petra comes over, sits on the edge of the couch. He doesn't say anything. He snuggles into her a bit.)

PETRA: Are you all right?

MARK: You won't tell Stephen what I tell you will you?

PETRA: Well. No.

MARK: Promise. He'll be mad.

PETRA: Are you all right?

MARK: Yeah. No. No, I'm not all right. Will you say a prayer with me?

PETRA: Sure.

MARK: My heart is just. I have to make all these—I almost—I almost—with Tan tonight—I just—what can I do about my heart? My heart feels like oh God. I hurt. I *hurt*. What can I do? What can I do?

PETRA: I think it's . . .

MARK: I'm—I want—I want so bad to touch him, I almost—I almost—

PETRA: You're shaking.

MARK: It feels—what can I do?—my *heart*—

PETRA: I think Mark. I think the only thing for you to do is stop. Seeing him.

MARK: But he—he has nothing he *needs me* and—

PETRA: He doesn't need you.

MARK: I've been so nice to him I can't—

PETRA: You don't need him and that's what you need to think about right now.

MARK: No

PETRA: That's—all I can say to you. You can't stop how you feel but you can change what you *do*.

MARK: It felt so good, Petra. It felt so good.

PETRA: What?—

MARK: I used to use drugs I don't do that anymore I stopped.

PETRA: I know you did and that was hard and I'm sure there was a time you never thought—

MARK *(Puts his arm around her waist)*: And I think I grew up and how—

PETRA: I bet you thought it was impossible—

MARK: —and my heart. It felt so good. I don't feel good. I don't feel good.

PETRA: Why don't we, Mark, why don't we say a prayer together.

(Mark moves away from her.)

Why don't we—
MARK: I need you to leave now.

(Pause.)

PETRA: What?
MARK: You have to go please.

(She sits up.)

PETRA: You want me to leave?
MARK: Yes.
PETRA: Well. Okay.
MARK: I'm sorry.
PETRA: I'll be in my room if you need anything.
MARK: Thank you.

(Petra exits. Mark stands. He goes to Stephen's room. He climbs onto the loft bed. He shakes Stephen.)

Wake up.

(Stephen awakens.)

STEPHEN: Wha? . . .
MARK: It's me.
STEPHEN: Wh—are you okay?
MARK: Hug me.
STEPHEN: Mark?

(Mark climbs atop Stephen and hugs him.)

Are you—okay?—

MARK: Shhh.

(Mark keeps hugging. Then starts rubbing against Stephen.)

STEPHEN: Whoa—

(*Stephen sits up, pushes Mark away.*)

MARK: What?
STEPHEN (*Still groggy*): Mark, what?
MARK: Hug me again. Just hug.
STEPHEN: Mark—are you okay?
MARK: You said I needed anything I could wake you up.
STEPHEN: I know—
MARK: I was remembering us—how good it felt—
STEPHEN: Well—yeah—
MARK: —so just hug me Stephen hug me.
STEPHEN: Oh God.
MARK: What.
STEPHEN: Oh God oh.

(*Stephen's face tightens.*)

MARK: What? *What?*

(*A beat.*)

STEPHEN (*Flustered*): I—I came.
MARK: You came?
STEPHEN: I—Mark—
MARK: You came without? —But you weren't touching your-
self—
STEPHEN: I—I know I . . .
MARK: I want to come.
STEPHEN: Mark—
MARK: I want to come now.
STEPHEN: Mark, please—oh God, please let's leave my bed—
MARK: Are you—come on I want to come, you just came—
STEPHEN: What's—what's wrong?
MARK: Stephen!
STEPHEN: Let's just go into the living room.
MARK: One night, once, Stephen.

(*Mark buries his head in Stephen's chest, kisses, fumbles with his jeans.*)

STEPHEN: No, Mark, no, Mark, we can talk, we can *talk*—

(Stephen pushes him away.)

MARK: I don't want to talk! I'm sick of I don't want to talk!
STEPHEN: Mark I want to help you I want—

(Mark jumps off the bed.)

MARK: I'm leaving, I'm leaving.

(Stephen climbs off the bed.)

STEPHEN: Mark you shouldn't go out—
MARK: I didn't touch him, I didn't do anything with him Stephen—
STEPHEN: You stay here, I'll go.
MARK: What are you doing? Go where?
STEPHEN: Just stay here.
MARK: Where are you—

(Stephen goes to the closet, takes clothes, begins putting them on.)

Where are you going? Stephen. Stephen. Stephen! Don't—where are you going? You can't leave. Stephen—answer me!—don't fucking leave me Stephen. Don't leave me here—

(Mark blocks Stephen's way.)

No. No.

(Stephen tries to go, Mark continues to block. Stephen pushes Mark out of the way, exits the bedroom. He puts on his shoes.)

Where are you going, answer me, answer me Stephen, Stephen answer me—why aren't you ANSWERING me—

(Stephen grabs his backpack. He begins to cry.)

Stephen—Stephen—I need you right now where are you—
come back here! Come back here! Come *back* here!

(*Stephen puts on a coat, still crying.*)

Don't—cry Stephen. Okay. Okay. Look I'm quiet now. Look
I'm quiet. I'm okay. You don't know what happened. We can
talk about it. We can talk about what happened. We can talk
just please don't. Come back to bed. Come back.

(*Stephen gets his keys, goes to the door.*)

It's late, Stephen, where—it's Christmas. It's Christmas. It's
Christmas. It's.

(*Stephen opens the door.*)

Stephen. Stephen!

(*Stephen goes. Door slams.*)

Stephen!—

(*Mark begins punching his leg. He stops. His face is blank. His
breathing is heavy. Petra comes out of her room, listens. Silence.
Mark walks to the couch. Petra quickly sneaks back into her room.
Mark takes the cordless phone and goes back to Stephen's bed. He
dials, presses the phone to his ear, curls into a fetal position.*)

Act Three

Scene 1

Petra sits on the couch reading. Stephen comes storming in.

STEPHEN: Hi.

PETRA: When did you get back?

STEPHEN: This morning. So listen. I got fired.

PETRA: Oh no.

STEPHEN: Yes because. Because someone, because I made up, I wrote the blurb for *Men in Black* without watching it, they *found* out, someone *told* them. Someone, I told some *intern* in the office who I guess *blabbed* it. And literally. They called me into the office and asked me if I'd watched the movie. And. And you know. What am I? —I laugh. I laugh. Because, because I did watch the trailer, I watched the trailer so— so—I mean, come on! So they said, and there's two of them there, my boss and the "other" boss, the boss I never see, you know, the one who's always out having *lunch* eight hours a day. So what am I going to say, Yes, I did watch it and what, take a POP QUIZ on *Men in Black*?

PETRA: So what did you say?

STEPHEN: I said I—*fast-forwarded* through it. And they said *That is not good enough.* And I said *Okay.* I'm sitting there. And they said *We're sorry.* And they sent me to *personnel.* And

I have credit card bills, you know, this is not—I'm a—walking down the street. I write blurbs. I am a blurb writer. And you know, I didn't want to watch *Men in Black* that day, you know, and—you would think they'd—find it *funny*. But. So. So. New Year's Eve, here we are. Thank God this year is behind me is all I have to say. *Whooosh.* Good-bye. Any word from Mark?

PETRA: I haven't seen him.

STEPHEN: Well, I guess that's it. I guess I'm going to the play alone tonight. Unless you want to . . .

PETRA: I can't, I have—I made some plans.

STEPHEN: Have you seen him at all since I went home?

PETRA: He's been here a lot during the day. On the phone.

STEPHEN: Have you been talking to him?

PETRA: No. Listen you got . . .

STEPHEN: Did I do the right thing? That night was just so—maybe I shouldn't have gone home, maybe I should have *stayed* and just forced him to talk . . . his stuff's still here

(Petra hands Stephen an envelope.)

Oh God.

PETRA: This is it?

STEPHEN: This is it. This came today?

PETRA: Mm-hmm.

(He opens it. He takes out a letter.)

STEPHEN: I got it. I, yeah, I got it. Oh my God. I got it, seven thousand dollars.

PETRA: Oh. Yes. Yes.

STEPHEN: Thank you. Oh my God. Wow! Oh God. That's great. Oh my God.

PETRA: Oh, I'm so happy for you.

STEPHEN: Wow. Wow! Well that's over. I got it. Done. Oh.

(Stephen grabs the large envelope from the top of the TV.)

Look.

PETRA: What?

STEPHEN: He still hasn't opened it.

(He puts the envelope back on the TV. He looks at his grant let-ter again. Petra looks at him and smiles.)

Scene 2

A sleek modern apartment. Man and Petra.

MAN: Before we go any further, I want to get this out of the way. *(Hands her an envelope. She puts it in her purse)* Now. Now that that's done I want you to know—you can leave anytime you want. Okay?

PETRA: Okay.

MAN: So. This is it. I know, it could use a woman's touch.

PETRA: It's very minimalist.

MAN: Well that's not really by design. My wife kept all the really great stuff. Have a seat. *(She sits on a couch)* Do I have plans for us tonight. What's better than a quiet New Year's at home?

PETRA: It's such a difficult holiday to do right.

MAN: You're telling me! Misery of miseries! I've never had a good New Year's Eve.

PETRA: You're kidding! Oh God, me either. There's not one New Year's Eve where I haven't cried.

MAN: Well, not tonight. That's the only rule, okay? Now: wine?

PETRA: I'd love a glass.

(He pours wine.)

MAN: So first off the bat, tell me how you are.

PETRA: I'm okay. Stephen got back today. He got that grant, which is very exciting.

MAN: Do you realize that whenever I ask how you are, you tell me about someone else?

(Pause.)

PETRA: I'm well, thank you.

MAN: I want this to be a good holiday for you. A good New Year's Eve.

(Petra sips wine.)

Tell me what you're writing. Tell me what you've been working on, how about that.

PETRA: Well, I've been reading a lot. This excellent book by Mary Gaitskill; and Dorothy Parker, who's very underrated I think. People dismiss her as some sort of alcoholic, you know, little funny poem writer, but. She wrote some devastating fiction. The class issues are . . .

MAN: Maybe you can lend me her book.

PETRA: Yes. Listen. I. I don't want to take your money. Not tonight.

MAN: Anyway. Listen. I want to read you a poem.

PETRA: I'm serious—

MAN: Not now. Here.

(Petra sips wine.)

Okay. This isn't easy. Okay.

The darkness of your eyes
pierces into my heart.
I cannot fathom the size
of the waters you part.
You contain such light
that I cannot even see.
But I shall take flight
in your utter beauty.

There. I said it. Okay. Be honest. Tell me. I know, rhyming's kind of passé, right?

PETRA: I'm—very glad you wrote that. I hope. I hope it gave you some joy.

MAN: It's about you.

PETRA: That . . . makes me feel good.

(The Man smiles.)

Scene 3

The apartment. Stephen's sitting, reading. Mark enters.

MARK: Hi.

STEPHEN: Hi. Are you . . . the play starts in half an hour, are you . . . ?

MARK: Oh no. I have this—party to go to. I'm—sorry, I forgot all about it.

STEPHEN: Well—we haven't spoken since—so . . . I um—I should get going but I thought—

MARK: I just came to pick something up.

(Mark crosses to the large envelope atop the TV, takes it.)

. . . Are you going to the play alone?

STEPHEN: Yeah.

MARK: Cool. You went home to see your folks Pet said, how um. How was that?

STEPHEN: It was good. Actually. As good as . . . you know.

MARK: Yeah. Well.

STEPHEN: Right.

MARK: Happy New Year's.

STEPHEN: You, too.

(Mark goes. Door slams. Stephen crosses to his jacket. He puts it on. He goes to the door. He waits some moments. And goes.)

Scene 4

The Royalton bathroom. They've set a TV and VCR up on the sink counter. Mark and Tan are watching, passing a cigarette between them. They sit in the giant tub. We can see they are bare-chested. Sounds from TV.

TAN: Man. Yeah. Yeah.

MARK: Hah. Yeah, I shot that, that was fun.

TAN: What was he like, in real life?

MARK: He was whatever.

(Mark uses an eyedropper to drop a few darkish drops of liquid into his nose. He hands the eyedropper to Tan, who gives him the cigarette.)

TAN: This is totally cool, man.

MARK: Yeah. I feel good. I feel good. Did I tell you about the bathroom in the place I looked at? Practically identical to this one . . . 'cept not mirrors like these but . . .

TAN *(Finishing with the drops)*: You know what I was thinking.

MARK: What.

TAN: I was thinking it'd be cool to come, you know, as the clock hits twelve or whatever.

MARK: Yeah?

TAN: Yeah. You don't think that's cheesy do you?

MARK: No. I think it's kind of hot.

TAN: Yeah.

(Tan takes Mark's hand with the cigarette, brings it to his mouth, inhales, then lets go.)

Whoa! Butch camera angle! Fuck! That dude, what's his name? He's cool.

Scene 5

Man's apartment. Petra's a little tipsy.

PETRA: You know what people want? I'll tell you, you, me, Quentin Tarantino, Bill Clinton, whether they know it or not, I'll tell you exactly what people want: love. As stupid as that sounds.

MAN: Hah, you're getting drunk, I've never seen you like this.

PETRA: No, we're all the same, in this, in just this one way, look, look: They have on videotape of, they have children, they did this in Britain, this study, okay, and little kids would get beaten up by their mothers, little, two and three years old, slapped, punched, disgusting—but when the nurse came into the room—they actually did this, secret videotape—when the nurse came in to stop the beating and take the baby from the abusive mother, the baby cried, the baby cried and tried to hang on to its mother. So. So whatever you want to call it, that's—the baby wants—love—so the love is inappropriate, so what, it's what the baby knows.

MAN (*Laughing*): And some babies grow up to make movies and run countries.

(*Petra laughs, refills her wine glass.*)

You sure about that?

PETRA: I'm not drunk. Okay. You asked me once, you said are you in pain? And I lied. I said no. And I'm in pain because I am not loved. You see. And artists—there's so little love to go around—the promise of love is so fleeting and inconsistent so to get noticed—people do—what they *do* is—just like you cheated on your wife, you see it in art too, the terror of not being loved, safe art, meaningless art, pandering art, commercial art, titillating art, outrageous art, can we sell it, can I sell myself, will I be rewarded with money, with prestige, with recognition—all those things which are, which are *perversions* of love—and let me tell you. If there were more love to go around. And more consciousness and less fear. People might make beautiful things. Beautiful things. What are all these horrible disgusting movies with violence and anger and, you know, I mean, they're cries for help! You look at a Quentin Tarantino movie, you know, this man has never been loved. He has had no experience of love in his life. Art, the art can never be better than the person who made it.

MAN: Well you have to love yourself, don't you? Isn't that the hardest part?

PETRA: You know what? That's New Age bullshit. You can't love yourself. You go and try. One is a fiction. Reality exists when the other person walks into the room. Life is other people.

MAN: So is hell, or so someone said.

PETRA: Well then so is heaven.

MAN: Do you think you'll be loved?

PETRA: I'd better.

MAN: Do you think you will?

PETRA: Hey, if I didn't, I'd put my head in the oven.

MAN: Me, too. Hah. That calls for one more glass I think. We're not even *close* to the ball dropping you know.

(Man pours himself a drink. Petra gets up, goes to a rack of CDs.)

PETRA: Okay, tell me you have more than Bob Dylan.
MAN: Van Morrison.
PETRA: Shut up, what do you have to dance to?
MAN: Oh God. Dance?
PETRA: Yeah, you're gonna dance with me.
MAN: Dance.
PETRA: Here we go.

(Petra puts on something like a slow, sexy Janet Jackson song. She starts to dance.)

MAN: Wow, look at you.
PETRA: Come on, get up here.

(He does.)

MAN: I can't believe I'm doing this.

(He starts to dance. Petra laughs.)

PETRA: See! You're great!
MAN: Don't mock me!
PETRA: You're great!

(Petra moves closer to Man, dances.)

Come on, just let go.
MAN: That's very hard for insecure people.
PETRA: You're good! God I love dancing.
MAN: You do, eh.
PETRA: The only orgasms I've had, the last two years—while I've been dancing.
MAN: You're joking.
PETRA: Only when I've been dancing. And I've been in plenty of beds in that time.
MAN: Really, when you're stripping?
PETRA: Mm-hmm. See, now you're dancing!

MAN: Don't condescend.

PETRA: I'm not. Here, you have to look at the person when you're dancing.

(Petra grabs him and slow dances.)

MAN: Whoa.

PETRA: When's the last time you danced?

MAN: My wedding night I think.

PETRA: So you don't have herpes, do you?

(Man stops a little, then starts up again.)

MAN: Well why do you ask?

PETRA: Answer the question, come on.

MAN: No. No, I don't. Have it.

(Petra laughs. They dance.)

Nothing gets by your artist's eye, does it?

PETRA: I want to go to your bed.

MAN: You want to go to my bed?

PETRA: Yes.

MAN: No you don't.

PETRA: Yes I do.

MAN: Well I don't want to.

(Petra smiles, dances a few steps longer, then stops. Man stops.)

I mean—you're gorgeous but. But. That's not right. You shouldn't—maybe you had a little too much to drink—

PETRA: You know, I'm not a child, three four glasses of wine, I am *conscious*. It's not like I popped a Rohypnol too.

MAN: I'm sorry.

PETRA: You're sorry? You're—fuck you.

MAN: Whoa, what?

PETRA: Fuck you you're sorry you—you invite me to your apartment and—New Year's Eve—and you tell me I'm beautiful and you write a—

MAN: Wait, I never said—I never, I was always up front—

PETRA: No, you manipulative you, no you made me—you made me—no.

MAN: —about what I wanted, I was always honest with you. I was always. Here. Sit. Sit. You're drunk. *(Petra sits back down)* I'm sorry. Oh God. *(She takes a deep breath)* Listen. Listen I just wanted to talk to you. I just—I never wanted this to—

PETRA *(Stands)*: You know what, I'm just gonna go home.

MAN: Are you sure?

(Beat.)

PETRA: Yeah. Yeah I'm sure.

MAN: I'll talk to you . . .

PETRA: Well, look at us. Look at this, you know.

(Pause. Man goes to the stereo, shuts off the music.)

MAN: You—you should be having a blast. I wanted you to have a good New Year's Eve. I'm sorry.

PETRA: No, this is. This *is* a good New Year's Eve. Actually. If you can believe it. *(Laughs)*

MAN: Let me call you a car.

(Petra reaches into her pocketbook and takes out the envelope.)

PETRA: Look, I can't, and I don't want to, take this.

MAN: No. No. You. I think you're valuable. I value you and you, you should go out there and. Make something beautiful.

(She looks at him. She puts the envelope back in her pocketbook.)

PETRA: You're gonna make me cry.

MAN: No! Don't cry! Listen, let me call you a car. *(Goes to the phone, across the room)* Hi, I need a car at 178 East 72nd Street. Yes. To the East Village. Yes. *(Petra begins to cry, silently)* To um—what's the street address? Petra?

PETRA: —199 East 4th.

MAN: To 199 East 4th. Yeah, 178 East 72nd. Thanks! *(Hangs up)* They'll be right there.

(Petra turns. She walks to him and gives him a hug.)

Oh—oh—you're crying.

PETRA: I'm okay.
MAN: You're sure?
PETRA: Yeah.

(She lets go. Laughs, wipes away tears.)

God, my accent comes out so bad when I cry. *(A beat)*
MAN: I am gonna watch me some Dick Clark tonight. *(They share a brief laugh)* The car'll be right down.

(Petra nods.)

PETRA: Good-bye.
MAN: I'll uh—I'll keep an eye out for you. In the papers, I mean. I don't imagine I'll be seeing you at the club. So. I'll. Good luck with everything.
PETRA: Thank you. You, too.

(Petra goes.)

Scene 6

The Royalton bathroom, postcoital, on the tile floor.

MARK: Oh God.
TAN: You fuck like someone who hasn't fucked in a really long time.
MARK: Yeah well. Before this . . . it was a really long time.
TAN: You're good.
MARK: You, too.

(Mark kisses Tan on the head.)

I'm cold. I'm gonna put on some clothes.

(Tan, naked, turns on the TV. Mark starts to dress.)

TAN: Hey dude, you're putting on my pants.
MARK: Oh yeah. Whoops. Oh well. See how I look. *(Putting on the tight jeans. Really tight)* I'm Tan. Hello.

(He takes Tan's wallet out of his pants, opens it.)

Let's see here.

TAN: Whoa, whoa—

(Mark stops. Takes out a small card.)

—Well. Guess um.

MARK: You go to NYU?

TAN: Well, yeah. Yeah.

(Tan grabs a shirt—Mark's—and throws it on.)

MARK: Huh.

TAN: Yeah, so.

(Tan grabs Mark's pants, puts them on.)

MARK: Whatever.

(Mark grabs Tan's shirt, puts it on.)

TAN: What, you're not—mad?

MARK: No.

TAN: You're not?

MARK: I figured as much I mean. It doesn't matter.

TAN *(Face erupting into a smile)*: Really?

MARK: Yeah.

TAN: Hey you know I major, I major in acting.

MARK: Yeah?

TAN: Yeah, so, if you make any more movies . . .

(Mark smiles, nods, hands Tan his wallet.)

(Looking at TV) Shit, it's ten minutes.

MARK: What?

TAN: Till the ball drops.

MARK: Oh.

TAN: We forgot. We finished too early.

MARK *(Chuckles)*: Oops.

TAN: Wanna see if we can come? At midnight, we can try anyway?
We can just, like, jerk off.

MARK: Um. Okay. What the hell.

TAN: 'Cuz I think that'd be cool. To come at midnight.

MARK: Fun.

TAN: We could even do it by the window. People could see us. No one could tell who we were, and it'd be a kick, right?

MARK: Do it by the window?

TAN: And then people could see us.

Scene 7

The apartment. Stephen's on the couch. Petra enters. We hear party noise from the street and from other apartments within the building.

PETRA: Hey.

STEPHEN: Why are you home? It's not midnight?

PETRA: I'll be right back.

(She goes into her room.)

(From offstage) I was thinking about what you said. About starting the New Year on a symbolic note. So I thought I'd come home and. Read or something.

STEPHEN: Oh. Well that's nice. I'm glad you're here.

PETRA *(Offstage)*: What?

STEPHEN: I'm glad you're here!

(Some moments pass. Petra comes into the living room, wrapped in a kimono. She sits on the couch.)

Was your night okay?

PETRA: Yeah.

STEPHEN: Yeah. Mine, too. I'm sad.

PETRA: Me, too.

STEPHEN: But it'll be okay.

PETRA: Yeah. It'll be okay.

(Pause.)

Will you be mad at me if I leave, Stephen?

119

STEPHEN: Leave where?

PETRA: If I leave here.

STEPHEN: You're going to leave?

PETRA: I'm going to leave this city.

STEPHEN: You are? *(Petra nods)* Where are you going to go?

PETRA: I don't know yet.

STEPHEN: When?

PETRA: Soon.

(Pause.)

STEPHEN: Wow.

PETRA: Yeah.

STEPHEN: You never said anything. When did you decide this?

PETRA: I've been thinking about it for a long time.

(Pause.)

STEPHEN: I'll miss you.

PETRA: I'll miss you. How was the play?

(Stephen shrugs. Pause. Noise from outside.)

STEPHEN: What time is it?

PETRA: Oh God, there's one minute.

STEPHEN: 11:59.

PETRA: Should we turn on the TV and watch all the people in Times Square and watch the ball drop?

STEPHEN: No.

(Pause.)

PETRA: I'm gonna go read.

(Pause. Petra gets up, goes to her room. Stephen stays seated. Outside, we hear continued sounds of people, shouting, honking, stomping around, screaming. Stephen does not move. We hear people counting down from ten. Stephen closes his eyes. The sounds increase.)

END OF PLAY

What Didn't Happen

Production History

What Didn't Happen was originally produced by Playwrights Horizons (Tim Sanford, Artistic Director; Leslie Marcus, Managing Director; William Russo, General Manager) in New York City, opening on December 10, 2002. It was directed by Michael Wilson; the set design was by Jeff Cowie, the lighting design was by Howell Binkley, the original music and sound design were by John Gromada, the costume design was by David C. Woolard and the production stage manager was Susie Cordon. The cast was as follows:

JEFF	Matt Cowell
EMILY	Suzanne Cryer
SCOTT	Matt McGrath
ELAINE	Annalee Jefferies
DAVE	Steven Skybell
PETER	Chris Noth
ALAN	Robert Hogan

Characters

JEFF
EMILY
SCOTT
ELAINE
DAVE
PETER
ALAN

Place

A house in upstate New York.

Time

The play back-and-forths between 1999 and 1993.

Children picking up our bones
Will never know that these were once
As quick as foxes on the hill . . .

—WALLACE STEVENS
from "A Postcard from the Volcano"

Scene 1

*In the darkness, a light flickers in a window. Lights rise. The house.
1999. The last light of day is murky, there are clouds in the sky. A
large handbag is next to one of the chairs on the porch. Emily enters
from the lake path. A boy, Jeff, is on the roof.*

EMILY: How's the work going?

JEFF *(Turning sharply)*: Oh—you say something?

EMILY: How's it going up there?

(Jeff comes to the edge of the roof, with a brown bucket.)

JEFF: Almost done here Actually I am done . . .

EMILY: Right . . . He didn't happen to tell you where he was *going*
did he?

JEFF: Where?

EMILY: Yeah. My cell phone doesn't work out here so I can't
call . . .

JEFF: There's a phone in the house.

EMILY: The door is locked, I tried it.

JEFF: It's locked? Jaime's home. Jaime's in her room, I can hear the
TV.

EMILY: Right . . .

125

JEFF: Are you Jaime's mom?

EMILY: No, I'm—so Scott didn't tell you when he might be back?

JEFF: He just went.

(Emily moves across the lawn.)

EMILY: He just went. Right.

(Beat.)

(Changing tone) It's beautiful here.

JEFF: Where, the lake?

EMILY: The lake—the whole town.

JEFF: I think it sucks. My best friend moved to Clifton. My mom's like Don't be on the computer It rots your brain But what am I supposed to do. He moved to Clifton. His dad got a new job.

EMILY: Have you lived here your whole life?

JEFF: We used to live in Newburgh. My dad was from Newburgh but not my mom. Then me and my mom moved here.

EMILY: Do you remember the man who used to live here?

JEFF: Where?

EMILY: In this house. A man used to live here—five or six years ago maybe?

JEFF: I don't know. It was empty a wicked long time. This road doesn't go anywhere. My mom said it's the most expensive house. No one would ever buy it because it's so expensive. And also 'cuz it's weird—

(We hear a car pull into the driveway. Jeff leaps up, runs to the far side of the roof, looking off. Emily moves to the porch. Waving.)

Hi! All done!

(Scott enters. He has a bottle of wine in one hand, and a box marked amazon.com in the other.)

SCOTT: There she is!

EMILY: Hi.

JEFF: —All done up here!

EMILY: Jeff's been keeping me company.

SCOTT: Has he? *(To Jeff)* Come down, I'll give you your money.

JEFF: I think I might stay up here!—
SCOTT: Trip okay?
EMILY *(Wryly)*: Your directions were adequate.
SCOTT *(Laughs)*: "Adequate"—
JEFF: If I stomp on the roof will Jaime hear me?
SCOTT: I don't know, but please don't try it.
EMILY: Jeff and I had a nice long chat about *anthrax* earlier.
SCOTT: Ohh . . . his favorite topic.

(Jeff comes to the edge of the roof.)

JEFF: Remember how I was telling you before?
SCOTT *(Pleasantly)*: Of course I remember.

(Scott smiles at Emily. She sits on the porch.)

JEFF: I found a new one. On the web. It's called marburg. You die slow. Slow like. You sweat blood from your pores? serious blood—all your pores—and like your nose and your mouth and your eyes and even like your nips and stuff. It goes from one person to the next so you can't tell you got it till it's too late. Passes invisibly. It'll hit the cities first.
SCOTT: Wow. So we're lucky to be here, so far away from the cities.
JEFF: Definitely, but it can travel here, fast.
SCOTT *(Opening wallet)*: I have your money here—
JEFF *(Smelling hands)*: —My hands smell like gutter—when's the last time they were cleared?
SCOTT *(Offering him cash aggressively)*: I'm not sure, but thank you, that really needed doing.
JEFF *(Taking money quickly, going)*: So—I'll see you tomorrow I'll come by.
SCOTT: Actually—Jeff. I don't have any more work for you.

(Pause.)

JEFF: What?
SCOTT: At least for a while. You've done so good a job!
JEFF *(Looks at Emily)*: But—the path to the lake. *(To Scott)* You should clear that. I could clear that. *(To Emily)* Did you fall or anything, it's tricky, right?

SCOTT: Oh, you went down to the lake?

JEFF: —There's snakes in the lake.

EMILY: —Had to occupy myself somehow. I said I'd be here at four. It's almost five.

(During the following, Jeff looks up to the window—perhaps we can see a slight flickering light—and falls, flash-fast, into a daze. He picks up a fair-sized piece of gravel.)

SCOTT: Five? I'm sorry, I got held up at the bank. At closing, they told me about some acres they own around the lake. I'm thinking about buying them

EMILY: Really. It is pretty.

SCOTT: —I built that dock myself, you know.

EMILY: Did you. Can we— (hurry this up.)

JEFF *(Quietly, to himself)*: —Jaime.

(Jeff throws the rock at the window, narrowly missing. Scott turns and sees.)

SCOTT: —Yeah, I'm—Jeff!

JEFF *(Back)*: Wha?

SCOTT: Don't do that! You could break the window!

JEFF: Just wanted—to Jaime—I wasn't—I thought she might hear it, it just hit the side.

SCOTT: I have work to do now, okay?

JEFF: Does Jaime swim in the lake?

SCOTT: No.

(Jeff bends down and picks up another piece of gravel.)

Jeff!

JEFF: No I'm not gonna throw it, I was just—holding it. You hafta . . . work.

SCOTT: I have to work.

(Jeff looks at Emily, and goes. Emily smiles.)

I'm sorry.

EMILY: Love the outfit.

(Emily takes a bottle of water from her handbag. Scott sits down opposite her, puts the wine on the table.)

SCOTT: Yeah, gangsta culture reaches the hinterlands.

EMILY: What hinterlands? I passed a Home Depot and a Bob's a few miles out.

SCOTT: Well, that's the main road—this counts as hinterlands.

EMILY: So many of the houses have satellite dishes, it's amazing.

SCOTT: —You're here!

EMILY: A right at the American Legion!

SCOTT: I see you rented a Bug . . .

EMILY: Yeah. I might have to get one. They're so fun.

SCOTT: They are. *(Taking wine in hand)* I'll just go in and get some glasses.

EMILY: Actually—I'm fine with my water.

SCOTT: Oh. Well come in, take a look. And I bought some steaks, are you hungry?

EMILY: You know—I'd rather we just get started.

SCOTT: Started—you mean with work?

EMILY: What else would I mean?

(Pause.)

SCOTT: Okay. Work. *(Returning to table)* —You look really good!

(Emily smiles, takes a PowerBook from her handbag, and opens it.)

EMILY: So, we need to figure out how to handle Ellen's exit. They want it over three episodes, so it's not too abrupt. We outline the story, they approve, I write the scripts, and we're done. —Now what I pitched, and what everybody liked, is the idea of Tom going to D.C. What I'm playing with is that he—it's sort of like a modified Sid Blumenthal thing: Tom leaves the magazine, goes to Washington, to work for a senator he's admired, a "provocateur," a "man of many ambitions," libidinous and otherwise, et cetera et cetera . . .

SCOTT: Really?

EMILY: What?

SCOTT: Isn't D.C. a little—you know—aren't people a little tired of politics right now? With the whole impeachment, and the election next year . . .

EMILY: Well, what would be great is that we could squeeze in social issues. We could do, like, the "Columbine episode"—it wouldn't be all politics.

SCOTT: —Right. Okay.

EMILY: Now. Ellen.

SCOTT: Ellen.

EMILY: I think it's best to be simple about it. She's an actress, she doesn't want to go to D.C., she needs to stay in New York. She and Tom call it quits reluctantly. Bittersweet. The network doesn't want any bad guys, you know, they want to keep the door open in case she comes back. —I mean Ellen's "your" character. What do you think?

SCOTT: Should I keep him away from Jaime?

(Pause.)

EMILY: How is she doing?

SCOTT: Better! Since we got here. I think it's definitely helped. —I finally took her to a shrink.

EMILY: Oh?

SCOTT: Three of them. The first guy talked to her for an hour, came out, said to me, "Your daughter is well-adjusted. She misses her mother, and is coping with change. But essentially she's fine. You have nothing to worry about." Easy two hundred bucks!

EMILY: But—that's great—that he thought she was okay.

SCOTT: Well. The next one—a bald man with big cheeks, very goofy looking. Did all these *doodlings* with Jaime. He said I should feel lucky—Jaime's smart, pleasant, alert. Since all he had done with her was *draw*, I laid it out very clearly—I said, "She's a zombie. She sits in front of the television and doesn't leave her room. Does her homework in front of it, reads books in front of it. And not MTV, you know, TRL, Limp Bizkit tour special—no, CNN, the war in Kosovo. At night she can't sleep unless the television is left on. How is this okay?" "Children growing up today have a very different relationship to 'technology' than you or I did. Jaime's very wise, very mature for a ten year old. She has a real sense of emotional texture and ambiguity." —I took her to an art critic! *Finally*, the last one—

EMILY: Wait, what did she draw?

SCOTT: The doctor wouldn't show me—"confidential." I asked Jaime later, she said, "Abstract stuff."

EMILY: Hm. She's probably feeling very abstract. Her mother's been in Europe almost a year now, she's away from her friends, out here, uprooted . . .

(Beat.)

SCOTT: So finally—I take her to a woman. Sees Jaime for three sessions, recommends *I* enter therapy. "What did Jaime say to make you think that I need to be in therapy?" I ask. "She tells me you've taken her to two other doctors. She described your impulsive purchase of a remote home, your emotional distance from your ex-wife, and your depression about your career as a TV producer." I said, "Did she get to how much I hate my mother?" *(Pause)* And in the car I say, "Jaime, do you think something is wrong with Daddy?" "You miss Mommy." "No, I don't. I wonder about her sometimes, but the divorce was a good thing, you know that." And she says, "Do you miss Emily?" I ask her why she thinks that. "You don't have anyone to talk to anymore." "I have you," I say. "No you don't!" she says—as her hand reaches to turn up the radio, some Spice Girls travesty. And her eyes glaze over in that distant way . . .

(Pause. Emily puts her hand on Scott's. A moment between them. Then:)

EMILY: How is she better?

SCOTT: What?

EMILY: You said since you got here—she's better.

(Scott breaks, rises, moves to the citronella candle, takes the Zippo out of his pocket.)

SCOTT: Just—a sense I have. —She's excited you're here.

EMILY: Yeah?

SCOTT *(Lighting candle)*: I haven't said too much to her because I— *(Turning to her)* don't know how long you're staying . . .

EMILY: Well. *(Beat)* I'm glad she's doing better.

SCOTT: I'm so glad you're here, Emily.

(Pause.)

EMILY: We should—they want this tomorrow—
SCOTT: —I'm sorry. A month up here alone—I'm just—
EMILY: It's awkward. But we have to—
SCOTT: Begin. Let's begin.

(Pause. Scott goes to Emily, kisses her on the head. She allows this, and there is an intimate moment between them. Then Scott takes the bottle of wine, goes into the house. Emily closes her PowerBook and looks around.)

Scene 2

1993. Scott is squatting, looking at the ground. We hear a car pull in the gravel drive. Scott stays squat, turns briefly to the sound, then back to the ground, eyes focused. He has a small shovel in his hand and a small sheaf of papers rolled up, sticking out of his back pocket. We hear a call:

VOICE *(Offstage)*: Hello!

(Scott looks quickly off again, then back to the ground. Elaine enters. She sees Scott, stops, watches him a moment. Then:)

ELAINE: Hi.
SCOTT *(Not looking up)*: A millipede!
ELAINE: A what?
SCOTT: It's been ages since I— *(Looking at her)* Come look.
ELAINE *(Moves closer)*: It's a—
SCOTT: —millipede—
ELAINE: —I'm not a fan of bugs—

(Elaine takes another step. Scott lets the bug crawl onto his finger.)

SCOTT: "Hello, little man." *(Lifting finger)* It's a miracle this thing survived evolution.
ELAINE: Yes. All those legs, and look how slowly it moves.

(Scott shakes the bug off. He rises.)

SCOTT: You gotta be Elaine.

ELAINE: "I am Elaine."

SCOTT: I'd shake your hand but— *(Holds up dirty hands)* I'm disgusting.

ELAINE: "A rain check."

SCOTT *(Wiping hands across shirt, laughing)*: Wicked.

ELAINE: Forgive my—unease there. *(Lightly, smiling)* When I was a little girl I had a horrible experience with *worms,* and ever since I've not been what you'd call a "nature girl."

SCOTT: —I'm Scott?

ELAINE: Yes. —Oh, I'm sorry, no, of course. Dave's told me your name and . . . Scott. I didn't know I'd actually be meeting you. But here you are!

SCOTT: I was just making sure—I'm Scott!

ELAINE: Yes. —Dave speaks often of you, so highly.

SCOTT: Well lucky for him I'm a better handyman than I am a writer.

ELAINE: Oh no, no.

SCOTT: He's just inside, think he's trying to—I think actually he's almost done with the whole—

DAVE *(From off and up)*: Chapter Fourteen!

(They look up and laugh. Dave pops his head out of the window.)

Ladrica's ex-boyfriend has finally found her, and it's heartbreak at the Wendy's! Hi!

ELAINE: So, are you in there eavesdropping, is that what you're up to?

DAVE: I can't help it, you project so well!

ELAINE: Come down!

(He disappears inside. A beat.)

So . . . Dave tells me he works you to death, is that true?

SCOTT: He said that? Naw, I'm having the time of my life! He's exaggerating.

ELAINE: Ah.

SCOTT: You know Dave. *(Beat)* But—I should get back to work, have some stuff to finish. *(Yelling loudly toward the house)* He pays me way too much money!

(They laugh, and he's off. Elaine has a beat to survey the surroundings, when Dave emerges, holding some paper-clipped yellow pages of a manuscript draft and a red pen.)

ELAINE *(An old joke)*: Oh, he has the red marker out.
DAVE: I hope you brought a few up with you. *(Holds up the pages, marked insanely in red)*
ELAINE: Ah, it's going to be a long night.

(He puts the pages on the table, moves to Elaine. They embrace.)

DAVE: "At long last."
ELAINE: "The country house."
DAVE: I'm officially "A Man with a House."
ELAINE: I have to say, my imagination had had it much differently.
DAVE: How so?
ELAINE: I don't know—I was picturing it—more—"damp." Darker, more overgrown somehow.
DAVE: Well, it used to be. And now you've met Scott.
ELAINE: Yes—finally.
DAVE: Where's your stuff, is he getting it?
ELAINE: No—
DAVE: Do you need money for the taxi or—?
ELAINE: Actually—a wonderful coincidence:

(Peter enters, with Elaine's bag in one hand, a bottle of wine in the other.)

PETER: —Ten years! Ten years we have known each other and never once! —David, this is *extraordinary*!
ELAINE: —Peter was coming up to see Mary, and offered to give me a ride.
DAVE: Wow—how about that!
PETER *(Moving to Dave)*: What's it been, a year since I've seen you? Unacceptable!
DAVE *(Laughing, hugging him)*: Good to see you, Peter.
PETER: —I was just on my car phone trying to reach Mary, but I have a sneaking suspicion we're "out of range." Elaine did the whole three-act drama of the house for me on the way up. Now, I never took you to keep secrets.
ELAINE: *I've* never even seen it till today.

PETER: At least you knew about it! —Oh—now, I didn't want to arrive empty-handed for your big debut, but we were running late in the city, so we had to stop at a—what would one call it, a liquor *stand*? It's a '93 merlot, from Bubba's Vineyard, Little Rock!

ELAINE: It's not that bad.

(Peter hands Dave the bottle, puts Elaine's bag on the porch.)

PETER: You have to look there at the— *(Smiles at Elaine. They laugh)*

DAVE: What?

PETER: —look there at the label, read it aloud.

DAVE: Ahh . . . "Let this wine breath after opening." Let it *breath*.

PETER: If you should instead wish to suffocate it, I will not take offense.

DAVE: I never whine about wine. Thanks!

(Dave puts the wine on the table as Peter takes in the view.)

PETER: You've really carved out your own little Eden here. Down where Mary and I are—everyone looks like us, wears the same *shoes*—"rustic" antique shops for boobs like me on every corner. You must be the only city boy in this town—if you can even call it a town.

DAVE: Yeah—I really just wanted a place for me to work, far from the, you know, the phone calls and the cocktail parties, all that city crap. *(Beat)* I got the place for a steal—ten years ago, 1983, when my dad died.

PETER: Elaine told me.

DAVE: The house was actually once a building where they'd shear and slaughter sheep.

PETER *(To Elaine)*: Didn't tell me *that*.

ELAINE: Didn't *know*. *That's* pleasant. "Slaughterhouse sweet slaughterhouse."

DAVE: Ha—so—obviously it needed a ton of—over the years I'd do this and that but I had to wait till I had the *money* which, when I got the advance for the *novel* . . . You're right about the town, but it wasn't so bleak when I bought the place. Now, there's only one working farm still left here.

PETER: So—because of the book—you decided to yuppie it up, all the amenities.

DAVE: The book's paid for me to finish the house to write it in. Hey, I should run to the store for an extra steak, it closes at five.

PETER: Oh, I'll just stay for a cocktail.

DAVE: —Very well. What'll we have?

PETER: Vodka on the rocks, or white wine.

DAVE: Are you on some ridiculous diet?

PETER: You know the pattern: get fat while writing the book, get skinny for the book tour.

(As if this drink symbolizes a shared history between them:)

Screw it: scotch on the rocks.

DAVE: Very good! Elaine?

ELAINE: Nothing for me, actually.

DAVE: Really? Why not?

ELAINE: Water will be fine.

DAVE: Water. Okay. Well, have a look around.

(Dave goes into the house. Peter and Elaine sit at the table. Confidential tone:)

PETER: How are you holding up?

ELAINE: I'm all right. I was more nervous driving up than I am now. Thank you for holding my hand.

PETER: Please. —He's not as lugubrious as you anticipated.

ELAINE: Well, *you're* here. He won't appear depressed in front of you.

PETER: Mm.

(Beat.)

So. This is it.

ELAINE: Yes . . . Siberia.

(Elaine nods toward the manuscript. Peter glances at the pages.)

—All those boarded-up homes and empty storefronts . . . and I knew, I told you he's been thinking of spending time up here during the year. "All that city crap."

PETER: A few months alone in the country isn't proof of a crisis, especially for a writer.

ELAINE: —But he hasn't been alone.

(Beat. Dave enters with three glasses of ice, scotch, water.)

DAVE: So! What are we talking about?

PETER: —My fabulous wife!

(Elaine laughs. Drinks are poured.)

DAVE: Oh? How is fabulous Mary?

PETER: She is in our fabulous home with our fabulous son. I should call to let her know I'm on my way. I've seen so little of her all summer with the book tour.

DAVE: How's that going? Any funny "book tour anecdotes" to report?

PETER: I did put a sanctimonious local NPR reporter in his place. Other than that it's been rather staid.

DAVE: I'm sorry I haven't had a chance to read the book yet. It's on the top of the pile.

PETER *(Laughs)*: Not to worry, it's just like the ones you *have* read, only with a better jacket photo. Wait till you finish writing yours.

(Scott enters from lake path.)

DAVE *(Taking drink, laughing)*: Who knows when that'll be.

SCOTT: Hey!

(All look to Scott.)

—Sorry to interrupt.

DAVE: —Nonsense. Scott, this is my dear old friend Peter! Scott's a student of mine at Columbia. A wonderful writer.

SCOTT *(Laughing)*: I am?

PETER: "Abandon all hope ye who entertain." That's my advice to you, never forget it, ha!

SCOTT: Hi. I'd shake your hand but—fertilizer.

PETER: I smell that.

SCOTT: Right—um, if it's cool, Dave, I'm just gonna grab a quick shower, then run home—what time? . . .

DAVE: Oh, an hour and a half, two hours.

SCOTT: I called Carol but—says she's "painting" tonight.

ELAINE: Oh— *(Looking to Dave)* you're joining us for— *(To Scott)* Good.

DAVE: —That's a shame she can't make it. Dedicated to her art, Carol! Always working!

SCOTT: Also Carol isn't really cool with leaving Jaime with my mom, which I don't blame her. *(Makes "drinking" motion with hand)*

ELAINE: Oh, you have a son?

SCOTT: A *girl*—Jaime. Four years old, breaks my heart every day.

DAVE: Yeah, she's an angel. She and Carol spent the afternoon at the lake a few weeks ago.

(Pause.)

ELAINE: How wonderful.

(Pause.)

SCOTT: Hey uh—for the path to the dock—I want—did you make up your mind? It's all cleared out now so . . .

DAVE: Wood chips or stones?

PETER: Stones! Stones!

DAVE: The stones are kind of pricey.

PETER: Stones!

DAVE: And the windows are costing so much more than the estimate . . .

SCOTT: So . . .

DAVE: Yeah, let's say wood. You eat steak, right?

SCOTT: What a treat! Carol's a vegan. We compromised with Jaime, she can have eggs but no chicken.

PETER: Ah, the postmodern age—a pro-choice vegetarian toddler.

SCOTT: Yeah. *(Beat)* So I'll phone that order in.

(Scott starts to go.)

Oh—I keep forgetting—my new draft.

(Scott whips the coiled manuscript out of his back pocket and hands it to Dave.)

DAVE: I look forward to reading it.

(Scott goes into the house. Peter nods to his manuscript.)

PETER: Does he have it?

DAVE: He does. He has a sense of rhythm—a sense of feeling— with language that's rare. What he needs is to rein it in, find a social context, a metaphor for all that young male rage of his.

ELAINE: Why is he—I mean, what is the rage? He seems so— thrilled.

DAVE: He tends to punish his characters, especially the most vulnerable ones. I don't know what the rage is personally— I guess, I mean, we all remember what it was like in our twenties.

PETER: I don't. *(Laughter)* It's such a different time, though, there's not really a parallel, is there?

DAVE: What do you mean?

PETER: Well, we grew up with the Kennedys, Vietnam, Women's Lib. What did he grow up with?

ELAINE *(Laughing)*: Trickle Down and the Gulf War!

DAVE: No, exactly—Reagan and Spielberg! Most of my students—their angst is all domestic because the social and the political have become so diffuse.

ELAINE: But that's their context. Maybe that's what makes what they have to say valuable—that it's a product of its time.

PETER: All you can ever be is of your time.

ELAINE: Alas. *(Laughs)*

DAVE: Yes and no. Scott may be of his time, but—what he has to say is unsatisfying to *him* I think, and he's looking to history— to us—to help place him. I think Scott writes in order to figure out—exactly what you said, Elaine—"what the rage is."

(Beat.)

PETER: You know—it's been too long. Let me call Mary and see if she'll suffer my absence a few more hours. The phone? . . .

DAVE: —Upstairs, last room on the right.

PETER: Wish me luck.

DAVE: Oh—a house rule both of you should know: if the phone rings, please allow the machine the honor.

ELAINE (*Smiling*): Yeah, I've inferred that rule.

DAVE (*Laughs*): Oh—right.

PETER: —I've heard you don't pick up the phone: Robert's not pleased.

DAVE: Yes—Robert—ha. How times have changed—now my agent's mad at *me* for not returning *his* calls.

(*Peter exits.*)

(*Confidentially*) Well I can't *exactly* say I'm in the mood.

ELAINE: Oh, it's good to see him. He's so up. Fun.

DAVE: Oh, sure, sure, just . . . This new book's really broken through, huh. That movie opened him up to a whole new audience.

ELAINE: Well, he's still smarting about his reviews. Though I told him at the least they've been getting a little more exuberant in their ambivalence.

DAVE: Was he complaining about them?

ELAINE: I don't know about "complaining"—he spoke about it on the drive up.

DAVE (*Laughing*): Whatever.

ELAINE: What-what?

DAVE: What?

ELAINE: No, it's just funny—I've never heard you say, "Whatever."

DAVE: Oh.

(*Pause. Elaine puts her hand on Dave's head, musses his hair a bit.*)

You should have seen me yesterday. Three months, since I got here, without a haircut and just—mad scientist kind of thing, hair every which way.

ELAINE: You are kidding.

DAVE: The barber kept mumbling in Italian, he was not pleased.

ELAINE (*Tousling his hair*): It must have been a little hot with all that hair.

DAVE: It was, but—I got in a groove with the book, downhill, end in sight, so any kind of little errand or responsibility—to think I'd have to stop writing for even ten minutes . . .

ELAINE (*Not entirely unserious*): So—Scott kept you fed, took out the garbage . . .

DAVE *(Laughing)*: I'm exaggerating a little. I did manage to feed myself.

(Beat. Peter pops his head out the window.)

PETER: Charming phone!

(A beat.)

DAVE: —It was the only thing here when I bought the place!
PETER: Is that red paint or sheep's blood speckled all over it?
DAVE: —Yes!
PETER: Ha!

(Peter disappears inside. Dave angles back to Elaine.)

DAVE: Well—you look fantastic. You're here, in the flesh!
ELAINE: Here I am. —Ready for summer to be over.
DAVE: Yeah?
ELAINE: Everything gets so quiet. *(Beat)* I guess—you know—to speak "frankly" . . . I've been a little worried lately.
DAVE: Worried? About what?
ELAINE: You. Us. You. *(Smiles)*
DAVE: Why?
ELAINE: Just—the distance . . . literally . . . metaphorically . . .
DAVE: The book. I know. I've felt it, too. This is the longest we've ever been away from each other.
ELAINE: It is.
DAVE: But we're together now. Right?
ELAINE: And you're almost finished up here—the house and the book . . . Back to the city . . .
DAVE: —The good life resumes.
ELAINE: Life resumes.
DAVE: Not the good life?
ELAINE *(Gently)*: Oh, I dunno. The same life, how's that. But— you're okay? Not "us" but—
DAVE: Yeah.
ELAINE: It's just—I don't really know.
DAVE: I'm fine. —How was your audition?
ELAINE: Everything's all right?
DAVE: I said I'm fine.

(Beat.)

How was your audition?

ELAINE: *That. (Beat)* The play— *(Shifting tone, more casual; she takes bug spray from purse, applies it)* was so bathetic and juvenile. I read for this kind of bitter, histrionic society lady named Veronica, who torments her shiftless homosexual son.

DAVE *(Sipping drink)*: —She's got a Valium prescription in one hand—

ELAINE: —and the telephone number of her handsome young masseur in the other, exactly. Now, the director is this thin little reed of a man, this little wisp—a *boy*—and he stops me in the middle of my speech. "Too hard," he says. "Too harsh." *(Laughs)* He can't even give me a complete sentence—just fragments! "Softer around the edges."

DAVE: Six weeks out of grad school . . .

ELAINE: So—I take the adjustment, I do "softer around the edges," and I see from the corner of my eye that he's eating a big *carrot*. Really crunching on it.

DAVE *(Laughing)*: Onwards and downwards!

ELAINE: This will sound ghastly, but I'm on the subway going home, and I start thinking about TV . . . and I have this horrible image of me—going in for an eye tuck.

DAVE: Oh God, Elaine. That's grotesque!

ELAINE: I think so too, but . . .

DAVE: It's that you're too smart for these people, that's why they won't cast you.

ELAINE: You know, I hate when people talk that way about themselves. I hate it. "I'm too threatening." It's so presumptuous. How am I "threatening"? I'm just a person.

DAVE: But that's just it. You're real. They have to look at you and see what it means to be a real person in this world, and it's intolerable to them.

ELAINE: Well . . . I haven't told you the best part: I get home, my agent's called: there's an offer for me . . . a tenth anniversary production of *'night, Mother*—in Syracuse.

DAVE: Oh no.

ELAINE: I mean—who wants to see *'night, Mother*? I mean, really, at the end of the day . . . Anyway. *(Smiles)*

DAVE: I'm sorry.

ELAINE: —I might be able to get a sitcom still, maybe.

DAVE: Really?

ELAINE: Why not? I can do that "suburban spunk," right?

DAVE: Well, in that case, you're doing the dishes tonight.

(Peter enters from house.)

PETER: Good news! Permission from mother!

DAVE: That was quick; Mary's losing her touch.

PETER: Actually, I just left her a message.

DAVE: Well—I should get that steak then.

PETER: Oh, finish your cocktail.

DAVE: No time. If we don't get there before it closes, I'll have to scoop up some venison from the side of the road. Are you up for a drive?

PETER: Absolutely! *(Finishes drink with a gulp)* Off to market!

ELAINE: My men are leaving me? To "stave off" Mother Nature all on my own?

DAVE: —The potatoes are all boiled; you can cut them up for the salad if you want.

(Dave and Peter start off.)

PETER: Let's take that big scary truck of yours, I'm tired of driving my stupid Volvo.

DAVE: Do you need anything at the store?

(Elaine doesn't respond for a moment, as if lost in thought.)

Elaine?

ELAINE: Oh—I have all I need.

(A beat. Dave moves to Elaine, kisses her gently on the head, and exits with Peter. Pause. Elaine looks down at Dave's manuscript. We hear the car pull away. She starts to scan, turns some pages. Scott emerges from the house, shirtless, in an old pair of athletic shorts and sneakers. He's holding his work clothes and boots under one arm, a bottle of beer in his other hand.)

SCOTT *(Un-self-consciously)*: Hey.

ELAINE: Oh—hi. —You got your shower, I see.

SCOTT: Yeah—unfortunately didn't bring anything to change into—grabbed these shorts from Dave's dresser, hope he doesn't mind. (*Looks at them, laughs a little*) —Whatever. (*Elaine smiles*) What do you think of it?

ELAINE: —Oh, I've only just—picked it up.

SCOTT: There's this scene he showed me the other night, with this welfare case worker who's basically torturing Ladrica— this single mother on welfare—it's like Kafka meets Marx in the Bronx. Blew me away.

ELAINE: That's good to hear.

SCOTT: Yeah—so—enjoy yourself.

ELAINE: I hope to.

(*Pause.*)

—Drive safely!

SCOTT: Yeah—see you in a flash. (*As he goes*) —I'm looking forward to tonight!

(*Scott is off. We hear his car start—with difficulty—and pull away. Elaine sees Scott's manuscript. She looks at it a moment, then puts down Dave's pages, picks up Scott's—coiled, stained with dirt—and begins to read.*)

Scene 3

1993. Nearing sundown. A large plate wrapped in tinfoil is on the grill, where Dave stands, preparing. Place settings and ice bucket are on the table. A small, square, wrapped package sits on the table also. Scott is laying out silverware. Lights rise.

SCOTT: I feel so stupid that I didn't know.

DAVE: Oh, it's fine.

SCOTT (*Like he still can't believe it*): Peter Lawson!

DAVE: That's what his driver's license says.

SCOTT: Fucking A. I'm so nervous I'm gonna start sweating.

DAVE: —It's not like it's Philip Roth.

(*Elaine pops her head out the upper window; we can partially see Peter behind her.*)

ELAINE: So this is where the magic happens!

DAVE: If only it were magic!

(Peter squeezes through.)

PETER: How quaint that you still write it out longhand. Al Gore has your name on a list somewhere!

DAVE: How do you like your steak, Peter?

PETER: As I like my women: pink on the inside!

(Elaine laughs, mock-hits Peter, and both disappear inside. Scott, finished setting the table, picks up the package and approaches Dave.)

SCOTT: So—um—table's all set.

DAVE: Thank you.

SCOTT: Yeah—so—I'm gonna be done, like—in a couple days. Totally done. All that's left is just the path really—I hope I did all right.

DAVE: You're kidding. You know what this place looked like before.

SCOTT: No—yeah. Just—I guess I have something to ask you—

(Peter and Elaine enter.)

PETER: Calling *Architectural Digest*!

DAVE: Oh! Ha.

PETER: No, really Dave. So open and airy, you'd never tell looking at it from the outside. Genius!

ELAINE: It really is remarkable.

DAVE: You guys have to go down to the dock and take a look at the lake—and redirect your compliments. Scott did all the "down and dirty" stuff.

SCOTT: —Dave and I did it together. He's just a modest guy.

DAVE: So—Peter's rare, Elaine's medium. —Scott?

SCOTT: Steak! It's been so long.

(Elaine moves toward lake path, looks down it. Peter pours himself another scotch.)

DAVE: How do you like it?

145

SCOTT: Burn the bitch!

(Peter looks at Elaine.)

DAVE *(Embarrassed by Scott's language)*: Well done, I can do that for you.

(Pause. Scott looks around, catches Peter's eye.)

PETER: So, Scott . . . —What are you gripping so severely in your hands there?
SCOTT: —This. Yeah, just waiting for the right—awkward. Here.

(Scott hands the package to Dave.)

DAVE: Oh, thank you. Should I open this now?
SCOTT: Sure, go for it.

(Dave begins to open it.)

PETER: Would you like a drink, Scott?
SCOTT: Yeah—beer's cool.
PETER: Be a writer; have a scotch.
ELAINE: —Peter.
SCOTT: —Sure—scotch is cool. *(To Elaine)* Hey, I brought pictures of Jaime with me.
ELAINE *(After a beat; realizing this was addressed to her)*: Oh.

(Dave has the package open and is looking at what we see is a small painting, simply framed.)

DAVE: —Wow—did Carol? . . .
SCOTT: She said I could take one, yeah.
DAVE *(Struck by the seriousness of the painting)*: My God.

(Pause as Dave looks at the painting.)

SCOTT: I should light these citronellas.

(Scott takes a Zippo out of his pocket, begins to light the three citronella candles at the corners of the porch.)

DAVE: Is it?—it looks a little like—you.

SCOTT: Yeah—me, in the abstract. That's been her theme all summer—me!

(Elaine moves to look at the painting.)

PETER *(Holding Scott's tall glass of scotch)*: Why's that?

SCOTT *(Laughing)*: I don't know, maybe it's 'cuz we've been fighting a lot.

PETER: Ah yes, art, fantasy, control . . .

ELAINE: —Very striking. Did you pose for her?

SCOTT: I can't sit still like that, she's given up trying to make me. Anyway, by now she pretty much knows what I look like naked.

PETER: Let me have a look.

(Peter crosses to the painting. If we can see it at all, we see that it's a male figure, somewhat abstracted, nude; the figure holds something in his right hand, dark and amorphous.)

You have a talented wife.

(Beat.)

What's that you're holding, your cock?

DAVE: —Peter.

ELAINE *(Similarly embarrassed)*: He's—that's not—no—

PETER: Well what is it then? Oh, *there's* the penis—well, Jesus, take your prick!

DAVE: Scott, what is the figure—holding, this vague dark shape here?

SCOTT: It freaks me out a little, actually. Carol says she doesn't know what it is, just that it's "something"—something "getting in the way" when she looks at me.

PETER *(Crossing to Scott, giving him scotch)*: Can't do that in prose—too bad, too, it would make things a lot easier. "What's that you're holding?" he asked quizzically. "I don't know," she replied, "but it has some significance."

(Scott takes the drink, sits. Elaine drifts back to the table, sits. She and Peter are on either side of Scott.)

147

DAVE (*Moving to house*): Well, I'm honored to receive this. Thank you, and thank her for me.

SCOTT: Will do!

DAVE: If anyone needs anything—I'll be in the kitchen making potato salad.

(*Dave exits.*)

PETER: You did a fine job in there, really. That bathroom!

SCOTT: Yeah. The two showerheads was my idea. (*To Elaine*) Gotta build that man some romance!

(*A moment. Scott takes his drink, sips a bit too much, gasps.*)

Whoa, bartender!

PETER: Small sips. Have you never had scotch before?

SCOTT: No—I drink beer . . . (*Turning to Elaine*) Hey, pictures.

ELAINE: That's right.

(*He takes about twelve loose pictures out of his pocket and hands them to Elaine. He looks at Elaine till she says:*)

—Awwww.

SCOTT: Yeah. (*Turning to Peter*) So I just have to tell you—how totally great I think your books are? The last two, *Tall Grass* and *Laura on the Jitney*—whoa. And the movie of *Laura*, it rocks. —I mean, the book's better . . .

PETER: You think? I preferred the film myself.

(*Pause. Scott laughs.*)

SCOTT: I sound stupid here don't I.

PETER: No, I was just trying to be self-deprecating. Though I did prefer the *paycheck*.

SCOTT: Yeah. (*To Elaine*) Isn't she the best?

ELAINE: Oh—gorgeous child—

SCOTT (*To Peter*): It's just—what I like about them is—they're totally trashy—in a good way trashy—sexy and alive, just, bursting, like—and I love books about successful people screwing their lives up.

PETER: *Schadenfreude.*

SCOTT: Yeah.

PETER: Do you know what *Schadenfreude* is?

ELAINE *(Lightly)*: Oh Peter.

PETER: What?

SCOTT: Is it um . . . it's a philosopher, right, or? . . .

PETER: Schopenhauer is a philosopher. *Schadenfreude* is a noun: the pleasure one takes in someone else's misfortune.

SCOTT: Oh. *Schadenfreude*. Cool word.

(Pause.)

ELAINE *(Rescuing Scott a little)*: Carol is—stunning.

SCOTT: Oh—yeah. And that's my house—that I grew up in. Me and Carol are staying up here with my mom for the summer. Like a half hour north. Saving some money.

PETER: You're *from* here.

SCOTT: Near. That's actually how I got this job. I write a lot about growing up. Dave said he had a house nearby, I told him I was gonna be around this summer . . .

PETER *(To Elaine as well)*: So it was fortuitous.

(A beat.)

SCOTT: Fortuitous, yeah . . . Dave's the best, just—showed me so much about my work. He's so brilliant

PETER: Brilliance worth forty thousand dollars?

SCOTT: —Try sixty by the time I graduate. Student loans crawling out my ass.

ELAINE *(Genuinely touched)*: Look at her face—she is loved!

SCOTT *(Turning to see picture)*: Who, Carol or Jaime?

ELAINE: Oh—well, both. —You must have had Jaime so young.

(We hear a car pull up. All turn vaguely toward the sound.)

SCOTT: Yeah, Deerhill High sweethearts, me and Carol.

PETER: —Who's that?

SCOTT: We were together almost six years when she got pregnant, and it was like—*yeah*, let's do this. She's my rock.

PETER: What have you two been fighting about?

SCOTT: Oh—you know, usual ball-and-chain stuff.

(Alan enters inconspicuously; only Scott sees. But he does not acknowledge him. Alan has a loaf of bread half-sticking out of a brown bag. He crosses to Elaine.)

Anyway. She's a reason to live, right?

PETER: —Just wait a few years. My thirteen-year-old son thinks he should have *no* curfew—Manhattan.

SCOTT: Yeah, I know, it's like—I love her too much. When she has her first date I'll meet the little dude at the front door with a Glock or something.

(Alan takes a few more steps into the yard.)

ALAN *(Shyly)*: Hello; my name is Alan, and I'm looking for Dave Ardith.

ELAINE *(Looking up)*: —Oh—hello. I'm Elaine. Dave is making "potato salad."

(Scott grabs his drink, avoids Alan's eyes.)

ALAN: I hope I was expected.

ELAINE: Dave's so casual about this kind of thing—but welcome. Yes, I was wondering who the extra steak was for.

ALAN *(Squinting a bit)*: Hello . . . Scott?

SCOTT: Hey—Dr. Richards.

ALAN: Please, call me Alan.

SCOTT: —Alan. Hey.

ELAINE: You two—

SCOTT: —yeah actually—had a class.

ALAN: We know each other academically. It will be a pleasure to entertain you in a new context.

SCOTT: Right.

PETER: —I'm Peter, and I'm looking for love in all the wrong places.

ALAN: Very nice to meet you.

ELAINE: So you know Dave from Columbia.

ALAN: Yes, I'm a training analyst there, as well as a professor of psychoanalysis. —I have bread.

ELAINE: I see that. Have a seat.

ALAN *(Approaches chair)*: And I must say, it's an honor to meet you—a celebrity of the stage!

ELAINE: Oh yes—a "celebrity."

ALAN: I won't embarrass you now, but before the night is out we must discuss your sublime Madame Arkadina in *The Sea Gull* last year.

ELAINE: You're kidding, you saw it?

ALAN: Oh, magnificent. I have a few questions for you.

SCOTT: —I'll just run in and get Dave.

(Alan sits.)

PETER: Have a drink, Al. What would you like?

ALAN: I think I'll experience this nature unmedicated, actually. A glass of water would be lovely.

PETER: Water's for dogs! Have a scotch!

ALAN: Well—I'll be driving later and these roads are rather— tortured, aren't they?

PETER *(Pouring scotch)*: Just one. A nice steak will sober you up easy.

ALAN: I suppose just one . . .

(Dave enters from the house. Scott begins to move toward the house, inconspicuously.)

DAVE: Alan! You made it!

ALAN: Dave, thank you for having me! —I baked this myself. Twice!

DAVE *(Taking the bread)*: We'll slice it up and have it! I'm so glad you could come.

ALAN *(Nervous, but affable)*: Driving to your house is like entering a Grimm's fairy tale! The day's last light, the twisting road, the dense spread of forest. And a delightful little town from what I could see.

DAVE *(Moves to the grill, to do more prep work)*: I don't know about delightful—the economy's been eroding for a decade now.

ALAN: Ah . . .

PETER: —What was Alan's class like, Scott?

SCOTT: Oh—it was psychoanalysis and Shakespeare? It was called "Shakespeare on the Couch."

ALAN: —*They* gave it that title, claiming that my preference was too esoteric: "Harmonious Breath and the Rude Sea." One of my favorite passages.

PETER: So what then, you all talk about how Hamlet wants to bone his mother?

ALAN: God save us! No, no; we *did* read *Hamlet,* and the question I asked was, "How does the play reflect and challenge our *own* narcissism and paranoia, here in the year 1993?"

PETER: That's interesting. What's your take, Scott? Is Hamlet a Gen-X hero, the Kurt Cobain of his day?

SCOTT: I don't know about that. Um.

(Beat.)

—I actually promised Carol I'd call—can't let a night go by without checking in on Jaime!

(Scott gets up, goes into the house.)

ALAN: Yes. Well. You know, a lot of writers are unmoved by psychoanalysis—suspicious even—which is understandable. Theory is often reductive, while art examines the essential mysteries, without pathologizing them.

PETER: Speaking of pathology . . . I'd like to lay David on the couch for a moment. May I, David?

DAVE *(Smiles)*: Uh-oh.

PETER: Thank you. We're in the market just now, buying some meat, and I remark, "That's a very nice shirt, David." "Yes," he says, "isn't it? But I bought it from Banana Republic, and I can't shop there anymore because they use sweatshop labor."

DAVE *(Laughing)*: Feel free to decline to respond, Alan.

PETER: —It's the same thing at cocktail parties, when I hear people speaking in serious hushed tones about Bosnia: "I can't believe we're not doing anything more," they say. "We should be doing something." We, *we*? It's "they" who do things— governments, corporations— "we" have no "power," no effect on history that way, what's all this "we" talk?

DAVE: Peter, but—it's nihilism to refuse to imagine yourself as an actor in, I mean—sure obviously there's "history" but there's also *history,* which is life, and to proclaim that personal behavior has no *effect*—

PETER: —But we just elected a president who went on *60 Minutes* with his wife in a headband and told us he was a bad man in his "personal behavior," and we voted for him anyway. I think that's progress! (Lucky she wore that ugly castrating thing, else people might not have sympathized.) But really, it's a new age, and you just have to resign yourself to it, David— we're small creatures in a vast, unfathomable world, a world that spins forward despite us, and whether or not one buys a shirt at Banana Republic is a superfluous dilemma. The shirt is made! What we don't have control over: *that* is history. What we *do* have control over: that is *pleasure*.

(Pause.)

ALAN: I must say, Elaine, one of the things I was thinking as I was—
PETER: —The shirt is in the store!
DAVE: *Peter*. I purchased the shirt in the context of, "Oh, that would look good on me." When I learned what I learned— you know, that some ten-year-old "brown" girl is making forty cents a day working sixteen-hour shifts, her hands bleeding and her fingernails falling off and her back stiffening into knots the size of my fist and—you know, the context changes. It becomes, "I won't give my money to the people who are torturing that little girl."
PETER: You can contextualize it till the cows come home— I mean, that's probably the best job that little girl can find. —It's just guilt, right Alan? The terror of pleasure!
DAVE: How is denying global capitalism—it's *morality*, Peter—
ELAINE: You two just have different quirks of self-dramatization, that's all.

(A beat. Dave and Peter smile.)

ALAN: —I can't hold it back any longer, Elaine. I must congratulate you on your heartbreaking Madame Arkadina.
ELAINE: Thank you, Alan, you're very kind.
ALAN: On my drive up I was recalling the way you—or she—you *as* she, you—er—well—how delicate when calling Boris from the house! Not nearly as histrionic as I've always seen it done. Although—you—were grandiose, there was also the sense that you were—*she* was—striving to survive this collection of pompous men.
DAVE: —Hear that, Peter?

PETER: Ha!

ALAN: —What a muddle I made there! —How *does* one speak to an actress about her performance? Third or second person?

ELAINE: Well, I—

DAVE: —Have I ever told you the story of falling in love with Elaine, Alan?

(Elaine exhales theatrically.)

What?

ELAINE: This *story. (Beat)* How many times do we have to hear it? —Come on, please?

DAVE: Well—*I'll* never tire of it. What's wrong with my telling it?

PETER: —The country does make men nostalgic. All this space to fill.

DAVE: All right?

(Elaine doesn't quite respond.)

(To Alan) About four years ago, I saw Elaine on stage. Now, I'd never met her in real— *(At Elaine)* what?

ELAINE: Now what?

DAVE: That look you're—is there some reason you'd like me to not—

ELAINE: —*Tell* the story if you want, I'm just—are you sure you haven't heard it before, Alan?

ALAN: Oh—I don't believe I have . . . perhaps—

DAVE: Well. —I was devastated by this performance—in an otherwise undistinguished new play—and I ended up writing a story about a man who falls in love with a woman he first sees on stage. When I met Elaine socially a year or so later, the first time I met her, I didn't recognize her as the actress from the play— *(Elaine takes a sip of water)* —but as I was talking to her, I had this *sense,* the strangest feeling of— *(Stops; a good beat; then)* You know what—fine, I won't tell the story, it's obviously upsetting you.

ELAINE: —It's fine, Dave.

DAVE: Is it?

ELAINE: You already started.

DAVE: I'll tell Alan later, privately.

ELAINE: Dave—

154

DAVE: It's okay, whatever.

(Pause. Dave goes back to the grill.)

PETER *(To Alan)*: What I don't understand about the theater is—why don't people just walk out?

ALAN: Oh, but that's such a rude breach of the implicit contract! To be a member of an audience, to participate in a narrative collectively, and not carry the burden of a purely individual response—that's the privilege of attending the theater.

ELAINE: Do you see plays often, Alan.

ALAN: I do. Being in the academy offers constant opportunity to see plays—though it's often graduate-student nonsense—Armageddon, homosexual *Virginia Woolfs* and the like.

DAVE: Hey I saw that one!

ELAINE: —How interesting that you'd mention that play. I've been rereading all the old standards this summer, the "classic" American plays. And it really struck me—it's kind of funny actually—but almost all the female roles in these plays are different shades of *shrew*. Have you ever noticed that?

ALAN: Which plays?

ELAINE: Start with Williams—Blanche and Amanda and Maggie, practically the whole *oeuvre*, just *buckets* of hysteria and cruelty. Albee—Martha on down the line, all those women, so brutal and severe.

ALAN: Perhaps that is so . . .

ELAINE: Even Mary in *Long Day's Journey*—she's lost but at her core she's vicious really—

DAVE: —I keep trying to convince Elaine to go back to regional theater, where she might be cast in roles she'd never get to do in New York—Lady Macbeth, Mother Courage—plays in cities where people actually go to the theater to be told a story, not just confirm their status as masters of the universe.

PETER: You know, there *are* some good people in New York, David.

(Scott enters.)

—Daddy dearest! Does Jaime miss you?

155

SCOTT: Yeah. Hey—found this flashlight, thought I could take all of you down to the lake before dinner. Afterwards we might be too tipsy to make it.

PETER: Good idea!

(Scott moves to the lake path, Peter following. Elaine takes bug spray out of her bag, starts applying it.)

SCOTT: Coming, Alan?

ALAN: I'll come down in a minute.

SCOTT: A minute. Right.

(Elaine starts to follow Peter and Scott.)

DAVE: Elaine.

ELAINE: What?

(She turns. Peter motions Scott on, and they exit. Elaine moves to Dave, who guides her off a bit. Alan looks busy on the porch for a moment, then goes inside.)

DAVE: What's going on?

ELAINE: What?

DAVE: You're acting out.

ELAINE: *I'm* acting out. —Look, the evening's begun. "The epic dinner party." So this is not a discussion we're going to have now. It's obviously a discussion you hoped not to have at all.

DAVE: I don't think I'm following.

ELAINE: It's been *three months*, Dave. So what's the—have you invited anyone else up? Will we be entertaining all week?

DAVE: I—thought you would like to meet Scott and Alan.

ELAINE: Tonight? That's honestly and truly the thought that went through your head? After three months of not seeing each other, of barely speaking because you're so wrapped up in your book and—whatever else, this would be exactly what I . . .

DAVE: Whatever else? *(Pause. Elaine looks away)* Alan's—lonely. He doesn't go out a lot. He always brings up your performance—

ELAINE: Then why have I never even heard of him? Never once have you spoken of him. And Scott, you portrayed him as some bumbling, screwed-up kid—when he's obviously *very* shrewd.

DAVE: What does that have to do with? . . .

ELAINE: You've obviously been talking to *him* all summer, taking a great interest in *his* "rage" and his lack of "social context." Your book hasn't kept you from *that* relationship.

(Pause.)

DAVE: Okay. I'll shoo them along the best I can. —Unfortunately, Peter *never* leaves.

ELAINE: Peter's fine, we *know* Peter. It's these strangers—these polite getting-to-know-you conversations.

DAVE: Did something—happen—I mean, is something else going on here that you're not? . . .

ELAINE: What, I'm not allowed to be upset for the reasons I've articulated?

(Short pause.)

DAVE: Of course you are.

(A beat.)

ELAINE: Look, people are hovering, let's not. We'll talk in the morning, tonight obviously is—I'm going to go down to the lake now.

DAVE: I . . . I'm sorry, Elaine—

(Elaine exits. Dave stands stiff for a moment. Alan returns to the porch. Dave turns to Alan.)

ALAN: Everything all right?

DAVE: Oh—Elaine is—feeling under the weather.

ALAN: Sorry to hear that.

DAVE: And you—know how I am.

(Pause.)

ALAN *(Removing bottle of pills, extending them to Dave)*: I stayed back because—as promised—I brought the pills for you.

(A beat; Dave crosses to the pills.)

DAVE: Thanks.

ALAN: Have you . . . given any more thought to reentering therapy?

DAVE: I know how to talk to a therapist, it's talking to everyone else that . . . Could you top off my drink, Al? It's on the table—pour another for yourself.

ALAN: I'd better not.

DAVE *(Looking at the prescription bottle)*: How pathetic.

ALAN: What's important is that you feel well.

(During the following, Alan pours Dave a drink—as Dave goes on, he pours himself another drink as well. At some point Dave comes and takes his drink from the table.)

DAVE *(Looking at pills)*: Could it really be biological, chemical? That explanation leaves so much out. But what else is it? *(Laughing)* I have no interest in being unhappy! I should be— Elaine is the most wonderful woman, I'm writing, I'm teaching—I have every opportunity, every privilege—

ALAN: Now, don't do this to yourself.

DAVE: You know, when I'm writing . . . I feel so alive, so connected—to the world, to my politics. And the moment I put down the pen . . .

ALAN: Isn't that common? That the world you're creating becomes more compelling than the world you live in?

DAVE: No, I know what that is. It's something about—being here, away. When I think of my life back in the city, my community . . . you know, no one talks anymore about politics, morality—anything except the most boring domestic minutiae. There's a sense that with Bush gone, the political battle's been won and everyone just . . . people who started out believing there could be social change in the world, Peter— now he's writing about how tragic married life is. *(Laughs)* He's de-educated himself to justify his own indulgences. And this—this is the world I have to return to now. Summer's over. And—I don't think I want to go back.

(Pause.)

ALAN: It's painful to be in a place of not-knowing. But progress doesn't always happen in a straight line. We tend to look for something unequivocal, an "end to the story" to explain how we're feeling, but . . .

DAVE: That sounds like something I said to Scott.

ALAN: Oh?

DAVE: Invariably his stories end with acts of aggression. I've been trying to show him how to live with his characters' pain, without making them act it out . . . *(Takes sip of his drink)*

ALAN: I confess, I was surprised to see Scott here.

DAVE: Yeah. I hadn't expected such a—I just thought he'd do some work for me this summer, but as time went on, it evolved into a real friendship. Scott hasn't become preoccupied by the "game" yet; it's still about the art for him. Talking with him, I've been reconnecting with parts of myself that have become dormant—the political stuff, the reasons I became a writer. He actually wants to listen.

ALAN: That pleases me to hear. *(Pause)* I've had a very different experience of him.

DAVE: How so?

ALAN: The only assignment in my class was a paper on *Hamlet*, to be handed in at the end of the semester. Scott didn't turn it in. We met and he explained that he would complete the paper by the end of July. So I passed him. Well, a few weeks ago, I got the paper in the mail. I read it, and instantly recognized the essay he'd copied.

DAVE: Oh . . .

ALAN: I have to say—I feel exploited.

(Pause.)

DAVE: But Alan—Scott—he's not one of these trust-fund kids up there, you know, he's a real person, from a—a place where—this stuff, Shakespeare and psychoanalysis—it's a foreign language. It's almost like—for him, even *learning* this stuff is a betrayal. Of the values he grew up with, in his family, his community . . .

ALAN: But—certainly that's why he's at Columbia. To discover new values.

DAVE: But it's still—what's *Hamlet* to him? —The story Scott's working on—it's about this violent kid who has a sadistic father. It's taken me all summer to show Scott that it's not just a story about a kid who's violent because his father is abusive—but it's *also* a story about a man who, because he's been treated callously at work, becomes abusive towards his son. And even getting Scott *there* has been difficult— Shakespeare and—paranoia, narcissism? It's completely outside of his—Scott's a troubled kid, you shouldn't take it personally—

ALAN: He's hardly a kid.

(Pause.)

DAVE: No, you're right, he's . . . *(Pause)* Elaine—said something similar . . .

ALAN: What did she say?

DAVE *(Really making a discovery here)*: She said—that I described Scott as a kid when he's obviously—"very shrewd." Maybe . . . maybe I've gotten—lost in him—the way I've gotten lost in my *book*. Maybe—what I've taken as his interest is in *part* . . .

(Scott appears in the path, Dave sees him.)

So—you know—how do you like your steak, Alan?

ALAN: Go on, don't lose your train of thought.

DAVE: No, I just— *(To Scott)* —Hey!

(Alan turns, sees Scott. Then, back to Dave:)

ALAN: —Medium.

DAVE: Medium.

SCOTT: —How are those dead cows coming?

DAVE: Oh—hey—just a couple more minutes. Where are uh— Hänsel und Gretel?

SCOTT: Peter asked me to go get the scotch. They're sitting on the dock. He's teaching Elaine some song about the sea.

(Pause. Alan looks at Scott, with some compassion.)

ALAN: —Why don't I go tell them dinner's about to be served. I'd like to see the lake myself.

SCOTT: Path's dark—take it slow.

ALAN: I will. —And you said Peter asked you to fetch him his scotch?

SCOTT: He can wait.

(A moment. Alan nods, then exits. Scott grabs his drink.)

So. What's up.

DAVE: Just trading some "psychoanalytic gossip" with Alan—the things shrinks have heard!

SCOTT: Like what?

DAVE: Just—some amazing stories. As you could imagine.

SCOTT: Right. *(Beat)* When I was at SUNY, when people'd get really drunk, I'd ask 'em what the worst thing they'd ever done was?

DAVE: And?

SCOTT: And it turned out basically that most people hadn't ever done anything really bad.

(Dave laughs.)

Hey, I think Elaine liked the two showerheads. Could tell by the look on her face.

DAVE: Oh yeah?

SCOTT: I told you. Here, let me finish the steaks, you take a break.

DAVE: —Okay.

(Scott takes over the grill, giving Dave a jocular slap on the ass as he crosses to the table, to his drink.)

SCOTT: I'm really excited about the rewrite.

DAVE: I'm looking forward to reading it.

SCOTT: I trimmed down the sex scene? Like you said? And I added all this stuff about the boy, I have him working in a snack bar at this ritzy summer resort place. I think it's a lot more about class now. It's more about—how poor people need rich people and—how powerless you are when you're poor. —The only part you still might not like is what the boy—does to the girl in the end . . .

(Scott shrugs, flips a steak. He looks at Dave, who nods. Then:)

DAVE: I'll get to it this weekend.

SCOTT: Yeah, so . . . —you know, now that I got a drink in me I can say this . . . there's not too much work left and I'm sure

when I'm done I'm gonna feel all torn up and awkward, so—
I just thought I'd tell you now that I really—appreciate all of
this, you know. Just, the job, and your helping me with my
stories.

DAVE: Well, it's been a pleasure.

SCOTT: But there's—one question I never asked you. Do you—
and you can—do I have a future?

(Pause.)

DAVE: God. What a question! Who can say. *(Beat)* What's important is that you love to do it, and continue to do it, with
discipline . . .

SCOTT: Uh-huh . . .

DAVE: You have to keep writing. And reading, all the time—
and—then you'll find your own way. Your own path. But
you're very young, Scott, so much will happen to you. Your
life, your writing, will change in ways you can't fathom right
now and—

SCOTT: —I know I'm not dumb, but—whatever it is that
makes—like, I tell myself I should cut out TV and never read
magazines and I think of all the books that I haven't read and
it's like When Will I Read Them? Because I—like I *lack*
something you *need* . . .

DAVE: I can relate! Everyone's full of doubts, trust me, we're all
afraid we'll be found out for frauds—

SCOTT: —Aw, this is neurotic shit, isn't it?

DAVE: No—no. Of course you're going to wonder about the eco-
nomic viability of writing as a career, it's practical thinking—you have Jaime, and Carol has *her* art and—

SCOTT: No, not just that. It's like I'm lacking something—that
you have . . .

(Pause. Dave smiles, then turns away, toward the path.)

DAVE: What are they doing? *(Calling)* Come on you guys! Dinner!

SCOTT *(With conviction, rushing just a little, moving toward Dave)*:
Like—when I do fucked-up things, I feel I'm fucked-up, as a
person, but I'm here and it's like: No. I can be an adult. I *can*
have a, an adult life, I can be your age and have this—books
in bookstores, a house and this amazing relationship and—
this *happiness* . . .

DAVE: Uh-huh . . .

SCOTT: When I think of where I *come* from, what I grew *up* in, and here—since I got here—how much has opened up for me—because—where I'm from—there's never been a—an *adult* before who—cared, who showed me that. This.

(We hear a distant mingling of laughter and song, increasingly nearer.)

DAVE: Well. Wow. I appreciate your sentiments.

(Pause.)

SCOTT: But—no. I—do you know what I'm—?

DAVE: —I get what you're saying—

SCOTT: That feeling, of *lacking*, not having that *thing*—since we started this I feel that *less* now—

DAVE: That's great.

(Pause.)

SCOTT: Right. It's not like I *have* it, but—

DAVE: Right—

SCOTT: But I'm leaving soon and—

DAVE: Yeah—

SCOTT: And I just—I want to know we can keep this going—

DAVE: —Uh-huh, uh-huh—

SCOTT: —Why do you keep interrupting me?

(Short pause.)

DAVE: I'm not—interrupting—

SCOTT: Yes you are.

DAVE *(Laughing)*: Calm down, Scott.

SCOTT: —Calm down?

DAVE: Yeah, just—

SCOTT: —Calm? —*What?*

DAVE: Whoa—buddy—relax, it's okay—

SCOTT: Stop talking to me like I'm a child.

DAVE: *Scott.*

(Pause. They stare at each other. Scott breaks.)

SCOTT: Sorry, just—wasn't the right time. Don't worry about it.

(Laughter and song enter; Peter with his arm around Elaine, Alan trailing.)

PETER AND ELAINE:
> I'm a hard man
> And the old seas are mine
> When I take to ship
> I bring tobaccy and wine . . .

PETER: —Grrrrr, we're pirates, Scotty!
SCOTT: —You are blasted, man!

> *(Dave returns to the grill. Peter and Elaine reach Scott and embrace him.)*

PETER *(To Elaine)*: —That's very good, you're getting it now. Do you remember the next part?
ELAINE: I think so, I think so.

(Peter hums the melody and Elaine tries to hum along.)

PETER: Do your best, here we go—

(Alan watches Dave. Dave watches the three. They reach the table. Scott, smiling, downs his scotch.)

PETER AND ELAINE:
> Waitin' in each port
> Like heaven to my sight
> Is a girl with blond tresses
> I have for the night . . .

(Everyone claps.)

DAVE *(Brightly)*: On that note—dinner is served!

(Peter hums the next verse as he retrieves and refills his drink. Scott uses his Zippo to light the candles on the table. Elaine moves to Dave at the grill. A moment between them. Scott eyes

this; Peter eyes Scott; Alan eyes the entire scene. After a beat, Elaine smiles, and briefly but affectionately kisses Dave.)

Scene 4

1999. Dark. The porch light is on, casting a sulfuric wedge of light onto the lawn. Two empty wine glasses are on the table, the bottle of wine between them. Emily's PowerBook is also there. The flickering TV light in the room upstairs is visible, but less than it might be because of the porch light. A citronella candle burns, glows. Scott and Emily, under a light blue sheet, are on the lawn. The sheet is pulled up over their chests; both their shoulders are bare. We can sense, beneath the sheet, Scott's hand moving slowly along Emily's leg. Scott looks at her; she looks up at the night sky. Then, playfully:

SCOTT:
> The fault, dear Brutus, is not in our stars,
> But in ourselves . . .

EMILY *(Laughs a little; then)*:
> My star was unspeakable.

SCOTT: What's that from?

EMILY: *Oedipus at Colonus.* I think. Who can remember. They're so pretty they look fake.

(A silence.)

(Tenderly) What are you thinking?

SCOTT: Jeff.

EMILY: Oh?

SCOTT: The day I arrived—I'm at the gas station, and he comes up to me and literally tugs on my shirt—asks if I want to buy some "bait." Do I look like I fish? And he's holding this, like, styrofoam cup that he's filled with soil and a couple worms. I say no thanks. He follows me *all* the way down the road, asking, Where am I from, What do I do . . . I end up telling him about Jaime, who he still hasn't ever actually *seen* . . . Then he gets really quiet—but keeps walking with me, all the way back here. He looks over the lawn, tough-guy style, and asks if I have a lawnmower. Says he "mows lawns." *(Laughs a little)*

EMILY: At least you found a friend.

(Laughs.)

—That's still my favorite story of yours.

SCOTT: Which one?

EMILY: The one with the woman? After the flood?

SCOTT: Right.

EMILY: . . . Where "she stepped over the worms gingerly, regarding them with detached sympathy, unlucky victims of a modest plague. Then, catching one particularly thick worm's final twitch, she was seized, and the wet sidewalk began to writhe and curl: it was as though her memory had merely misplaced itself for a moment."

SCOTT: How do you remember that?

EMILY: It's so beautiful.

SCOTT: Yeah, if you like your prose in purple. "Check, please."

EMILY: Stop.

(A beat. Then Scott presses his lips to Emily's neck, kisses her gently, and runs his hand beneath the sheet across the inside of her leg.)

I thought Paxil was supposed to *diminish* your sex drive.

SCOTT: —Felled by a mere antidepressant? *Moi?* I think not!

(She laughs. He continues kissing her.)

EMILY: . . . Maybe D.C. *is* wrong. It is sort of monochromatic. *(Scott keeps kissing her)* It's so male too. Such a male energy, D.C.

SCOTT: Shhh. *(Continues kissing her)*

EMILY: Where else is there? Chicago's too *ER*y. L.A. hasn't worked since *L.A. Law*—

SCOTT: Shhhh.

EMILY: What?

SCOTT *(Stops kissing her)*: You're ruining it.

EMILY: Ruining what?

SCOTT: Why do you have to talk about this now?
EMILY: It's due tomorrow.

(Perhaps we hear a slight rustling sound; perhaps not.)

SCOTT: —Did you hear that?
EMILY: Hear what?

(Scott listens. Silence. Then he pulls on his underwear.)

SCOTT: I'm gonna check in on Jaime.

(He rises, goes into the house. A moment. Emily looks around. Then, decisively, under the sheet, puts on her underclothes. She dresses. The light in the upstairs window goes off. Emily folds Scott's pants and shirt and places them back on the ground. She picks up the sheet and folds it. She brings the sheet to the table. She picks up one of the books on the porch, looks at it. As Scott emerges:)

Sleeping like an angel.

(He sees that Emily is dressed. She puts the book on the table.)

You're dressed.

(Pause.)

EMILY: It was an impulse. *(Pause)* I think—I thought maybe you weren't *really* here. But you are.
SCOTT: You're gonna go?
EMILY: Scott . . .

(Scott takes the sheet from the table, wraps it around his shoulders, takes a few steps onto the lawn.)

I don't want to fight—
SCOTT: Please don't leave.
EMILY: You're the one who left, Scott.
SCOTT *(Turning to Emily)*: I'm not doing well without you, Emily.

(Pause.)

EMILY: Then come home.

(Scott moves to the table and sits.)

Come home, Scott—
SCOTT: You saw how unhappy I was, Emily! What was I—for the rest of my life, what? Supervise *scripts*, take *meetings*? Do a *line*, talk about did I like *The Matrix* at parties?
EMILY: Our life isn't the problem.
SCOTT: She knows, Jaime, she could see, she *saw* how unhappy I was, and I know that's one of the reasons she's so sad. Because she had seen me, she had known me when I was happy—
EMILY: When was this, this happiness, because it seems like "happiness" has eluded you for most of your life—
SCOTT: I don't mean happiness—I mean—*me*, who I *was*, who I wanted to *be*—
EMILY: God, it isn't your prose that's sentimental, it's your *life*.
SCOTT: —Oh, nice. That's one for the season opener. Did you think that line up on the plane?
EMILY *(Genuinely hurt)*: —No, Scott. That's just how I think. That's just—who I am.

(Emily goes to the table, closes her PowerBook.)

SCOTT *(Changing tone)*: Can't you see—here: there is time—this sky, this space—this *potential*. Can't you *feel* that?
EMILY: Can you? *(Beat)* Do you need me here to feel that? Because if you do—how could you think this is where you should be?

(Pause. Emily puts her PowerBook in her bag. Scott rises, walks back onto the lawn, the sheet enveloping him, ghost-like.)

SCOTT *(Almost mumbled to himself)*: There is so much I feel.
EMILY: What?
SCOTT: There is so much *inside* me here—that is *happening* and I—
EMILY: Scott, exactly— *(Moving toward him)* "inside," which is— inside. And I'm out here. Here *I* am, here's the entire world, where all the people live, right here.
SCOTT: I am here too!

EMILY: Yes! Here— *(Looking up at the sky, throwing her arms up)* Here! And what, *what* is here. You'll read all these books and *what.* And you'll take walks in the woods and then *what.* While I'm left to *write* the script and *do* the work, alone, while you, you dig around in your profound "inner life."

SCOTT: If an inner life isn't profound, what is, doll?

EMILY *(With finality)*: How many times can I ask you. What happened here. *(Pause)* What happened that makes me and my feelings and our life so impossible, so wrong, our *good* life. We were *fine.* Everything was *fine*—

SCOTT: I wasn't "fine," Jaime wasn't "fine"—

EMILY: Children get sad, they suffer loss, they go on, they grow up. People get depressed, they get in a rut, they get past it—

SCOTT: All the history I have left is *here*, Emily—

EMILY: What about *our* history—

SCOTT: My *soul* is here—

EMILY: Jesus! What "soul"—

SCOTT: *My* soul, will you *listen*—

EMILY: Will you please use a word that makes some *sense*—

SCOTT: What can I do to convince you. What. Would you like to see me—how can I show you what's inside *(Pounds fist against his leg hard, repeatedly)* —What can I do to make you understand—

EMILY: I know you're in pain—

SCOTT *(Still pounding)*: What?

EMILY: Scott—stop—

SCOTT: I am lost, I am lost and I don't understand, I am sad and *lost* and I do *not* understand—

(A final pound, so hard his leg gives out and he falls.)

EMILY: That's—that's awful what you just did.

(Pause. Scott looks up at Emily.)

SCOTT: Maybe I don't know how to say it but I have to *live* it, I have to find a way to *live* it, Emily. If you'll stay with me I can *live* it . . .

(Pause. Emily moves toward Scott.)

EMILY: You had something here and you lost it. A man who was your friend and you lost him. And lost "something." But it's not "here" somewhere. It's not in "books." It's not in "time." And it's certainly not in "me." I hope you find it. But I can't help you here. Because you can't love me here.

(Pause. Emily gathers her things. Scott staggers to his feet and limps to the table. Emily gets her bag, removes from it a book.)

I found this under the bed. With your dirty socks. I thought you'd want it.

(Scott sits down, ignores her. She places the book on the table. She starts to go, then turns.)

(With difficulty) Can't you see there are tears in my eyes?
SCOTT: No. There are tears in my own.

(He shoots her a brutal glance. They lock eyes. She quickly exits. He looks as though he may rise from his chair. Her car starts. He gasps, runs to the driveway, shedding his sheet.)

Scene 5

1993. Dark. Food is eaten, plates are stacked atop each other on the table. Two open, empty bottles of wine. The almost-spent bottle of scotch. The citronellas still burn and the lights in the kitchen are on. Scott sits in one of the sun chairs. Lights rise. Dave is taking dishes into the kitchen, as Alan collects empty glasses. Peter supervises vaguely, with a drink in his hand.

ALAN: Are we through with the scotch?
PETER: I'm grand. *(To Scott, a bit too loudly)* Do you need more liquor, Scott?
SCOTT: More? Sheesh.

(Alan takes the bottle of scotch and starts to go.)

PETER: Are you married, Alan?

ALAN: Am I married?

PETER: Yes.

ALAN: My wife passed away—three years ago.

PETER: Oh.

(Alan smiles awkwardly and goes inside. Peter walks to Scott.)

Whoops.

SCOTT *(Drunkenly)*: Hunh?

PETER: Could you believe Alan's prattling on all through dinner about *narrative* with David? So much fluffy, pseudointellectual nonsense. And David reading from his book! Ladrica the welfare mother adopting a stray cat! Thank God there wasn't a dessert course.

SCOTT: I thought it was beautiful.

(Peter rises, goes to the bushes.)

(Looking to Peter) —What are you doing?

PETER: I have to take a piss.

SCOTT: —There's a bathroom inside.

PETER: I don't want to go in there and get trapped in another conversation with Dr. Ding Dong.

(Scott laughs a little. Peter unzips. Then:)

Come over here and show me your cock.

SCOTT: 'Scuse me?

PETER: Your wife made it to be very big in that painting.

SCOTT: S'abstract. God, I'm—

PETER: I have a problem, very common among writers. I like to stare. At everything.

SCOTT: Maybe Dr. Ding Dong can help you with that.

PETER: You brought the thing, made sure we were all on the porch when you handed it over. They're doing dishes, it's dark. Come on, I haven't seen another man's dick in years.

SCOTT: Should go to the gym.

PETER: The gyms are full of fairies. Fine then. Keep your cock to yourself, Tease. Ahhh . . .

(Peter urinates. Scott waits a beat, looks at the house, then comes over.)

SCOTT: Maybe I can put this in a story.

PETER: That's right! Pissing on the trees with Peter Lawson!

SCOTT *(Justifying the action as he unzips)*: It's not that big a deal, right?

PETER *(Looking; a low tone)*: Oh yes it is. —Jesus.

(Scott urinates.)

SCOTT *(Laughs)*: Shut up.

PETER: How big does it get when it's hard?

SCOTT: You're a writer, use your imagination.

(Scott laughs, bounces his legs a little, shakes off, then ostenta-tiously puts himself together, goes back to the chair, falls into it. Peter, zipping up, approaches.)

Feels good to piss outdoors. Something primal.

(Peter sits down.)

PETER: You're not drunk.

SCOTT: —You're weird, dude.

PETER: I'm profoundly normal. It's the literary life, better get used to it—readings and panels and colonies, "artistic" friends, cultured conversation—but still *dirty inside.*

(Peter has a laughing-coughing fit. A beat. Scott rises.)

SCOTT *(Decisively)*: Could use some coffee I think.

(Alan enters onto the porch. Scott has to pass him.)

Hey.

ALAN: Hello there.

(A beat. Alan smiles politely. Scott's off. Alan moves toward Peter.)

PETER *(Sort of absently, to himself more than Alan)*: Children.

ALAN: Excuse me?

PETER: —You. Hello.

ALAN: We're about to break out the ice cream. Perfect way to cap off a late summer's evening, eh?

PETER: —I spent my whole life trying to be an intellectual, you know that? Ponderous conversations with Professor Ardith about all the stuff that "furrows the brow." It's like being alone in the middle of the ocean—it's infinite, and all there is to do is swim and swim and swim—and *drown*.

ALAN: Well—art isn't easy, isn't that what they say?

PETER: I read Shakespeare once upon a time, all of it—even *Troilus and Cressida*—all those shitty ones! I thought to be a writer I had to read everything!

ALAN: Well. If one's ambitions tend towards creating work of—

PETER: I envy you—talk to people all day about their darkest most unappealing shit. You have no idea *none* what it's like sitting alone in a room for twelve hours a day. It is *lonely* and un*bear*able. "Words, words, words . . . "

ALAN: Everyone always quotes *Hamlet*.

PETER: Is that where it's from? I forgot.

ALAN: Why does everyone like *that* one so much I wonder?

PETER: Because it's the truth—he dies at the end, too many words, that's what you get! So what if Dave is smarter than I am—what's the use of an inner life anyway? Can't see it, can't touch it, can't—might as well not have one.

ALAN *(Genuinely)*: It can also be very lonely sitting in a room, the only witness, and a mute one really, to someone's most significant and terrifying—

PETER: —for a hundred fifty an hour. And they have to leave when the fifty minutes are up—unlike a piece of paper, *staring* at you and *mocking* you and going *nowhere*.

ALAN: Nevertheless. I chose to enter a profession where, as someone sits a few feet before me weeping, I cannot reach out with my hand to touch them. There's a terrific masochism in that.

PETER: Or sadism, depending on your perspective.

(Elaine comes onto the porch, with a coffee mug.)

Regardless, you're still a chipper little idealist.

ALAN: Chipper? Really? Do I appear to you, quite seriously—a chipper fellow?

PETER: —The way you speak. It's very funny. "Fellow." Who says that?

173

(A beat. Alan places his hand on his stomach.)

I have to go to the bathroom.

(Peter rises, walks to the porch, clinks his glass of liquor with Elaine's coffee mug as he passes. From offstage:)

David, where are you?

(Elaine approaches Alan.)

ELAINE: How are you doing there, Alan?
ALAN: Oh—Elaine. Yes—I think I'm having a bit of trouble digesting. Also I'm used to just a single glass of wine with supper, I'm afraid.
ELAINE: I'm sorry.
ALAN: Perhaps I caught a bug in the city—university students are always ill—
ELAINE: Is it nausea or—?
ALAN: Can I tell you why I began to teach, Elaine?

(Pause.)

ELAINE *(Somewhat exasperated)*: —Sure.

(Elaine sits. Alan's too worked-up to notice her disinterest.)

ALAN: I desired an adventure of public—rather than private— exchange—lively, engaged debate between generations— mine, theirs, and the writers of past ages!
ELAINE: Of course.
ALAN: Well they don't read the books! It's as simple and as devastating as that! There they sit—gaping mouths, blank stares, fiddling with their little bottles of water and such— while I am alone before them, talking, talking, endlessly *talking!* —No wonder people give classes on pornography and rap lyrics—the students are sure to attend, and with enthusiasm!
ELAINE: I'm sure you're a wonderful teacher, I'm sure your students love you.

ALAN: At Columbia they've given us these—do you know my wife died three years ago?

ELAINE: Um—no.

ALAN: She died. Some days I manage to forget this. —Well, the *internet!* Do you know it?

ELAINE: I'm not sure I follow . . .

ALAN: It's this mysterious invention, and Columbia has given it to us.

ELAINE: Right—I don't have it, but I've skimmed a few articles.

ALAN: One day, there it appeared, not a word of debate or warning—"Here you are, process or perish!"

ELAINE: Yes?

ALAN: Well, my students: my Ivy League, graduate students: there they sat, before class, in the brand-new computer lab—chins at their chests, eyeballs ablaze, entirely at attention!

ELAINE: Well—hold onto your hat, Al, I mean, this is just one class, one group of kids, right?

ALAN: Read nothing, know nothing, but give 'em a mouse and clickety-click, clickety-click, there's no tearing them away! Do you know one of my students thought World War II happened in the 1920s? To get through my lecture without a snowballing sense of absolute *doom*— However will our world survive with a bunch of smug, ignorant *fools* inheriting—

ELAINE: So now you're moving from some lazy students to the apocalypse.

ALAN: Oh—you're right. I've had far too much to dr—it's merely change—and thinking of my life—my wife—usually she'd accompany me on a night like this—I'm just worrying over my *own* morality—*mortality*—the world will be just fine I'm sure—progress doesn't always happen in a straight—but—people who once upon a time would have come to me—and spoken to another human being about a dream they'd had—now they may just take a pill . . . —And what, what if everyone agrees that it *is* merely chemical? Worse, what if it really *is?* Then it's—the end—of all I have devoted my life to, all I *believe* in—art—the soul—memory—contemplation . . . What dark times we live in! Darker for the fact that no one acknowledges how dark indeed they are!

ELAINE: I don't know . . .

(Elaine pauses, looks up at the sky as if struck by something.)

The last regional job I took. I did *Hedda* in Hartford. It was a respectful production, but it wasn't a museum piece—it had life and spontaneity to it. Well. I got miserably depressed. Getting into that tight dress every night I thought—why do I have to wear this? I want to wear normal clothes. What the hell do I know about Hedda Gabler? It all began to feel vaguely humiliating. And I would walk around Hartford and think, I want to tell *that* story—that woman at the Dunkin' Donuts with her three kids—women who are alive today. So I came back to New York and I said, "That's it. Only new plays from now on."

(Pause.)

ALAN: What happened?

ELAINE: They didn't cast me. *(Beat)* The MFAs started pumping out pretty young things, new directors with new girlfriends came up . . . I got older. *(Beat)* You know, what Dave does—novelists—they get "better" with age, they increase in esteem in society's eyes. No one tells Saul Bellow he's irrelevant. There's respect. What *I* do—the more I know, the less I matter. I'm finally old enough that I have something interesting to tell the world, and no one wants to hear it.

(Elaine looks at Alan. A beat. She looks up at the sky.)

Beautiful night.

ALAN: . . . My whole life . . . sitting. Sitting here, sitting there . . . perhaps if I'd get out more, stand up, walk about, roll up my—do tangible, concrete . . . "I won't buy shirts at Banana Republic"—what a—mysterious statement!

(Scott appears on the porch, with a coffeepot and mug.)

ELAINE *(Calling to Scott)*: Hey—are we having ice cream or what?

(Alan turns, sees Scott.)

SCOTT *(Stepping onto the lawn)*: —Um—

(Alan rises, starts to move toward the drive.)

ALAN (*Clutching his stomach*): Ohh—I think I just need some air—well I'm outside ha—but if I just—walk around for a bit by myself—I'm sorry, forgive me.

ELAINE: Go—right ahead.

(*Alan passes Scott. He stumbles a bit, Scott goes to reach for him.*)

ALAN: No, no, I'm fine, I just—clear my head a bit—

(*Scott looks at Elaine as Alan goes to the driveway. We hear rising voices in the house.*)

ELAINE: Oh God, now what?

SCOTT: I think um—yeah I came out 'cuz they were starting to get into it—

(*Dave and Peter's voices getting louder, closer to us.*)

ELAINE: Don't tell me—

(*Dave bursts out of the house.*)

DAVE: —I don't want to talk about this, Peter!

(*Peter follows, with a pint of ice cream, which he puts on the table.*)

PETER: It was a harmless comment; what's this response now, come on—

DAVE: Always poking, poke poke, cause a reaction—well you have your reaction, drop it and shut *up*!

PETER: What, do you think what I said was unreasonable?

ELAINE (*Moving toward them*): Okay boys, not tonight—

DAVE: —Everybody just *stop*.

ELAINE: I'm only—

DAVE: —Just *end* this now No more *talking*! (*A beat*) You know, and of *course* you waited all night, perfect timing, here's the climax, and then you'll denouement home to Mary, intensely satisfied.

PETER (*To Elaine*): I merely suggested that David write about his own life. His own concerns. So I said he's smarter, more interesting than his books, that's not a *criticism*—

ELAINE: I think both of you, you both want to have this conversation obviously, so if you're going to have it, maybe—

DAVE: No, I do not want to have this conversation actually, I would like in fact to have a life that does not consist of conversations such as these.

PETER: What *would* you like to talk about, Dave? Haitian refugees? "Don't ask don't tell"? Why is the subject of "you" off—

DAVE: God this shit turns you on!

PETER: What turns *you* on? You're a straight white male, David. Very few people left upon this earth care a whit about what people like us have to say, and they are not going to turn to you to learn about the "Latino with a problem on the Lower East Side." I don't give a shit how *compassionately* it's written.

DAVE: My life is a good life, Peter, and it is a good and worthy and *moral* thing to try to imagine something you can't, or, or don't—*know*, or *feel*—a book for America, a—

PETER: "America"—

DAVE: It is *entirely* valid to write a democratic novel, okay? A novel that confronts a wide range of personalities and dilemmas, and I'm *sorry* if you're not interested in certain cultures, in conflicts of survival that don't "touch" you—

PETER: They don't "touch" you either!

DAVE: But they *do*, because those, those neglected lives are lives people *live*, small uncelebrated troubled lives, and it's important that there be an artful record of those lives, an attempt to understand what is not immediately—I mean this smug solipsism is just—

PETER: Bring out the big words!

DAVE: I thought you liked those! Those big words "Latinos on the Lower East Side" don't understand!

ELAINE *(In a conciliatory tone)*: —Both of you now, this is not the great ideological debate you're making it out to be— it's too much to drink and it's a long history . . .

DAVE *(Turning sharply to Elaine)*: What, "I'm not allowed to be upset for the reasons I've *articulated*," is that it, Elaine?

(Beat.)

ELAINE *(Taken aback)*: I just think that perhaps—

DAVE *(Laughs)*: —that's just a little cynical, I mean of course you don't care about any of this stuff, *you* want to be on a *sitcom*!

—Didja see *Seinfeld* last night, *Elaine*? Oh that wacky *irony*, that's *just* how life is!

(Pause. Elaine takes a few shocked steps away from the porch as Scott rises gently with the coffeepot and says:)

SCOTT: —Could all have some coffee?

(All look at Scott. Dave spits out a hard laugh.)

(Smiling) What?
DAVE: "Could all have some coffee?" Behold the *fucking* future!

(A genuinely stunned silence. Scott sinks down, puts down the coffeepot. Dave looks at Elaine. She looks away.)

PETER *(Gently)*: Why can't we have a dialogue, David?
DAVE: Because you're stupid.

(Pause.)

PETER: I speak out of concern for you.
DAVE: No, you speak out of concern for yourself, that's *all* you worry about and all you *think* about—
PETER: That *is* what people do, David, they think about themselves—you should try it!
DAVE: No, we're just different that way.
PETER: The only difference between you and me is that I don't believe the definition of an upper-middle-class person is "someone to whom nothing significant can happen." What do you honestly have to say about those communities you know merely from your trips to the bodega on 121st Street? Why *won't* you write about where you live?
DAVE *(With gravity and feeling)*: I do. This is where I live. Extending into new frontiers, imagination and empathy as *one*, for if we can't imagine another—if all we can imagine is what we can *see*—
PETER: —But you can't get rid of yourself in the process, for it's through your self, your very *life*, that you can see at all! *(Beat) That's* why you're having trouble with the novel.

(Pause.)

179

DAVE *(A confused tone)*: Where's the trouble? It's been difficult to write, like anything, but . . . *(His tone changes)* What do you mean, "having trouble"?

PETER: —Nothing. I don't want to talk about your book until I've read it anyhow.

DAVE *(Quietly)*: Pete. *(A beat)* What do you know? What have you heard?

PETER: You—know how it is—gossip, nonsense.

DAVE *(Putting it together)*: Robert. They're optioning out of the contract. He sent them the first few chapters months ago. Is that it? They're not going to? . . .

PETER: You should call him back. *(Pause)* He called me because he wanted to know what was wrong. Why you'd—disappeared.

(Dave looks to Elaine. She does not look at him. Peter makes a movement toward Dave, who turns and goes into the house. The kitchen light cuts off. Peter looks at Elaine.)

I'm sure it will be published—a number of houses will jump at the chance—

(Elaine turns and walks into the house. Peter looks at Scott.)

Christ.

(Peter gets up, walks onto the lawn, looks up at the house. To Scott:)

Come over and talk to me, I'm sad. *(Scott doesn't move)* You really read *Tall Grass*? *(Scott nods. Peter begins an approach to Scott)* When they were arranging my book tour, I told them I wanted to branch out—develop a bigger audience, so I told them not to send me to Boston and L.A. and Chicago. The real reason was that I was ashamed of the book. I went to cities like Pittsburgh and Ann Arbor, where I knew no one. I was also really fat. —Oh, hey. He didn't mean that. He was angry at *me*. *(Scott shrugs it off)* Well. I am in. Minneapolis. I give my reading. Afterwards, a middle-aged woman—a bit softer than middle-aged actually, but no longer young—this woman—who is black—approaches me. With a big bright nervous face. And tells me how much my books mean to her.

I'm aghast, as I've never before been approached by a black reader. I ask her why she likes my books and she laughs as though it's just a preposterous question. "Because they're good. They make me cry," she says. I want to know more, so I say, "But why?" I'm thinking, What does this woman relate to in my work? My books are about rich white people. She says, "Same shit goes on where I work, people hurting each other, stabbing each other in the back, this one slept with that one, this one's treating that one wrong, and everyone's doing their best but it just falls apart, and it's left like that, no way to put it back together."

So, I invite her to walk with me to my hotel. She does. I say, "Come to my room and have a cup of tea." She comes in. I make tea. We sit at the cheap shiny coffee table. I say, "I'd like to kiss you."

And, quite calmly, quite sweetly, not an ounce of condescension in her voice: she says, "I think you'll be just fine in a few minutes for not having done that." And she smiles an extraordinary smile. As do I. And she is gone.

Because. Do you? . . . For so many years I felt. Doubt. And. *Guilt.* Over my work—over my life. And to see—as I sat there with her—ghost—in the room. I thought of her wisdom.

Which so eclipsed mine.

Do you see?

SCOTT: I'm not . . .

PETER: That all of "this" *(Gesturing to the porch)* —these "questions" of—I had written a book from my heart, and that— that made it a good and worthy book. And me a good and worthy man. I have a beautiful wife and a beautiful son. And a loyal reader, somewhere in Minneapolis. I am blessed. My silly life—"The Bourgeoisie and Me." A blessing. And it is so easy. It is that easy to be—*fine. (Pause. Scott looks at him)* In my best moments, I still feel that way. And that's—that's all I really wanted to say.

(Peter turns around briefly, looks at the silent house.)

A wise man would make his exit now. *(Turning back to Scott)* I'll pretend I am one. *(Moves to Scott, smiles)* If you see Elaine, say good night for me. It—was a pleasure to meet you, Scott.

SCOTT: Yeah—definitely.

PETER: Good luck with your writing.

(And Peter goes. Scott gets up, sits down on the ground, stretches out, unties his sneakers, kicks them off. We hear Peter's car pull out of the gravel drive. Moments later, Elaine comes out of the house. It is very dark, the citronella pots throwing a bit of fiery glow onto the lawn.)

ELAINE: Was that Peter?

SCOTT: Hunh?

ELAINE: Peter left?

SCOTT: Oh yeah—he says g'night. —I just gotta sober up a little before I go.

ELAINE: Want some ice cream?

SCOTT: Sure.

(Elaine tosses the pint of ice cream to Scott, who catches it. She brings a spoon from the table, hands it to him. She sits near, but not next to him.)

ELAINE: I'm sorry about that.

SCOTT: Naw, yeah. I think we all just had way too much to drink tonight. *(Elaine looks off)* You didn't even have wine at dinner, did you?

ELAINE: It's a depressant. It depresses.

SCOTT: Right. And I was already depressed.

ELAINE *(Turning back to Scott)*: Oh? I thought you were having "the time of your life."

SCOTT: I'm so sad this summer. Back home. I forgot how much I hated it.

(Pause. Scott shrugs it off, opens the ice cream, digs in. Elaine looks at him a moment. Then:)

ELAINE: I read one of your stories.

SCOTT *(Doesn't yet take a bite)*: Oh yeah?

ELAINE: Like—a scream or a bullet. Stunning. Really.

SCOTT: Oh—wow. *(Putting down the ice cream)* Yeah—I try to make my stories like—pop songs. 'Cuz pop songs—they hit that emotion. Like when something happens to you and you just get in your car and drive and the perfect song comes on the radio and you hafta sing along, top of your lungs, 'cuz you have all that emotion rolling through you, that crazy rage. You know?

ELAINE: I do . . . *(Laughs)*

SCOTT: Yeah. *(Picks up ice cream, takes a bite)* Wonder where Dr. Richards went.

ELAINE: Alan? He seemed to be having an episode of some kind.

SCOTT: I really fucked-up with that guy.

ELAINE: What do you mean?

SCOTT: I work during the school year? I bartend four nights a week and—we had to write this—for his class—I didn't have any time to write a final paper on *Hamlet*—I didn't even have time to read it actually.

ELAINE: Ah. *(A beat)* You'll like *Hamlet*.

SCOTT: Yeah? *(Pause)* Hey, I almost forgot—the worms.

ELAINE: What?

SCOTT: You told me before? that you weren't a "nature girl" because of something to do with worms when you were little? I wanna know what happened.

ELAINE: You really want to know? *(He nods)* Well. I was walking out the door to go to school, the morning after these very heavy rainstorms. I went to the bus stop and—I looked down—and on the sidewalk, this long stretch of sidewalk, there must have been—it looked to me like a hundred worms. All shriveled up, some still alive, wriggling around, and I ran inside and—my father explained that they'd been flooded out of their little homes in the dirt. I refused to go outside until he got rid of them. Then. He went into the closet and got a big broom, and took my hand and sort of dragged me to the sidewalk, and I was crying—I was crying—and . . . we—swept them off onto the road.

SCOTT: Wow. Cool image. *(She smiles)* Hey.

(Scott puts down the ice cream, sticks his hand out.)

ELAINE: What?

SCOTT: Rain check.

ELAINE: What?

SCOTT: "I'd shake your hand but" *(Flexes palms)* "I'm disgusting." Then you said—

ELAINE: —"A rain check."

(She laughs, takes his hand. They shake. A moment. Then he takes his hand and strokes the top of her hand.)

SCOTT: . . . I think you rock, Elaine.
ELAINE *(A whisper)*: You're so sweet.
SCOTT: Which story of mine did you read?
ELAINE: The one about the boy . . . he works in the snack bar?—
SCOTT: —Would you like to fuck?

(Pause.)

ELAINE: Sure.

(He smiles. Brief pause. Then Elaine leans into him and they kiss. It becomes passionate rather quickly, Scott particularly aggressive. Elaine breaks. A moment.)

Not here.
SCOTT: The dock?

(A beat.)

ELAINE: You have a car here.
SCOTT: Yeah. *(Beat)* I know where we could go.
ELAINE: And in the morning you'd drive me to the train station?
SCOTT: —Sure.
ELAINE: Okay. *(Remembering)* —My bag. Get my bag, it's at the bottom of the stairs.
SCOTT: What if he? . . .
ELAINE: He's upstairs, in the bedroom. I'll meet you at the car.
SCOTT: Okay.

(A beat. She goes to the driveway. Scott rises, looks to the house, adjusts himself, laughs a light disbelieving laugh, then goes inside. Time passes. Sounds of nature. Alan enters from the woods, the other side of the house, sees no one. House is dark, save for the porch light and the light in the upper window. Alan looks around toward the porch, down the lawn, toward the lake path. Then he trips a little over Scott's sneakers. He looks down, and sees the open pint of ice cream beside them. Then:)

ALAN: What? . . .

(The porch light cuts off and Scott comes out of the house, holding Elaine's bag. He sees Alan, drops the bag. Alan hears and turns.)

SCOTT: Hey. Party's over.
ALAN: Oh.
SCOTT: Dave was feeling under the weather, called it a night.
ALAN: I see . . . —I should pop my head in and say good night.
SCOTT: —He's already in bed.
ALAN: Oh?
SCOTT: Have a good one.

(A short pause. Alan nods, goes to the driveway. Scott goes to his sneakers, puts them on. We hear Alan's car start and pull away. Scott rises, grabs Elaine's bag, starts to go. The porch light cuts on. When Scott is almost gone, Dave emerges from the house.)

DAVE: Scott.

(Scott stops, drops the bag, comes in some distance toward Dave, who hasn't seen the bag.)

SCOTT: Dave, what's up.
DAVE: Have you seen Elaine?
SCOTT: No—actually, I was just—I was taking off, um. Peter left. That was Alan just now, Alan left.
DAVE: Did Elaine—she didn't leave with Peter?
SCOTT: No, no, I think—I saw her go down to the lake a while ago.

(Dave takes a few steps off the porch.)

DAVE: Scott, I should—you deserve an apology. I don't—know that it's appropriate right now.
SCOTT: No, I don't need an apology.
DAVE: You do. Come by tomorrow and we can have a proper talk—
SCOTT: Had too much to drink—all that shit, it's not real, but it comes up, it just—I think Elaine's down on the dock, you should go there.

185

DAVE: Right.

(Dave begins to walk toward the lake path.)

SCOTT: Hey you know—it'd be great, I don't—it'd be great to get, like, a recommendation from you, something I could keep in my files.

(Dave turns. He sees the bag. Pause.)

DAVE: —Where is she? *(Short pause)* Scott?
SCOTT: No, I don't—I know she went down to the lake . . . *(Dave doesn't respond; keeps his eyes fixed on Scott)* I'm just—taking her to the train station. *(Short pause)*
DAVE: There's no trains now, Scott.
SCOTT: There isn't? I thought—

(Dave turns away. Pause.)

Just a bad night, happens . . .

(Scott takes a few steps toward Dave.)

So . . . you want me to come by tomorrow or—?
DAVE: No. Scott.
SCOTT: You don't—want me to come back?

(Dave moves slowly to the porch. He finds Scott's manuscript there, takes it, turns back to Scott.)

DAVE: You should take your story.
SCOTT: I—s'okay, I have it on disc.
DAVE: I understand that.
SCOTT: I don't need it, throw it out, I don't—

(Dave extends his hand, holding the story out to Scott. Scott slaps it away. The two stare at each other.)

Take all that shit out, just, just gonna go back to the old draft, I wrote—wrote it from my heart, *my* world.
DAVE: I know. I'm sorry.

SCOTT: Keep saying you're sorry, 'hell are you sorry about? *(Pause)* So you don't—want me to come back here?
DAVE: No.

(Pause. Abruptly, Scott turns, goes to Elaine's bag, takes it and exits to the driveway. Dave takes in the evening's landscape—the lawn, the porch, the house, the sky. We hear Scott's car start, with difficulty. It takes a few tries. Finally, it starts, revs. Dave stumbles. Moves to the house, finds his footing, disappears into the house. Porch light cuts off. We hear Scott's car pull away. After a moment, we see Dave in the upper window. He looks out of it, then backs away. The light in the room goes off. The house is in complete darkness.)

Scene 6

We hear Emily's car pull away. Scott returns from the driveway, moving toward the house, limping slightly. It's 1999. As he's about to go into the house, Jeff moves slightly toward him from the bushes.

SCOTT: Who's there? *(Comes off the porch, unable to see)* Hello?
JEFF: Hello?
SCOTT: —Christ, Jeff. Jeff what are you doing?
JEFF: Just walking around Mom's Mom's at work.
SCOTT: How long have you been here?
JEFF: I-I-I was gonna go swimming In the lake but it's dark and the snakes Can't see the snakes in the dark.
SCOTT: That's right. It's dark. It's time to be in bed.
JEFF: Did Emily go to work?
SCOTT: —Yes.
JEFF: Are you going to work?
SCOTT: —No. Go home.
JEFF: Is Jaime going with her mom?
SCOTT: No—not—Jaime's mom is away.
JEFF: Where?
SCOTT: In—far away—in Europe.
JEFF: Why?
SCOTT: She's—an artist.
JEFF: No.

SCOTT: What.

JEFF: No you're mad at me.

SCOTT: Jeff—

JEFF: I just came I wanted to say I'm sorry I'm sorry.

SCOTT: Why are you sorry?

JEFF: You were nice to me and I I wanted to say you were nice and you gave me these jobs. And I threw the rock and you got mad—

SCOTT: Jeff, I'm—

(Jeff rushes Scott, hugs him hard.)

Whoa—

JEFF: I'm sorry don't be

SCOTT: Jeff

JEFF: Don't be mad

SCOTT: Shh, shh—it's okay, Jeff. I'm not mad. *(A beat. Jeff looks up to Scott)* Come—here, have a seat. We'll talk for a minute.

(Jeff walks to the porch, sits in the chair Emily was sitting in. Scott redrapes the sheet over his body, covering himself fully, and sits. Jeff picks up a book from the table.)

JEFF: Reading this?

SCOTT: I read it recently.

JEFF: What is it?

SCOTT: It's a play. By Shakespeare.

JEFF: Who?

(A beat.)

SCOTT: Shakespeare. An old writer.

JEFF: Old . . . *(Opens it)* What's it about?

SCOTT: It's—about a young man. A prince. And . . . his father is killed. By his own brother. And then the prince's mother, she marries the brother. Then, the prince's father comes back— as a ghost—and tells the prince to kill the brother.

JEFF: Ghost. Then what.

SCOTT: Well . . . the prince talks to himself a lot, trying to figure out what to do.

JEFF: Does he cry?

SCOTT: —Yes.
JEFF: Does he kill him?
SCOTT: He does.
JEFF: Then what.
SCOTT: . . . He dies.

(A beat. Jeff puts down the book, picks up a second book.)

JEFF: What's this one?
SCOTT: Let me see? . . . Oh. I was—looking all over for this.
JEFF: Shakespeare?
SCOTT: No. It's a new book.
JEFF: Who.
SCOTT: A man named Dave Ardith wrote it.
JEFF: Who's he.
SCOTT: He's—a man I used to know, who lived in this very house when you were a little boy.
JEFF: Where'd he go?
SCOTT: He moved away a long time ago.
JEFF: Why?

(Scott flicks his Zippo, looks at the book by the light of its flame.)

Why'd he go?
SCOTT: Sometimes people go away . . .

(Scott shuts the Zippo.)

JEFF: Like a ghost?
SCOTT: —Yes. Like a ghost.

(Pause. They look at each other.)

JEFF: I can paint. Still mow the lawn. I can get weeds out. In the fall I can rake? *(Scott rises. Jeff follows)* Then the winter I can shovel and stuff. We have a ghost.
SCOTT: You do?
JEFF: Because when I ask about him Where he is My father. She says All she says is He's a ghost Jeff. Man's a ghost. *(Pause)* But he doesn't come to me and tell me things and she's not married to anybody now and he just left, nobody killed him.

(Just then, a flickering light in the upstairs window goes on. Neither notices the slight light it spills.)

SCOTT: Come back in the morning, Jeff.
JEFF: Yeah?
SCOTT: And we'll clear the path to the lake.
JEFF: Cool yo! Gonna do some *work*.
SCOTT *(Moving to house)*: Now I have to get some rest.
JEFF: Okay.

(Scott lightly taps Jeff on the head with the book.)

SCOTT: Good night, little man.

(Scott goes to the door. Before going inside, he turns to Jeff:)

Sweet dreams to you.
JEFF: Good night, Scott.

(Scott exits. Jeff surveys the lawn from the porch for a beat. Then he moves off. As he crosses to the driveway, he sees the light flickering in Jaime's window. He stops and looks up at it. Quietly, as if to himself:)

Good night, Jaime.

(Hold.)

END OF PLAY

The Coming World

Production History

The Coming World was originally produced by the Soho Theatre (Abigail Morris, Artistic Director) in London, opening on April 3, 2001. It was directed by Mark Brickman; the design was by Michael Pavelka, the lighting design was by Jason Taylor and the stage manager was Lorraine Tozer. The cast was as follows:

ED/TY	Andrew Scott
DORA	Doraly Rosen

Characters

ED
DORA
TY

Note: Ed and Ty are played by the same actor.

Place

A beach on the coast of New England.

Time

Summer 2001.

The Design

I am not a designer but it is, I think, worth noting that as I wrote this play, I imagined it taking place on a bare stage (no sand!), with no costume change or use of makeup effects, etc. While the play may benefit from a careful nod toward more traditional design elements, it's important that they not overwhelm the text which, I think, can tell us more than showing can.

In the London production there were no sound effects or music; no makeup effects; basic lighting, bright (though the play takes place largely at night); and a mostly bare stage made of gray wooden planks. Scenes in the ocean were created by taking out all lights; the actors held thin flashlights which washed light over their bodies. What I would stress most is that the play mustn't get lost in darkness and night. The text tells the audience it's evening; the lights should let us see clearly those evenings play out.

The Text

Dialogue in the play often overlaps. A slash in the text (/) indicates where the character who speaks next begins.

In the second scene, I use punctuation to convey a distinct sense of the unspoken. The meaning should be clear to both the actors and the audience, while maintaining the idiosyncratic and intimate system of communication the lovers use in their distress. Sometimes it's used to portray a gap in communication, a pregnant nonspoken moment different from a flat pause. Other times, a manner of speech is conveyed. For instance, if the dialogue in the text reads:

DORA: (You said) What?

The actress would speak, and the audience would hear:

DORA: What?

The parentheses are meant to clarify the meaning of what is actually spoken (rather than implied), to avoid a situation where an actor would say:

DORA: What?

And the audience would understand it to mean:

DORA: What (do you mean)?

Sure, what do you care for money?
You'd give your last penny to the first beggar you met—
if he had a shotgun pointed at your heart!

—EUGENE O'NEILL
A Moon for the Misbegotten

. . . this music's almost unrecognizable,
so utterly of the coming world it is.

—MARK DOTY
"Tunnel Music"

Scene 1

The beach. Dora and Ed are laughing.

ED: Come on, dare me.

DORA: "Dare" you!

ED: Fifty more! *(Flicking a little handful of sand at her)* Come / on!

DORA *(Laughing)*: Ah! Don't throw sand at me! —Go ahead, torture yourself.

ED: Here we go. One . . .

(Ed does push-ups. Dora brushes sand out of her hair.)

DORA: Hey, the DVDs are coming in a couple weeks, they called today.

ED: No shit!

DORA: They're starting slow, building them in slow. They did a survey I guess, and not that many people here have DVD players yet.

ED: Yeah, 'cuz there's no fucking place to buy DVDs! What am I at, forty?

DORA: Yeah, *right*. That's gonna be a pain, though, building them in, we're gonna have to totally rearrange the store to make room for new shelves.

(Ed stops and catches his breath.)

ED: What are we doing tonight?
DORA: I dunno. Why don't we just stay on the beach, it's nice.
ED: You're not working tomorrow, right?
DORA: At night I am. I'm closing.
ED: Get some drinks?
DORA: We could watch a movie . . .
ED: Go out, have a couple gin and tonics . . .
DORA: When is it ever "a couple." All night.
ED: I'm not saying all night. Plus—Martin's gonna be out tonight.
DORA: Martin?

(Ed starts doing push-ups again.)

ED: You remember Martin.
DORA: Yeah, no shit. Why, what about him?
ED: They're hiring. He said—at the—they need money / runners
DORA: You're not gonna fucking work at the casino.
ED: Maybe—not, like, right away. But—enough time's passed, right?
DORA: Every day going there?
ED: The pay is so good. They're hiring. Where / else
DORA: So, if you gamble it, so, who cares how much the pay is, you know?
ED: Gambling wasn't—it was the coke that was the thing. The gambling wasn't—I don't even like gambling. Plus I feel *so* much better now—
DORA: That's what I'm saying, you're feeling so much better, so why put yourself back there?

(Pause.)

ED: It's just drinks, I mean—I don't even know—it's not like I got the job.
DORA: No, I don't wanna go out drinking tonight.

(Pause.)

ED: All right. The thing is . . .
DORA: You told Martin already. *(Pause)* So cancel.

ED: Dora—
DORA: No, I worked all day, I don't / wanna
ED: I can't just / blow him off
DORA: So go without me.
ED: No . . .

(Pause.)

DORA: Why not?
ED: 'Cuz I wanna be with you tonight.

(Pause.)

DORA: All right . . .
ED: Uh-oh. Dora's got an idea.
DORA: I'll go out for drinks if you call Ty and invite him out.

(Pause.)

ED: Why?
DORA: I wanna meet him! Eight months, your twin brother and
    I have no idea what he's / like
ED: He's not gonna come out.
DORA: Why not?
ED: He doesn't go out.
DORA: Tell him I want to meet him. —I wanna meet the guy!

(Pause. Ed looks at the ocean. Then turns to Dora and smiles.
Grabs Dora's foot and kisses it, bites it a little. She moans quietly. He licks her foot. She begins to laugh.)

ED: What's so funny?

(He tickles her foot, she shrieks, laughs.)

DORA: No!
ED: No? No?

(He embraces her.)

DORA: Stop! You're all smelly!

ED: I'm smelly?
DORA: Yes!
ED: Then I guess I'm gonna make *you* all smelly!
DORA: No!

(He tickles her, she shrieks with laughter. Then he stops. Then he tickles her again, she shrieks with laughter. Then he stops. He starts to tickle her again, she laughs less, as though exhausted. He stares at her a beat, then looks out at the ocean. She follows his gaze to the ocean.)

ED: Beautiful.
DORA: It is . . .

(Ed turns to her.)

ED: No. You. You have the most beautiful face.

(Pause. Dora smiles, then turns away.)

Okay. *(Ed playfully smacks Dora's thigh)* Call my weirdo brother for you.

Scene 2

The beach. Dora approaches Ed. She startles him; he jerks.

DORA: Ahh!
ED: Shit!
DORA: Ed!
ED: Sorry.
DORA: Jesus.
ED: Sorry.

(Ed looks at Dora, smiles.)

DORA: ( ).

(Pause.)

ED: ( )?

DORA: I don't wanna be here.

ED: I know—

DORA: I can't get in your shit now—

ED: Nothing for you to get into . . . Sit.

DORA: I'm just—if you want something . . . (just tell me now)

ED: All I want—serious—all I want is to just . . . ( ) . . . *(She doesn't sit)* Miss you. —Okay that I say that?

DORA: (You) Just did.

ED: Yeah.

DORA: You look bad.

ED: I look *bad*?

DORA: Yeah.

ED: It's dark!

DORA: What.

ED: I look bad (in the dark)?

(Dora sits.)

DORA: Circles under your eyes, unshaven . . .

ED: Really?

DORA: Are you . . . (on drugs)?

ED: No.

DORA: No?

ED: *You* look good.

DORA: I worked all day, I look tired.

ED: How was work?

DORA: (You wanna talk about) Work?

ED: What movies came in today?

DORA: They come in Tuesdays.

ED: You put them up Tuesdays, but you get them before.

DORA: ( ).

(Pause.)

ED: (I'll) Rub your feet.

DORA: (No.)

ED: Shoulders. You look tense.

DORA: I don't (want a massage).

ED: Stressed-out, standing all day, the kids, annoying, come on.

DORA: Not everyone hates their job.

ED: Thanks.

DORA: "The kids, annoying" —(actually) I like my job.

ED: Good for you. ( )?

DORA: —I'm just saying, you're making it like I hate my job.

ED: I just said do you want a massage that place stresses you out.

(Pause.)

DORA: You have to stop calling me.

(Pause.)

ED: Who's talking about this.

DORA: We broke up.

ED: Okay.

DORA: Okay?

ED: I just wanted to talk. Am I doing anything?

DORA: "Can I rub your feet."

ED: ?

DORA: You don't do the same things after you break up. You don't (give massages)—

ED: —I don't even feel bad.

DORA: ( )?

ED: Not about you. Something else. I mean I do (feel bad) about you. But I don't know if I (feel bad) about this other thing. Maybe after I say it I'll feel bad. —No one knows (what I did).

DORA: What are you talking / about

ED: Why do you think Ty won't talk to me?

DORA: ( ).

ED: He won't call me back. Since we hung out. Which. That was a fun night. He had fun, right?

DORA: (Like) You remember (that night).

ED: It was only a month ago.

DORA: No. Because you blacked-out. (I was) Dragging you home.

ED: (You didn't) Drag me home.

DORA: Yeah (right)!

ED: He's probably just heavy into work. Computer shit. Big money. I thought it was maybe the money (he lent me) but that doesn't make sense. Why he would be mad about that.

DORA: ( )?

ED: He lent me money. I think he sent it, I think he sent it the next day, day after we hung-out. We were broke-up when

202

I got the check so I didn't tell you but. In the mail. Five thousand dollars. (I was like) Shit! Five thousand dollars! Just in
my mail! No note, no anything, and so—I called him, to
like—I don't know, to thank him or to say (why did you send
me five thousand dollars) . . . (I keep) Calling, but he won't
call me back. —Why did I get so drunk that night?

DORA: He just—(sent you) five thousand dollars.

(Pause.)

(I hope) You don't need more.

ED *(Laughs)*: Why do you say that?

DORA: Because—you don't look so good, you don't look like a guy
who has five thousand dollars, so—(do you need more?) . . .

(Ed reaches into his pocket, takes out ten singles.)

What (are you doing).

ED: Ten dollars.

DORA: (I know) But (why)?

ED: (This is) All I have left.

(Pause.)

DORA: ( )?

ED: It went.

DORA: I don't (understand).

ED: Paid bills, paid—not like five's a fortune, I mean, what I owe.
I was just trying to set things up, climb outta this hole—

DORA: The thousand (I gave you, is that gone too)?

ED: I paid off the credit card (with that).

DORA: Where did it (go)?

ED: . . .

DORA: I'm not (giving you anything) —Nothing.

ED: I had a job.

DORA: ?

ED: (I got paid a) Thousand a week.

DORA: . . .

ED: You want me to jump to the end of the story or start at the
start of it?

DORA: I don't (care).

ED: It's just, I don't know which way (makes more sense)—starting and going forward or going to the end and then back. Makes sense—(not the story, but) telling you.

DORA: I'm not going to get all (wrapped up in it) . . .

ED: But do you want to hear just the outcome or how I got there . . .

DORA: It's not gonna make me *do* something (I'm not gonna do).

ED: (Do you know) I'm the only person Ty ever showed his tattoos to? I ever tell you that?

DORA: This (relates how?)? . . .

ED: I'm just—trying to talk like—like there's none of this shit in between us.

DORA: (So you lost) Five thousand dollars.

ED: You think I should get a tattoo?

DORA: —They're gross.

ED: Why?

DORA: It's like self-mutilation, they're ugly.

ED: Ty showed me his. I'm the only one.

DORA: Ed. Come on.

(Ed looks at her. Pause.)

ED: Okay. All right. (I'll tell you) What happened.

(Pause.)

DORA: I don't need all kinds of details.

ED: All right.

(Pause.)

I just—there's this one question to get—out of the way—so I can tell you what happened because, just—I . . .

(Pause.)

DORA: ?

ED: . . .

DORA: . . . ?

ED: No, I know (why you broke up with me). I had no money. What you (said), I have no (money), I'm in debt, I have no job, you can't be with someone (with) no money (and) no job . . .

204

But—if there's (another reason)—you can tell me, I just (wanna know)—

DORA: No, there's no other reason, Ed.

ED: All right, okay, that's all I wanted (to know) . . .

(She looks out at the ocean.)

Okay. Okay. So. There's this (guy). I'm in the (casino)—at the least, I promise you, this is a good story.

DORA *(Turning back to him)*: Then (start telling it).

ED: No, because you look like (you don't care)—

DORA: I'm (listening, just tell me).

ED: I'm just (saying)— . . . Okay. —I haven't even told this (to anyone). Okay. I'm in the casino chilling, and this guy says there's this guy he knows. And the guy, the guy I'm talking to—

DORA: ?

ED: (Okay,) Martin.

DORA: Martin (great).

ED: Don't get all stupid.

DORA: Fucking Martin.

ED: Martin and John.

DORA: (I don't know) John (who is he)?

ED: They just know each other. John's at the casino all the time, Martin knows him from there. Okay. So Martin tells me John, John needs somebody for something—under-the—quick-buck thing. Puts me in (touch)—Martin—with John—in touch so—okay? Okay. So: what do I have to lose? I figure (what the hell, who knows)—so—okay. I call John. Hello, hello, come over, so. I go over. House, *his* house, oh my God. It's (fucking amazing)—totally new, mile away (from the casino)—inside—big TV, flat-screen, DVD. Guys watching *The Matrix*—the scene (where Neo fights the guy in the subway)—John sits me down, this *other* guy, guy gets *me* a drink, and I'm—(sitting) on this like electronic plush chair—massage, adjust the—

DORA: (What are all) These details . . .

ED: (Sorry, I'm getting all excited.) Okay. So. Okay. So John's like, a big guy, maybe thirty, well-groomed, but, like, hairy back kind of guy. (He's) Mob— (and he's like—)

DORA: ?

ED: But (not scary).

DORA: Mob.

ED: (All right, but) He says, "It's a very simple thing, Ed." Simple. I'm like—(it's) like a movie, (I'm) sitting there, like—"I supply"—this is him—"I"

DORA: You don't have to get all dramatic—

ED: (You don't think it's funny?)—Okay. "I supply a local man with Ecstasy. He distributes it to his people at six schools. I don't like to be involved with drugs but it's a lot of money and this is as far as I go with it. It's safe, it's easy, it's very lucrative. What your job is is this:"—and I'm sitting there, with my drink, thinking like (is this really happening?)—"Your job is this:"—not would be, (but) *is*—"once a week, you'll deliver the Ecstasy to this man. You'll be paid a thousand for each delivery. All you do is come here, pick up a backpack with ten thousand dollars of pills, drive half an hour, hand it over, take the cash, bring it back, I'll cut you a thousand, and you'll go home." *(Pause)* I mean, problem solved! Before Christmas! Four thousand a month!

DORA: So you just (say yes) . . .

ED: (I know but) I think—what if he knows some other guy, more eager guy, I don't want to (lose the chance)—Martin (must know other guys but)—he thought of me first. John's like, "Martin speaks very highly of you."

DORA: Martin speaks highly of you. Which, he knows you from (what). "He's a good drinker. He sniffs coke and loses money really well."

ED: (Fuck you.)

DORA: ( ).

ED: ( ).

DORA: Five minutes (you know this guy) and you say yes.

ED: I thought—he needs his money—drugs need to get where they're going—(it's) simple how I fit in. John said he doesn't like his guys to do it because if you get caught it's mandatory minimum sentence, so he contracts it out to keep it out of his thing. He said no one ever got caught but it's better for him that he's not directly connected to it.

DORA: Fine, so. What (happened).

(Ed pauses, staring at Dora.)

( )?

ED: Okay. So. Next day. I get the backpack. They give me a phone number. (Of) The guy I'm handing over to. I'm supposed to go to the pay phone in the parking lot of the bank near the Burger King. I call and let it ring. I can only use that pay phone because what the guy is going to do is, is look at his Caller-ID, and when he sees that pay phone number, he's gonna come meet me at the bank. That way there's no talking on any phones. So. I get the backpack. I get in my car and go. Get to the Burger King, the bank, pull in, pull around back . . .

DORA: (Wait,) What time is it?

ED: What?

DORA: Is it dark? *(Short pause)* This is the phone, the one behind the bank, out of sight of the road?

ED: There's—the Burger King—

DORA: There's the fence between the bank and the Burger King. And it's dark. (Do you see?)

ED: What are you (saying)?

DORA: (You're sitting where) No one can see you.

ED: Why would you want anyone to see?

DORA: (It's a) Backpack—you could hand it over *in* the Burger / King!

ED: You wanna tell the story? You know what happens?

DORA: (   ).

(Pause.)

ED: (So I) Pick up the phone. Dial. Ringing. Then (I hear) a tap on the glass. (Out of) Nowhere. (I) Look. (It's a) Gun. Passenger side, guy with a gun, tapping on the glass. (I) Turn around, (my) window's rolled down, (I) still have the phone to my ear, sitting in the car, so my window is down, (I) turn. Another guy. (Guy) *Rips* the phone from my hand, hangs it up, slams it . . . (I) Give him the (backpack) . . . They just (go) . . .

(Pause. Dora looks away.)

So.

DORA: Do you know what happened?

ED *(Grabbing stomach)*: Fuck, my stomach. Can you hear that?

DORA: What?

ED: I guess only I can hear it, 'cuz of the vibrations in my body.

DORA: What are you talking about?

ED: My stomach is making weird noises, it hurts.

DORA: —Ed, they didn't see the Caller-ID, so how did they know what time you were gonna be there?

ED: I guess—I figure John probably told them around when to expect me. So they were probably just hanging out, waiting. Waiting for a car to pull in there, pick up the phone. Boom.

DORA: But . . . you don't see?

ED: ( )?

DORA: Okay. So—Martin and John know each other a little, they bullshit, whatever. One night John says to Martin, "Hey Martin, I need a favor." Martin's flattered, (he's a) bartender, (and a) mob guy needs his help. (He) Says, "Want you to find me some kid, some fuck-up who needs some money. I'll jerk him around, scare him a little, but I won't hurt him, you have my word. You know anybody?" (You.) Now, John's got this all planned out already with the guy—the distributor guy, the dealer. John fills him in, the *dealer* gives him nine thousand bucks. The dealer gets to save a thousand, and now John has an errand boy who thinks he owes him ten thousand bucks. Who'll do whatever he wants.

ED: What . . . ?

DORA: (They) Pumped you up, gave you a bullshit story—the whole thing was planned out. Robbing *you* works out for *both* of them, they *both* save all this money, meanwhile, *you* get a gun in your face, and now *you* think you owe a mobster ten thousand bucks. Which, if he says you do, you do. So now he'll make you work it off, doing all his dirty work or whatever.

ED: I don't . . . you think he set me up? But—no. No way. John— no, there's gotta be holes in there.

DORA: There's no holes.

ED: ( ).

(Short pause.)

Oh—oh fuck—

DORA: They're not stupid, these guys, they know what they're doing. This dealer is gonna rob a mobster? No one robs mobsters. They have a whole system, this whole thing together, and this guy's just gonna up and rob him? It's where he gets the Ecstasy from—like you said, they both need each other.

ED: Oh God.

(Pause.)

DORA: (Tell me the truth,) Are you doing coke?
ED: Not—really, I don't know, a couple of times—
DORA: Five thousand dollars partying.
ED: I haven't (been partying that much), I've been paying (off my debts.)—*you* doing coke?
DORA: (We're) Talking about me now?
ED: Don't be so angry.
DORA: Fine, (let's) talk about me, what do *you* want *me* to do?

(Pause.)

ED: ( ).
DORA: So I can just leave now.
ED: All right. This is what I came up with. I thought—I can move home, (that) kills my rent, (that) kills my bills. I gotta pay John, God knows what he's gonna make me do to pay it off. So, get the ten thousand out of the way, hold off my other debts—
DORA: So, what, this ten thousand is just gonna wash up on shore?
ED: Well—I gotta find a job. Obviously.
DORA: How do I fit into this.
ED: Well . . . I know I can't—stay with you.
DORA: You already figured that out, you're gonna stay with your folks.
ED: Right.

(Pause.)

I know . . . you don't have any money I could . . . ( ) . . .
DORA: ( ).
ED: I know.
DORA: So all that's left that I can do for you is fuck you, basically.
ED: (Seriously)?
DORA: !
ED: Kidding, Dora! I'm not (that dumb). But what's going on with you, you seeing anybody?

DORA: ( ).

ED: I hope he's good to you, that's all I hope.

DORA: (I) Got it.

ED: What?

DORA: Ask Ty for more money.

ED: No.

DORA: Why not?

ED: That's not right.

DORA: Why not?

ED: No!

DORA: He gave you five thousand.

ED: I didn't ask for it. He just gave it to me.

DORA: So?

ED: What I don't understand is. Because you said you loved me. So when. How do you just stop. Two people / who

DORA: ( ).

ED: If you loved me one month / ago

DORA: Ed

ED: Do you love me?

(Pause.)

Did you?

DORA: ( ).

ED: ?

DORA: Yes (but)—

ED: So when did you stop.

DORA: ( ).

(Pause.)

ED: I'm sorry.

DORA: I'm gonna / leave, Ed.

ED: Okay, wait. Wait. I got this idea. It's a way you can help me. It's a really good idea.

(Dora looks at Ed. Ed looks at Dora.)

I wanna. Okay. Ready?

DORA: ( ).

ED: I wanna rob the Blockbuster.

DORA: —What?

ED: How much is it before you put the final night's total in the safe?

DORA: Ed.

ED: Corporation, won't feel a thing. A couple thousand, right? At closing, so easy, just you in the store—

DORA: No, Ed!

ED: I know there's all those cameras and stuff, but I put on a mask or whatever, we make it look like an actual robbery, like, with a gun and stuff, simple!

DORA: A *gun*?

ED: I have one. I got one.

DORA: You have a *gun*?

ED: What if I get into trouble with John? (What if I have to do) Some ghetto shit?

(Pause.)

DORA: I'm going, Ed.

ED: You're gonna go. You're just gonna go.

DORA *(Rising)*: Yeah.

ED: All right. Whatever. *(Starts removing clothes)* Thanks for the help!

DORA: What are you doing?

ED: (I'm gonna) Take a swim. You wanna?

DORA: Fuck you.

(Dora starts to exit. Ed stands naked, laughs.)

ED: You know you want me. That's why you're leaving!

(She keeps going. Then she is off.)

(Calling) You know that's why you're leaving! Come on, come swimming with me. *(Pause. He yells)* WHY DON'T YOU COME BACK HERE AND COME SWIMMING WITH ME. WHY DON'T YOU COME BACK AND SUCK MY DICK LIKE YOU USED TO! *(Long pause. He's still watching. Screaming)* WHY DON'T YOU COME BACK AND TELL ME YOU LOVE ME.

(Hold.)

Scene 3

Ty approaches Dora on the beach, tentatively.

TY: Dora?

(She turns, startled.)

DORA: Oh—I didn't . . .

(She stands with some difficulty.)

Hey, Ty.
TY: Hi. —Are you okay?
DORA: I'm okay.
TY: Jesus.
DORA: It's not that bad. They got me on Vicodin, so . . .
TY: What happened?
DORA: You don't know? You didn't hear?
TY: No.
DORA: The Blockbuster got robbed.

(Pause.)

TY: Oh.
DORA: Didn't get any money actually. But I got roughed-up . . .
TY: Oh my God.
DORA: I thought everybody heard.
TY: No, I . . .
DORA: Don't talk to anybody?
TY *(Smiles)*: Right.

(Dora sits, with some difficulty.)

DORA: I figured your parents would have told you. Just some random thing—it happens—just happened to happen to me, so.
TY: Does it hurt?
DORA: Just normal pain.
TY: What's normal pain?
DORA: Just—you know. Pain you can live with.

(Short pause.)

I just—wanted to talk to someone.

TY: Sure.

DORA: Because—I didn't—feel like I could go to the wake. I was gonna, but. Your folks didn't—they always said to Eddie how I was "loud." And Eddie's friends . . . Eddie partied so much less when he was with me so they . . . I would have just gone in, fuck 'em, but—my face . . .

TY: Right.

DORA: They don't—the doctors don't know what it's gonna look like yet . . . *(Short pause)* Anyway, I just kept—all night, driving by the funeral home. His buddies outside smoking. Called information, got your number, left you that message, and just came here and . . . —What—was it—nice, or? . . . The wake, what was it like?

TY: Actually . . . I didn't go.

DORA: You didn't go?

TY: Same thing basically. Ed's friends, I can't stand those guys. And I guess Ed never told you, but I don't—I don't speak to my folks.

DORA: Oh. I didn't know that. Why not?

TY: We just don't get along.

DORA: Uh-huh. *(Pause)* I actually—I called you because—when I was driving by, like, the funeral home, I kept, I kept thinking about something you said. That night we all went out.

TY: What?

DORA: That's the thing. It's like, I can't remember it! You talk so good—I can't talk that good. But it was something like— remember, Eddie was getting drinks, or in the bathroom or something and you said—it was so loud and dark—in the bar—and I was like, Why, if you want to hang out with your friends, why would you come to a place like this? Where it's so loud you can't hear them and so dark you can't see them. —Do you remember what you said?

TY: I think . . . I said that guys don't like to talk.

DORA: Yeah. But you kept going.

TY: Well, that they go out because they're looking for a girl to sleep with or a guy to fight.

DORA: Yeah, no, it was after that.

TY: Right—that they communicate with actions. Not words. Guys.

DORA: Yeah! That was it. That's so right, like. And it came back to me—because I was thinking—what you said, with Eddie. Like—what was it Eddie couldn't say. That he would do this. *(Short pause)* That he'd—shoot himself. *(Short pause)*

TY: I don't know. Ed was never the most—rational guy . . .

DORA: No . . .

TY: Just—spending that one night with him. He was a mess.

DORA: Yeah. I actually broke up with him the next day.

TY: You did?

DORA: You didn't know that?

TY: No, I—no.

DORA: I didn't know if you talked to him in the time . . . between . . . then / and—

TY: Right.

DORA: Did you?

TY: What?

DORA: Talk to him at all or . . . ?

TY: I—a few nights ago—he showed up at my apartment sort of—out of the blue . . .

DORA: What was . . .

TY: Just. Um. Well. Really, he seemed just—basically like he was fucked-up on a lot of drugs. He didn't make much—sense . . .

DORA: That was it?

TY: Yeah . . .

DORA: That fucking night. After you left. It was horrible. Eddie kept drinking, right. Then this guy Martin showed up, like three hours later than he was supposed to. Do you know this guy?

TY: No.

DORA: Martin. Works at the casino, he's a bartender, and Eddie— thought he might help him get a job there, right? So we're talking and drinking and Eddie keeps, like, bringing up jobs and stuff, but Martin's not—he's not saying anything about jobs, right? Then Martin kinda leans in and says, "Wanna know a secret?" And Eddie's like, "Sure." And Martin says, "You know why you get so many free drinks in a casino?" And Eddie's like, "Because the drunker you are, the more you'll gamble." And Martin gets all quiet, like he's being all bad by telling us this, and says, "No." He says, "We want, we give out free drinks because we want you to feel like every- one here is your friend." *(Pause)* "We do it so you'll associate the casino with getting something for free, with generosity. That's what makes you gamble more. We actually don't want you drunk, we actually pump oxygen into the casino to keep you sober and awake." And Martin *laughs*. I think it's gross, this guy, talking about how they trick people into losing their money, but I look at Eddie—and Eddie's got this look on his face like—he's entranced. Like this is the coolest thing. But Eddie—I'm thinking, like—Eddie works hard. All his jobs, you can't fuck anyone over in those jobs, they can just fuck you. Eddie moves boxes. Eddie drives trucks, mows lawns, plows snow. Eddie gets fucked-over all the time, so— why does he think this is all cool? Anyway, the night goes on—Martin doesn't say a *word* about any job. Takes out a bag of coke, Eddie's eyes go real big, like—that was it. Dragged him out of there, drove him home, puking in my car, put him in bed, and left. *(Pause)* And . . . that was the last time I saw him. That night. Blacked-out, puking all over himself. Called him the next day and dumped him.

TY: I actually—sent him some money after that night.

DORA: You did?

TY: Just to—I don't know what. Something . . .

(Pause.)

DORA: I told Eddie to invite you out that night. I wanted to meet you. He was kinda weird about it. He didn't talk about you a lot.

TY: Didn't have much in common.

DORA: Eddie said you're like a genius.

TY: He said that? That's funny. He never really understood what I do. It's pretty simple.

DORA: You work really hard though, right?

TY: Not really.

DORA: Yeah right.

TY: No. I just have a skill most people don't.

DORA: What exactly do you do?

TY: You really want to know?

DORA: Yeah.

TY: It's pretty boring.

DORA: No, what *I* do is boring.

TY *(Laughs)*: I design educational programming for use in schools.

DORA: Uh-huh?

TY: Which means—I take what would have been a schoolbook, and put it on a computer screen. So what I'm really doing is taking what something is—the content—and changing the look of it—the form—to fit a different medium.

DORA: Uh-huh . . .

TY: I'm making it sound more complicated than it is. Like—all right: you have computers at Blockbuster, right? What do they do?

DORA: The computers. Just—keep track of your account. What you rented, if it's overdue, like that.

TY: Exactly. Those are primitive programs—meaning they do simple tasks—but even so—think about before those computers. Someone would have had to write down all the information, what you rented, when it was due, and store it in a file cabinet, and retrieving that information would have taken time and slowed down the business . . . so, now, instead of lots of file cabinets and paper cuts and hand cramps, you have a computer on a desk and sore wrists and tired eyes. What I do is, instead of a kid sitting in a classroom, with ink all over his hands and seven books in his backpack, and five notebooks for his different classes— instead, he's tapping away at a computer. I'm sort of the bridge between the past and the future—or the file cabinet and the computer.

DORA: I have no idea what you just said.

TY (*Laughs*): Meaning, we're not there yet. Kids still have books. They still write notes in notebooks with pens. But they won't always. Someday, they'll type notes onto a computer, and read lessons on a screen, and the teacher will type lessons during class, which they'll read on their screen, and be able to read when they go home, because they'll be doing their homework and going over their notes on their computers at home. I'm designing the programming that will make that happen.

DORA: Wow. What's the company's name that you work for?

TY: Education Alternatives. "Preparing Children for the Coming World."

DORA: The backpack companies won't be happy. (*Laughs*) I like my job. It's okay. People'll always wanna watch movies I guess.

(Dora clutches her jaw.)

TY: Are you okay?

DORA: The d-d-doctor said not to. T-t-talk too much. Nnnh.

(Pause. Dora holds her jaw, in evident pain. She reaches into her purse, takes out a Vicodin pill, dry-swallows it.)

I'm okay. Sometimes it throbs.

TY: What?

DORA: The pain. It just, out of nowhere, this throbbing. I'm okay. I'm fine. —You had a horrible night, too, right.

TY: What?

DORA: At the bar that night.

TY: No!

DORA: Come on, you hated it.

TY: No—it was really cool talking to you. I left because—I just couldn't watch him like that.

DORA: You were so uncomfortable like.

TY: In the bar. Yeah—it's that thing—like Eddie's friends. I just don't fit in.

DORA: Eddie loved taking me out to bars. I hated it, but. He said he always wanted to show me off. I thought that was stupid, but. I don't know, is that how guys are?

TY: Is that—are guys? . . .

DORA: Like, do you like showing off your girlfriends, or? . . .

TY: Um . . . I don't—I never really thought about it . . .

DORA: Like, do you like to go to the movies with your girl, or do you like to hang at home?

TY: I guess it—depends . . .

DORA: Yeah. Do you have a girlfriend now or . . . ?

TY: No, no, not at the— . . . / no.

DORA: Oh—secret's out—Ty's a player!

TY: Ha! / Right!

DORA: You are, for real. I see that little grin, that's a player grin.

(Ty laughs. Then clutches his stomach.)

Are you okay?

TY: Oh, I'm fine, just—my stomach.

DORA: Is it? . . .

TY: It's a—I'm fine.

DORA: That's funny. Eddie had stomach things all the time.

TY: He did?

DORA: I always thought it was how much crap he ate. Do you eat, like, Burger King every day?

TY: I'm a vegetarian.

DORA: That must suck.

TY: No—it's really easy being a vegetarian. I cook / my own

DORA: No, I meant, it must suck having people always assume because you have a twin, you're the same in all these ways.

TY: Oh. Yeah. When I was a kid—I hated it. Everyone thought I liked what Eddie liked—because what Eddie liked was what everyone liked.

DORA: Is that why you got tattoos? *(Pause)* To be different?

TY: How do you—?

DORA: Eddie told me. I hope it's okay that I—he was so proud, like—that you showed him your tattoos.

TY: That's—he said that?

DORA: Could I see? *(Pause)* They're—you can't see them on your / arms—

TY: I wanted them to be private.

DORA: Right.

TY: But. If you— . . .

DORA: It's just—I'm so curious.

(Short pause. Ty stands. Dora follows. A beat. Then Ty lifts his shirt over his head, covering his face.)

Oh my God. So many.

(Short pause. She takes his T-shirt and lifts it the rest of the way off his head, and gently lets his T-shirt fall to the ground. Ty smiles. She looks at his body.)

They're beautiful.

TY: Thanks.

DORA: What do they mean?

TY: They're j-just—abstract designs . . .

DORA: You're shivering.

TY: A little / cold

DORA: Did that hurt?

TY: What?

DORA: The nipple ring?

TY: Just— *(Laughs)* just normal pain.

DORA: All down just the one side . . .

TY: I wanted it to be ordered—not random, all / over

DORA: He didn't tell me they were all down just the one side.

TY: That's because—actually—he never saw them actually. *(Short pause. Dora looks at him)* He knew that I had them, but I never showed them to him.

(Short pause. She places her hand on his chest, slowly moves it down across his abdomen.)

DORA: Where did you get them?

TY: I—I did them myself.

DORA: Wait—*you* did them?

TY: Yeah, I—bought the tools and studied and . . .

(Pause. They look as if about to embrace; then, Ty turns away. Dora looks out at the ocean. Ty reaches down to pick up his shirt.)

DORA: Wanna go swimming?

TY: —Now?

DORA: You think I'm crazy?

TY: It's—a little / cold

DORA: You ever done it?

TY: Swim—in the / ocean at

DORA: At night?

TY: No.

DORA: Eddie and I used to.

(Short pause. She looks at him and smiles. Then she removes her clothes, to her undergarments.)

Coming?

TY: I . . .

(Dora smiles at Ty, then runs into the ocean. Ty watches her for a moment. Then he takes off his pants and rushes into the ocean. In the ocean, we see Dora; Ty appears far behind her, slowly and blindly finding his way to her.)

OH!

DORA: TY?

TY: IT'S COLD!

DORA: TY?

TY: IT'S FREEZING!

DORA: CAN YOU SEE ME?

TY: NO!

DORA: WHERE ARE YOU?

TY: BACK HERE!

DORA: COME TO WHERE I AM! I'LL KEEP TALKING! FOLLOW THE SOUND!

TY: OKAY!

DORA: HELLO HELLO HELLO! GOOD-BYE GOOD-BYE GOOD-BYE!

TY: . . . GETTING CLOSER.

DORA: I HEAR YOU BETTER. HELLO HELLO HELLO!

TY: HELLO HELLO HELLO!

DORA: SEAWEED! SEAWEED! SEASHELL! SEASHELL!

TY: Seaweed! Seashell!

DORA: Ha! Hermit crab!

TY: Hermit crab!

DORA: I think I see you!

TY: Barely!

DORA: You're here.

TY: Yeah—a hideous mistake but—here I am.

(They are a few feet away from each other, though both looking somewhat past each other, as though still indistinct.)

DORA: God it's so dark.

TY: No moon. No stars.

DORA: There's clouds.

TY: Are there clouds?

DORA: You can tell 'cuz the sky feels so low. Can you feel how low the sky is? Look up.

TY *(Looking up)*: It is low.

DORA: You can feel it, right?

TY: It's colder than I thought.

DORA: It gets warmer.

TY: Ha, does it?

DORA: You're really cold?

TY: Shivering.

DORA: Come closer.

(She moves somewhat blindly toward him, while he remains relatively still, groping a bit dumbly.)

Am I—I'm right / in
TY: Yeah, I'm right / here
DORA: Hold my hand to stay warm.
TY: Hold your—where—but I can't / see
DORA: Find my hand, in the / water
TY: I can't / even
DORA: Just move your hand around . . .

(Beneath the water, both hands search. And connect.)

There!
TY: Yeah!
DORA: Found it.

(Silence. They look at each other, still significantly obscured by darkness, so that though they are inches away from each other, they stare intensely as if far apart. Their hands stay clutched.)

Your face . . .
TY: My face?
DORA: I can't see you . . .
TY: I'm here . . .
DORA: You are . . . God.
TY: What?
DORA: Just feel it.
TY: What?

(Dora wraps her arm around Ty's waist, and moves behind him, clutching him. She sways with the gentle tide.)

DORA: There.

(Dora presses against Ty, swaying; he begins to sway as well.)

Do you feel it?

(Now they are swaying in unison to the tide.)

221

TY: I think . . .

DORA: Close your eyes . . .

> *(A beat. He does. The swaying grows more close, more intense, though it continues to be gentle.)*

Do you feel it? . . .

TY: Mmm . . .

DORA: Right? . . .

> *(Ty opens his eyes. He turns his head to look at Dora, whose eyes are closed. He stares at her a long while.)*

DORA: Can I tell you something, Ty?

> *(Ty turns back, closes his eyes.)*

TY: —Sure.

DORA: It's a secret . . .

TY: A—secret?

DORA: You don't have to say anything.

TY: Wh—what?

DORA: A secret from that night at the bar . . .

TY: What?

DORA: Shhh.

> *(Dora, eyes still closed, still clutching Ty, begins to kiss his neck. Again he opens his eyes and looks, as if about to speak. She continues to kiss him with great feeling. Then he closes his eyes and arches toward her. Their lips meet. Abruptly, he pulls away. Dora opens her eyes and looks at him. He stares back, somewhat inscrutable, as if about to speak but hesitant. Slowly their gaze entwines, and Ty turns away. She approaches him. She puts her hand on Ty's chest. He turns to her and with a sense of inevitability and deep communion they embrace. They kiss. Then Ty pulls back, ever so slightly, and whispers:)*

TY: I can't.

DORA: Shhh.

TY: Dora.

> *(She continues to kiss his neck.)*

I know, Dora.

DORA: Mmm . . .

(She runs her hand up and down his chest, toward his groin.)

TY: Oh God—

(She puts her hand beneath his boxer shorts.)

Dora—
DORA: Mmmm . . .

(She continues to kiss his neck.)

TY: I know—Dora—No—oh God—oh—

(Ty releases from Dora almost violently. Her eyes open. Ty strides back to shore, through the thick water. Dora watches him go. On shore, Ty dresses. In the ocean, Dora stares blankly ahead. Then suddenly she plunges herself under the surface of the water, and hangs there, lifeless, peaceful. Just as suddenly she emerges, almost violently, from beneath the ocean. She sucks in air and chokes, then takes in a monstrous, gasping breath. Slowly her breathing normalizes, and she starts her way out of the vast dark ocean to shore. On shore, Ty sits, dressed, his head between his knees. Dora comes onto the beach and moves to her clothes. Silently, she starts to dress. Ty picks up his head and watches her. She turns and sees. Conversationally:)

DORA: I do *not* wanna work tomorrow.
TY: What time are you working?
DORA: Morning. The corporate people are sending all these people down—it's this thing they do after a robbery, this whole fucking interview thing. But since they didn't get any money it shouldn't be that bad, hopefully.
TY: Right.
DORA: You should come in sometime. I got this stack of free rental coupons for dissatisfied customers, but we can use them for whatever.
TY: Cool.
DORA: Someone was telling me . . . *(She's fully dressed)* You can rent movies online now or something? Do you do that?

(Dora looks to Ty. His head is bowed again.)

Ty?

(Ty looks up to her. A beat.)

What's wrong?
TY: I know it was Edward that—did this to your face, Dora.

(Pause. Dora chuckles.)

DORA: What are you talking about?
TY: He came to me the night—he shot / himself.
DORA: You know—I gotta work tomorrow for like / twelve hours
TY: He told me he needed ten thousand dollars—he wouldn't say
   for what, / but he seemed really desperate—and
DORA: He always needed money—
TY: He told me he was going to rob you. *(Pause)* He was really
   high, he was fucked-up. I knew I should have done something but I just—wrote him a check and—I . . . they didn't
   find it on him so. I guess—after he went to the Blockbuster
   he—that's when he decided to—that's when he came to the
   beach and killed himself.

(Suddenly Dora clutches her jaw.)

DORA: Nnnnh. Nnnnnh. Nnnnnh.

(Ty rises. Dora breathes. Then another wave of pain.)

Ahhhh. Ahhhhhhh.

(Ty moves toward Dora.)

TY: Let me take you home—

*(Ty reaches out to her. Dora slaps his arm away, her purse flying
off her arm. Ty takes a shocked step back.)*

What's wrong?

(Dora doesn't answer. She slowly removes her hand from her jaw. She gains her balance, then starts to move to where her purse is. Ty takes a few steps as if to retrieve it for her, but she shakes her head no. She reaches her purse and, in agony, sits down. She takes out a pill. She manages to open her mouth ever so slightly; she bends her head back and drops the pill onto her tongue. She tries to swallow; gags badly, then forces it down. Ty takes a step toward her. She looks at him. They stare at each other for a moment. Then she turns away from him and looks out at the ocean. Ty watches her for a moment, and then turns and leaves the beach. Dora does not turn to see that he is gone.)

Scene 4

Day. Dora approaches Ty, who is sitting on the beach. He is wearing headphones. So is she. She sees Ty and takes off her headphones.

DORA: Ty.

(He doesn't respond. She sees he's wearing headphones. She moves in front of him and smiles. He looks up. Eventually he sees her, and takes his headphones off.)

Hey!
TY: Hi!
DORA: Sorry I'm late. I would have called but I don't have your cell.

(He rises.)

TY: It's okay.
DORA: What are you listening to?
TY: Oh—just—a mix I burned—different stuff.
DORA: Trade for a second?
TY: —Sure!
DORA: You're gonna hate this. Okay.

(They sit down and switch headphones. Both sit and listen to each other's discs. Dora rocks out a little. Ty laughs, grooves to Dora's music.)

IT'S GOOD. WHAT IS IT.

TY: IT'S THIS FRIEND OF MINE. CREATES IT ALL HIMSELF, JUST HIM, A KEYBOARD AND A MAC.

DORA: COOL. —DO YOU HATE MINE.

TY: WHAT'S THERE TO HATE ABOUT CYNDI LAUPER.

(Dora laughs. They listen a few more seconds. Then Dora takes the headphones off, and Ty follows. They hand headphones back to each other.)

DORA: Your friend is good. Is he from here?

TY: Yeah, he's in school here. Doesn't go to class much, spends all day writing songs on his computer. Big into Ecstasy, kind of a drug freak.

DORA: Tell me about it. It took me so long to get off that Vicodin.

TY: Yeah?

DORA: Do you know you can get it on the internet? My last refill ran out and I was freaking, and then this guy was like, I get Vicodin online. They have like online pharmacies and doctors talk to you on the phone and stuff, and just prescribe it. So then *he* got me some . . .

TY: But you're—you're off them?

DORA: Yeah. I'm basically fine. I still have a little back thing, but I do this water therapy, 'cuz the water helps it supposedly.

TY: Are you in a rehabilitation program or? . . .

DORA: No, they just showed me how, I do it on my own.

TY: In the ocean?

DORA: It's too cold now. I've been using the pool at the casino, actually.

TY: Oh.

DORA: I went to this acupuncturist too for a while, for my back.

TY: Oh yeah?

DORA: It really helped. They rake it in, those guys. Good line of business to be in. Everyone's back is a wreck, right? Nobody can walk in this country.

TY: Or sleep.

DORA: Ambien for that. You like Ambien?

TY: Never had it.

DORA: Ambien-Vicodin combo . . . like peanut butter and jelly.

(Ty laughs. Short pause.)

TY: You look—amazing.

DORA: I do?

TY: Like—nothing happened.

DORA: They did a good job, right? When they did the operation on my nose, they actually, I think they made it better than before. The girls at work are all like, "Did you get a nose job?"

TY: Wow.

DORA: I swear to God. I thought the rest of my life, people were gonna look at me, like, "What the fuck happened to her?" Like one of those people.

TY: Right.

DORA: 'Cuz I see those women. They come in to Blockbuster. Alone. The ugliest guy can come in, there's some woman with him. Ugly women, forget it. I got two new teeth too, see? Discolored, just like my real ones.

(She bares her teeth.)

TY: Watch out, she can bite.

(Short pause.)

DORA: What about you?

TY: What about me.

DORA: What's going on, player!

TY *(Laughs)*: Not much. *(Short pause)* I've—missed you. *(Short pause)* Been thinking of quitting my job.

DORA: You're kidding.

TY: Thinking about it.

DORA: Why?

TY: I'm just tired of it. There must be something else I can do.

DORA: Don't quit your job.

TY: No?

DORA: No. You have a good job, Ty.

(Short pause.)

TY: Just something I'm thinking about.

(Pause.)

227

DORA: I'm going to this therapist.

TY: Really?

DORA: Yeah. It's good, you know? We talk a lot about—we talk about everything that happened and.

(Short pause.)

TY: It's okay.

(Dora smiles at Ty and looks away. Then Dora's cell phone rings. She checks it, then shuts it off. Pause.)

DORA: I'm sorry about that night, Ty. And not calling you and. I'm sorry.

(Dora's cell phone rings again. She answers:)

Hey. Yeah. I'm running late. At the store, we're rearranging the whole store and it's taking forever. No. Soon. Okay.

(She hangs up.)

Sorry. Meeting someone later . . .

TY: It's okay.

DORA: The last thing I expected.

TY: —What?

DORA: Remember that guy I told you about? Martin? Who works at the casino, Eddie's friend?

TY: Yeah?

DORA: I guess he was all upset, like, that I wasn't at Eddie's wake, and so he called a couple days after to check on me. Turns out he's like this really cool guy . . .

(Pause. Ty looks away.)

My therapist thinks it's a really good thing for / me

TY: I'm sure it is.

(Pause.)

DORA: I'm not—I'm not gonna say some stupid thing to you that isn't true.

(Pause.)

    I don't / want to
TY: I actually—have to get somewhere, so.
DORA: Oh.

    (Ty rises.)

    Can I get your cell?
TY: Calling me at home is the best way / to
DORA: Well—give it to me anyway.
TY: Why?

    (Pause.)

DORA: —I don't wanna say anything stupid to you, Ty.
TY: So don't.

    (Pause.)

DORA: —I want what I have to say to you to come out right.
TY: Fine. Call me when you figure it out.

    (Ty starts to go. Dora rises.)

DORA: You know that's not how I—wait, Ty.

    (He stops and turns.)

    Forget all that, okay? There's one / thing.
TY: *Forget* it?
DORA: Just—there's something I need you to tell me. *(Pause)*
I need you to tell me the truth. 'Cuz I know you know it.
TY: What?

    (Pause.)

DORA: When I think about that night. I think about how you said
you should have done something. How you should have
done something but you just let him go. *(Pause)* Sometimes
I think about things *I* did to him. Things *I* said. And my ther-

apist, she says, she always says, "It's not your fault that he killed himself. It's not your fault, Dora." But. Like. What *I* think is, Whose fault is it then? *(Pause)* Because. In a way. It *is* my fault. *(Pause)* Is it?

(Dora and Ty look at each other. Pause. Dora turns away from Ty, and looks out at the ocean. Ty turns away, toward the shore. Then Ty turns to Dora. He is quietly crying. He watches her looking out at the ocean. Then, as if sensing his eyes on her, she turns to him. A long silence. Then:)

TY: (No.)

(Pause.)

DORA: (Thank you.)

(Hold.)

END OF PLAY

Where Do We Live

Production History

Where Do We Live was commissioned by and received its world premiere at the Royal Court Theatre (Ian Rickson, Artistic Director) in London, on May 21, 2002. It was directed by Richard Wilson; the set and costume design were by Julian McGowan, the lighting design was by Johanna Town, the sound design was by Paul Arditti and the music was composed by Olly Fox. The cast was as follows:

STEPHEN	Daniel Evans
PATRICIA	Susannah Wise
TYLER	Adam Garcia
BILLY, YOUNG BUSINESSMAN 1, YOUNG ART STUDENT	Toby Dantzic
SHEDRICK	Noel Clarke
TIMOTHY	Cyril Nri
LILY	Jemima Rooper
DAVE, YOUNG BUSINESSMAN 2, YOUNG WHITE MAN	Nicholas Aaron
LEO, VIOLINIST	Ray Panthaki

It received its U.S. premiere at the Vineyard Theatre (Douglas Aibel, Artistic Director; Bardo S. Ramirez, Managing Director) in New York City, opening on May 11, 2004. It was directed by Christopher Shinn; the set design was by Rachel Hauck, the lighting design was by David Weiner, the sound design was by Jill BC Du Boff, the original music was by Storm P, the costume design was by Mattie Ullrich and the production stage manager was Erika Timperman. The cast was as follows:

STEPHEN	Luke Macfarlane
PATRICIA	Emily Bergl
TYLER	Jacob Pitts
BILLY, YOUNG BUSINESSMAN 2,	
YOUNG ART STUDENT	Jesse Tyler Ferguson
SHEDRICK	Burl Moseley
TIMOTHY	Daryl Edwards
LILY	Liz Stauber
DAVE, YOUNG BUSINESSMAN 1,	
YOUNG WHITE MAN	Aaron Stanford
LEO, CELLIST	Aaron Yoo

Characters

STEPHEN, white, late twenties
PATRICIA, white, late twenties
TYLER, white, late twenties
BILLY, white, late twenties
SHEDRICK, black, early twenties
TIMOTHY, black, early fifties
LILY, white, mid-twenties
DAVE, white, late teens
LEO, Asian, mid-twenties
YOUNG BUSINESSMAN 1, white, late twenties
YOUNG BUSINESSMAN 2, white, late twenties
YOUNG WHITE MAN, white, late twenties
SECURITY GUARD, black, early forties
VIOLINIST, Asian, mid-twenties
YOUNG ART STUDENT, white, mid-twenties

Place

New York City.

Time

Late summer/fall 2001.

Note

Dialogue in the play often overlaps. A slash in the text (/) indicates where the character who speaks next begins.

Included in this text is my feeble attempt at an Eminem-like rap. In London some of the actors volunteered to make it better, and they did; better still, in New York, we hired a hip-hop artist who created a really extraordinary Eminem-like rap of his own. I encourage future collaborators to improve upon the rap written here, as long as it keeps to the context which the script makes clear. Stephen should always be right to object to it; no matter how entertaining and appealing the production, or clever the expression of homophobic sentiment, the rap must be ugly and hateful at its core.

Scene 1

A bar. Patricia works behind the bar. Stephen sits, with soda. Two Young Businessmen sit a few stools away, looking up at stock quotes on the television. Stephen is smoking.

STEPHEN: And he said, "Ooh, you don't want to be a caretaker."
PATRICIA: Oh. Of course.
STEPHEN: And I thought—I mean, the guy's missing a *leg*, what? . . .
PATRICIA: Of course you did.
STEPHEN: And he knew the facts.
PATRICIA: What are the facts exactly?

(Patricia listens while filling pretzel bowls.)

STEPHEN: Well. When I moved in, I just noticed—a family. There was a woman—and there was a man—and a kid—not a kid— maybe eighteen. So one day the woman disappears—I never see her again, and the father—when I see / him next
YOUNG BUSINESSMAN 1: One more round here, Patricia.

(Patricia pours two whiskeys.)

237

PATRICIA *(Nodding to TV, pouring drinks)*: You guys losing money today?

YOUNG BUSINESSMAN 2: You're a loser if you're losing / money

YOUNG BUSINESSMAN 1: You gotta be crazy to lose money in this market.

YOUNG BUSINESSMAN 2 *(Nodding toward Stephen)*: What's your boyfriend's name?

PATRICIA *(Laughs, gives whiskeys to men)*: Here you go. *(Goes back to Stephen, keeps refilling pretzel bowls)* So the woman disappears.

STEPHEN: Right. And then, the man, the father, he has no leg suddenly. I see him, he has no leg below the knee.

(The bar phone rings. Patricia answers.)

PATRICIA: Hello?

YOUNG BUSINESSMAN 1 *(To Patricia)*: Ah, *that's* your boyfriend.

YOUNG BUSINESSMAN 2 *(To Stephen)*: She have a boyfriend? She never tells us.

PATRICIA: Okay. *(Hangs up)*

YOUNG BUSINESSMAN 2: You ready to invest yet, Patricia?

PATRICIA: I'm already in the stock market—it goes up, I get good tips, if it goes down I know it's gonna be a bad day.

YOUNG BUSINESSMAN 1: You're lucky Bush got in.

PATRICIA: Right, yeah, thank God.

YOUNG BUSINESSMAN 1: More money for you!

YOUNG BUSINESSMAN 2: Three-hundred-dollar tax refund, what is that, how many tips is that? How many drinks you have to serve to get that?

(Patricia goes back to Stephen. The men laugh.)

PATRICIA: Okay, so.

STEPHEN: Anyway—I can't tell for sure but I think the kid, I think the kid is dealing drugs out of the apartment, because I see people go in there during the day—white people—so that's the / situation basically.

YOUNG BUSINESSMAN 1 *(Regarding the TV)*: Bingo. I told / you

YOUNG BUSINESSMAN 2: Yeah, yeah, it'll drop, just / watch

YOUNG BUSINESSMAN 1: I don't / think so

STEPHEN: Anyway—the father—knocks on my door maybe once a week and asks me for cigarettes, and I give him a few. This has never seemed to bother Tyler—*until*—

(The phone rings. Patricia answers it.)

PATRICIA: Hello?

YOUNG BUSINESSMAN 2 *(To Stephen)*: What do you do?

STEPHEN: —I'm a writer.

YOUNG BUSINESSMAN 1: Oh yeah? A screenwriter?

STEPHEN: No, not a / screenwriter

YOUNG BUSINESSMAN 2: You should write a story about us. I'm / serious

YOUNG BUSINESSMAN 1: Yeah, this guy's life is screwed up, let me / tell you

YOUNG BUSINESSMAN 2: —Two guys, one of them gets laid all the time, the other one can't / get laid

STEPHEN *(Amiably)*: Maybe I will.

PATRICIA: Okay, gotcha.

(Patricia hangs up and goes to Stephen, starts drying glasses.)

Sorry. This has never seemed to bother Tyler "until"—

STEPHEN: —The other night. So the father knocks on my door. He needs to go to the deli. It's raining outside and he's afraid his crutches will slip. He tells me if he falls on his leg—the amputated leg, the remaining part of it—he'll be in really bad trouble. So I help him—I go with him—to the deli. And as we're walking, he starts talking. Telling me he's worked his whole life, he can't work anymore, he's on Social Security . . . Anyway, so he buys his stuff, I help him back up to his apartment—the end. And I tell Tyler this, I tell him this, and his response is—and this is his *instinctive* response— "Oooh, be careful, you don't want to become a caretaker."

PATRICIA: I see. *(Beat; sincerely)* Do you love this person?

STEPHEN: Do I love him? Yeah—yeah. I do. I really / do. *(Stephen's cell phone rings. He checks the number, answers)* Hey sweets. Nothing, just stopped by to see Patricia. Yeah? Okay. Okay great. Bye. *(He hangs up)*

PATRICIA: It's funny—because from what you've told me about him, he's been taken care of.

STEPHEN: What?

PATRICIA: Was that him by the way?

STEPHEN: Yeah.

PATRICIA: You told me that he has a trust fund. He's never had to worry about money.

STEPHEN: Right?

PATRICIA: He's been taken care of. So why was he threatened by your taking care of someone?

STEPHEN: Oh—right. Hunh. *(Beat)* —It made me think about empathy.

(Patricia clears Stephen's empty soda, wipes down the bar.)

PATRICIA: Uh-huh?

STEPHEN: Just—what it is. How it comes to be. On an individual level, a societal level . . . how do you imagine other people, their lives—whether it's someone you love or someone you don't—a stranger—I should get going, we're "clubbing" tonight. —I guess it's really a small thing to get so worked up about.

PATRICIA: No it's not. *(Beat)* I mean—the way you spoke of it, it doesn't sound like a small thing to you.

(Pause.)

STEPHEN *(Lightly)*: Yeah. Okay. I'll see you soon.

(Stephen puts down money for his soda.)

PATRICIA: Shut up.

(Stephen laughs and takes his money back. He goes.)

YOUNG BUSINESSMAN 1 *(To Patricia)*: Blah blah blah, *Jesus* that guy can talk. —Is he gay, that guy?

PATRICIA *(Teasingly)*: What do you think?

YOUNG BUSINESSMAN 2 *(To 1)*: I told you he was.

YOUNG BUSINESSMAN 1: He's a writer like you, / huh?

YOUNG BUSINESSMAN 2: —You know Patricia, there's this whole trend of attractive women hanging around gay guys, I saw a thing about it on TV.

PATRICIA *(Laughing)*: Is that so? This is a trend now?

(The men rise, take out money, preparing to go.)

YOUNG BUSINESSMAN 2: Yeah, but it's not healthy, they're afraid of real men, they've been hurt too many times, so they take comfort in gay men. But it's bad, you're / cutting off from—

YOUNG BUSINESSMAN 1: —Don't listen to this / guy, Patricia.

YOUNG BUSINESSMAN 2: What? It's just an / observation.

PATRICIA: I actually have a boyfriend, but thank you for your concern.

YOUNG BUSINESSMAN 2: You *do*. Truth is out. —That's a lucky guy. What's his name?

PATRICIA: Frank.

YOUNG BUSINESSMAN 2: What's he do?

PATRICIA: He's a chef.

YOUNG BUSINESSMAN 2: A chef? What kind of money do chefs make?

YOUNG BUSINESSMAN 1 *(Starts going)*: We'll get out of your hair, Patricia.

PATRICIA *(Laughing)*: Take care, you guys.

YOUNG BUSINESSMAN 1: But I'm serious, Patricia, you'll be voting Republican by the time we're through with you.

PATRICIA: Yeah, right.

YOUNG BUSINESSMAN 2 *(Going)*: Hey, whenever you're ready to invest some money, you talk to me first, okay?

PATRICIA: Gotcha.

Scene 2

Stephen's apartment. R & B music plays. Stephen is dressing. A knock on his apartment door. Stephen turns down music and opens the door.

YOUNG WHITE MAN: Your elevator is *scary, yo!*

STEPHEN: Sorry?

YOUNG WHITE MAN: Oh, fuck *(Looks down hall)* —have the wrong apartment.

STEPHEN: Oh.

YOUNG WHITE MAN: Sorry!

STEPHEN: That's okay.

(Stephen shuts the door. He begins dressing and singing and dancing as he does. There is another knock on the door. He goes to the peephole and looks in.)

Hello?

SHED'S VOICE: Yeah, open up a minute?

STEPHEN: I'm sorry, who is it you're looking for?

SHED'S VOICE: I'm your neighbor, 'cross the hall.

(Pause. Stephen opens.)

STEPHEN: Hi.

SHED: Hey, 'sup.

STEPHEN: Not much.

SHED: Yeah. Naw, 'cuz I know you help us out over there.

STEPHEN: Right?

SHED: Yeah. You know, I just wanna say, we appreciate that, you helping us out.

STEPHEN: Oh. It's not a problem.

SHED: But—you know—we okay, we take care of ourselves.

STEPHEN: Uh-huh.

SHED: You know how it is, we all live together, we all neighbors.

STEPHEN: Uh-huh.

SHED: Naw, 'cuz it's good to know, you know—everybody let everybody live their lives up here . . .

STEPHEN: Right.

(Pause.)

SHED: That's all. Peace.

(Shed extends his hand. Stephen takes it. Shed shakes, releases.)

STEPHEN: Bye.

(Shed goes. Stephen shuts the door.)

Scene 3

Shed's apartment. He enters, goes to couch where Lily (who speaks with a British accent tinged with a black American urban sound) sits. They are sharing a joint. Shed resumes counting money; Lily is reading a movie magazine. The TV is on. There is a lock box on the table with cash and cocaine in it.

LILY: What'd the faggot say?

SHED: Did I put the money in here?

LILY: What money?

SHED: Where'd I put the fifty dollars?

(Shed's cell phone rings. He looks at the number, answers.)

What. No. Not here. I told you. No. Peace. *(He hangs up)*

LILY: Was that Dave?

SHED: No, it was the boys, looking to party.

LILY: That wasn't Dave?

SHED: I told them, find somewhere else. Keep calling . . . *(Reaches in back pocket, finds cash)* There.

LILY: —What'd the faggot say?

SHED: He harmless.

LILY: Is Dave with Maryanne tonight?

SHED: —He fine, just spoke a minute. He not gonna call anybody, he scared.

LILY: Is Dave with Maryanne tonight?

SHED: I don't know, Lily.

LILY: What did I do?

SHED *(Picking up cash, counting)*: —I gotta get that number from Dave.

LILY: What number?

SHED: He said, this one night we went to this hotel—he said he knew the guy who managed the bar in the hotel. You never went there with him?

LILY: No.

SHED: Amazing. I thought—way people spending money in / there

LILY: Fucking Maryanne.

SHED: 'Cuz I can't anymore—sitting here all day, never going outside, worrying about cops, people in the building knowing what's going on, calling the cops. In the hotel—watching people spend their money—so many people there, they gotta be / hiring people

LILY *(Looking back at magazine)*: Do you like Nicole Kidman?

SHED: You know? Out of hand with this. *(Gesturing to Stephen's apartment)* Like what if he called. What if he—what if he just called the police and said there's a kid in 6C dealing / drugs

LILY: You just said he's harmless. Do you like Nicole Kidman?

SHED: Next time Dave comes I just gotta tell him, find someone else. But if he could set me up with / that hotel guy

LILY: Dave likes you, he always talks about you, "Shed Shed, Shed's my boy."

SHED: That's why, you just gotta stop, you know, otherwise it keeps going.

LILY: You get paid crap. In hotels you get paid crap, they're all Mexicans / who aren't even

SHED: Whatever, I got money saved now. Saved, so I don't need to—what I need. That's the thing, you just gotta stop thinking you can just keep / making more

LILY (Giggling): "Shed's my boy, my boy downtown."

SHED: I fucking—I was a mover before. You know being a mover? Your back? In the summer? Fucking, people barking at you, elevators too small to fit all the heavy shit, people all freaking out you're gonna scratch their stuff, antique / whatever

LILY: I have to see *Moulin Rouge* again.

SHED: How many times you gonna / see that movie

LILY: Ewan MacGregor . . . Do you think Nicole Kidman's pretty?

SHED (Continuing counting): She all right . . .

LILY: She's pretty, but do you think she's sexy?

SHED (Putting down cash): Five. —It's like, people too ambitious—like all that shit the boys talk—"I'm gonna marry this girl." "I'm gonna get a recording contract." Why don't you lay down one song first. Why don't you try fucking the bitch more than two months.

LILY: Me and Dave were together for three months. Maryanne thinks she / can just

SHED: He fucked you for three months, you not together.

LILY: You've only known me one month, what do you know?

SHED: People don't—like—things happen for real, happen slow. People talking / shit

LILY: Can I play a game?

SHED: Whatever, I don't care.

(Lily turns on video game, gets controller. Shed counts money. Timothy enters from back, using crutches.)

TIMOTHY: Oh, you're not watching TV? I thought I heard the TV.

(Lily starts playing, Shed keeps counting, neither looks at him. Timothy exits.)

SHED: Five.

LILY: How many times you going to count the money, Jesus Christ!

SHED: Just making sure.

LILY: I can never get to the next level.

SHED: Just making sure he not skimming from me.

LILY: You keep it locked up, how's he gonna take any? I can't get to the next level.

SHED: Maybe he find the extra key. What else he do all day besides eat and fucking watch TV.

LILY: I don't know what I did.

SHED *(Looking up to TV)*: You gotta press down *then* up. You don't do a double leap to get / to the gold rings

LILY: No, Dave. I don't know what I did to Dave.

SHED: You didn't do nothing.

LILY: He's not calling me! Fuck.

(Lily puts down controller, goes to couch, cuddles Shed.)

Is it the same as the last twelve times you counted it?

SHED *(Laughs)*: Yeah. *(Lily begins licking his neck)* Lily. *(She reaches for his crotch)*

No. *(He pushes her hand away)*

LILY: "No."

SHED: Nothing happening.

LILY: I don't believe you.

SHED: You know, no.

LILY *(Moving to his chest, touching him)*: I just want to give you a blow job, what's the big / deal?

SHED: Stop, Lily. *(She sits up)*

LILY: You won't let me have a bump?

SHED: I'm done with that here, I told you.

LILY: One bump.

SHED: No.

LILY: "No." Just one.

(Timothy enters, eating.)

TIMOTHY: You done playing? You gonna watch TV?

SHED *(Not looking at him)*: Why you be awake all hours, at night you supposed to sleep.

TIMOTHY: I ran out of cigarettes.

(Shed calmly lights a cigarette and smokes. Timothy walks toward door.)

SHED: Now where you going?
TIMOTHY: Get a cigarette 'cross the hall.
SHED: He not there, he left.
TIMOTHY: How do you know?
LILY *(Laughs)*: Shed knows everything.
SHED: I heard him go out.
TIMOTHY: Maybe he came back, maybe he just went to the deli.
SHED: He not there.

(Pause. Timothy goes back to the bedroom. Shed goes to the door, looks out peephole.)

Giving him cigarettes and shit, giving him shit all the time—he need to mind his own fucking business. He thinks anytime he wants something he can just knock on the door. Prepared for nothing in his life, *(Turning back to Lily)* now he can't fucking—

(Shed sees Lily has her cell phone out, is dialing, oblivious.)

Scene 4

A (relatively) quiet area of a club. Stephen stands next to Leo, who is Asian. Pause.

LEO: It's so over, isn't it?
STEPHEN: What?
LEO: All of it.
STEPHEN: Oh.
LEO: You didn't look like you were having a good time, so . . .
STEPHEN: I'm just looking for someone.
LEO: Who?
STEPHEN: I'm trying to find my boyfriend.
LEO: Oh, you lost him?

STEPHEN: I just got here—I can't find him.

LEO: Are you on anything?

STEPHEN: Sorry?

LEO: Are you on any drugs?

STEPHEN: No.

LEO: Drugs are kind of over, too, aren't they? What are we rebelling against except our own feelings?

STEPHEN: Good question.

(Pause. Stephen looks around.)

LEO: What's your boyfriend like?

STEPHEN: What does he look like?

LEO: No—what is he *like*?

STEPHEN: He's sweet, he's sensitive . . .

LEO: Do you love him?

STEPHEN: I do. *(Looking)* There's so many people.

LEO: And the lights. And everyone looks the same.

STEPHEN: Uh-huh.

LEO: Or it's just that I look so different. What do you do?

STEPHEN: I'm a writer.

LEO: Cool—you're smart!

STEPHEN: I guess.

LEO: I'm in grad school—American studies. Whatever that is. Is your boyfriend white?

STEPHEN: He is.

LEO: I don't know why I keep coming here—I have no access. I'm totally ignored because I'm not blond and built and—it's like, it's so clear here, like— Who cares what we *do* in this world—it's all how you look. Who cares who *speaks* at our funeral. Just go to the gym and sign up, buy the right *clothes*.

STEPHEN: Uh-huh . . .

LEO: —I look at this and it's like— How can you even believe in homophobia? Gay people are supposed to be oppressed but—come *on*. I mean, I believe in oppression—I believe, like, that Iraqis are oppressed and whole continents are oppressed in brutal ways—but *this*? —But I guess oppression is tricky, it's invisible now, more indirect, harder to define. Who do you blame if you can't tell who's oppressing you—you can't have a rally against invisible forces. And why would anyone here want to believe they're oppressed? It's not a pleasant way to live. *(Stephen looks around. Leo's nose starts to bleed)* I guess I'm talking mostly about myself. I guess I just wish I could disappear like everyone else here. Or maybe it's the opposite—maybe I just wish someone would look at me. I'd like to have someone who says he loves me looking for me! Maybe I should just join the gym and dye my hair blond.

(Stephen looks at Leo.)

STEPHEN: Oh—are you okay?
LEO: What?
STEPHEN: Your nose is bleeding, I think.

(Leo touches his lip, feels blood.)

LEO: Oh fuck!

(Leo runs off. Stephen sees Tyler, rushes toward him. The music is deafening.)

TYLER: OH—HEY!
STEPHEN: HI!
TYLER: YOU'RE HERE!
STEPHEN: I TRIED CALLING! I GUESS YOU COULDN'T HEAR YOUR PHONE!
TYLER: WHAT?
STEPHEN: NOTHING. YOU LOOK GREAT!
TYLER: THANK YOU YOU TOO. SO—THE PLAN CHANGED A LITTLE. I WASN'T GOING TO—BUT I ENDED UP TAKING ECSTASY.
STEPHEN: OH.
TYLER: IT'S ACTUALLY BEEN TERRIBLE—NOT THE ECSTASY BUT—LET ME FIND BILLY AND TELL HIM I'M LEAVING. IS THAT OK?
STEPHEN: WHY ARE YOU HAVING A TERRIBLE TIME?
TYLER: LET ME FIND BILLY.

(Tyler exits. A Young White Man comes to Stephen and begins dancing, somewhat seductively, but with a ridiculous seriousness. Stephen dances with him, politely, avoiding eye contact. The Man demands to be seen, keeps dancing into Stephen's vision. Stephen smiles and dances away from him. The Man fol-

lows him. Stephen goes back to the quiet area of the club. The Man dances away. Leo returns, holding a napkin to his nose, pinching, checking.)

LEO: Thanks for telling me.

STEPHEN: Oh—yeah—

LEO: What do you write about? One of my areas of study is queer representation.

STEPHEN: I actually can't really talk, I found my boyfriend, so . . .

LEO: Oh, you found him?

STEPHEN *(Stephen sees Tyler, turns briefly back to Leo)*: Nice to meet you.

LEO: You're going?

(Stephen goes back into the loud part of the club.)

TYLER: HEY—WHERE DID YOU GO?

STEPHEN: WHAT?

TYLER: WERE YOU TALKING TO SOMEONE?

STEPHEN: NO.

TYLER: WHO WAS THAT?

STEPHEN: NO ONE.

TYLER: SO—UM. THERE'S A PROBLEM.

STEPHEN: WHAT?

TYLER: WHAT?

STEPHEN: WHAT'S THE PROBLEM?

TYLER: WELL—WE JUST STARTED PEAKING? SO BILLY'S LIKE, WHY AM I LEAVING NOW, WHEN WE JUST STARTED PEAKING.

STEPHEN: COME TO THE QUIETER PART!

TYLER: WHAT?

(Stephen pulls him; they go to the quieter part of the club. Leo sits some feet away, watching.)

STEPHEN: What's going on?

TYLER: It's kind of a long story.

STEPHEN: You said you're having a terrible time?

TYLER: Well it's this whole thing. Michael's here, and you met Michael, and his boyfriend Russell, and there are these two guys, Keith and Derek who you don't know I don't think.

STEPHEN: Uh-huh?

TYLER: Anyway, so we were all dancing, me and Billy and all six of us basically, and, Billy's had a crush on Keith for a while. So basically Michael and Russell start dancing in their own world, so it's me and Billy and Keith and Derek. So I'm dancing with Derek because it's clear Billy wants to dance with Keith. Then Derek starts dancing with some random guy, and he disappears. So it's me and Billy and Keith, and I don't, I don't mind dancing in my own world, so I just drift away a little so Billy can dance with Keith. Also we did some coke. Anyway. So I'm dancing in my own world, but Keith keeps dancing towards me—but not just dancing towards me, he's doing this move, this really, like, provocative move, this kind of "dance walk"?

STEPHEN: Uh-huh . . .

TYLER: Sort of . . . he'll dance-walk towards Billy, but at the last moment, at the moment he gets to Billy, it's kind of a diva move, just as he reaches Billy he turns away and dances back towards me. So he's going between me and Billy, but he's dancing more with me—he just, it's sort of like he's teasing Billy. And Billy says to him, he grabs him and says, "Why won't you dance with me?" And Keith's like, "What are you talking about?" So Billy tells him to fuck off. Just says, "Fuck off." And Keith just up and walks away. And I say, "I guess it's just me and you," and Billy says, "No, it's you and *Stephen* and *fuck* you too." And then I saw you—

(Billy enters.)

BILLY: —Hey.

(Tyler stands, moves to Billy; Stephen hangs back. Leo looks at him.)

TYLER: Hey.

BILLY: I can't believe you're going.

TYLER: I don't—

BILLY: You don't make a plan for an evening and then bail out.

TYLER: Billy, you told me to—

BILLY: Just stay, we made a plan. Come on.

TYLER: I just . . . Stephen doesn't want to stay, he doesn't really like clubs . . .

(Young White Man enters, sits next to Leo. Leo hides his napkin.)

LEO: Hi!

(Young White Man nods.)

BILLY: Fine. Go play boyfriend.
TYLER: *Billy* . . .
BILLY: And this fucking E I got sucks.

(Pause.)

TYLER: Bye.

(Tyler goes back to Stephen. Billy stays where he is. Stephen rises and Tyler and Stephen exit. Billy looks briefly at Leo, then makes sustained eye contact with Young White Man. Billy exits. Young White Man follows him. Leo watches, then looks around.)

Scene 5

Stephen and Tyler enter the hall, moving to the apartment.

STEPHEN *(Playfully)*: I have something to show you.
TYLER: You do?
STEPHEN: Yeah, but you have to be a good boy. *(Stephen opens door; they kiss briefly before going inside)* Okay, sit down.
TYLER *(Pulling Stephen down to couch, starts fondling him)*: I know what you have to show me.
STEPHEN *(Laughing)*: No, stay here.

(Stephen exits. Tyler glances down at an open book on the couch. Stephen returns, sits down on couch, takes out pictures.)

The weekend!
TYLER: Oh, you got them done! Yay!

(They look at pictures, flipping through.)

—They were so nice. We should send that to them.

STEPHEN: —And there's everyone.

TYLER: —God, that house.

STEPHEN: —And the cat.

TYLER: Evil animal. —Oh, you took a picture of the cute boy.

STEPHEN (*Laughing*): You were the one who said he was cute!

TYLER: I did not—oh, *there's* a cute boy.

STEPHEN: Isn't that great! I love that picture of you.

TYLER: My eyes are puffy.

STEPHEN: No! (*Rising*) I'm gonna put it in my frame, by the bed.

TYLER: Okay—hey, can I have the one of us that's in there?

STEPHEN: Sure.

(*Stephen goes to his bedroom. Tyler picks up the open book. Stephen returns with picture and frame, sits. Tyler reads from book:*)

TYLER: "In the end, a whole vast area of Central Africa was completely transformed, not by the actions of some power or international organization."

STEPHEN: It's such a good little book, this British historian Eric Hobsbawm . . .

(*Tyler reads with a bad posh British accent:*)

TYLER: "Everyone got involved: Paris, Washington and the United Nations. Everyone tried to mediate and, I am told, there were as many as thirteen different mediators in Rwanda. However, it all proved to be inadequate." (*He puts down the book*) Did I tell you about this audition tomorrow?

STEPHEN: No. What's it for?

TYLER: This TV show? Want a massage?

STEPHEN: Sure!

(*Tyler massages Stephen.*)

TYLER: It's not terrible. It's about this kind of loser kid in a small town who learns he has special powers.

STEPHEN (*Derisively*): Special powers? Who are you auditioning for?

TYLER: The kind of loser kid in the small town who learns he has special powers. (*Stephen laughs*) Here, I worked on my special power pose all day. What do you think? *(Does special power pose)*

STEPHEN: You're hired. *(Picks up book)* Listen to this.

TYLER: I love you.

(Stephen turns page, reads:)

STEPHEN: "A Marxist interpretation / suggests . . ."

TYLER: —I said I love you!

STEPHEN: I love you too! *(Tyler resumes massaging Stephen)* "A Marxist interpretation suggests that, in having understood a particular historical stage is not permanent, human society is a successful structure because it is capable of change, and thus the present is not its point of arrival."

TYLER *(Mockingly)*: Marxist!

STEPHEN *(Laughs)*: Interpretation, though. There's a difference.

TYLER: That *is* beautiful. —You're tense.

STEPHEN: I am?

TYLER: Super tense.

STEPHEN: —I guess I got a little freaked-out tonight.

TYLER: What happened?

STEPHEN: It's not a big deal really.

TYLER: Am I hurting you?

STEPHEN *(Laughing)*: I can't tell, I think you might be. Yeah, the— kid from across the hall knocked on my door.

TYLER: —Why?

STEPHEN: Well, this other kid—this white kid—who I assume was here to buy drugs, but he went to the wrong apartment—knocked on my door. Anyway—he must have told this to the kid across the hall, and the kid—the black kid— must know I help out his dad or whatever, so he must think that maybe I know what's going on in there, and he just sort of wanted to let me know that he knew I knew what was going on—that he's dealing.

(Pause.)

TYLER: Did he threaten you?

STEPHEN: No, no. I'm sure he's harmless, but . . .

TYLER: Be careful, Stephen.

STEPHEN: No, I know.

TYLER: —Okay, now me. *(Stephen massages Tyler)* I got a little freaked-out tonight, too.

STEPHEN: Yeah?

TYLER: I was talking to some people at the club. I talked to this one kid who said he was sixteen? He said he was a pig bottom and was looking for someone to fuck him.

STEPHEN: Uh-huh.

TYLER: Oooh, right there. Yeah. I don't know, it started to depress me. The pig bottom kid was so—beautiful and innocent looking. How did he get like that, you know? —And did you see this? In the *Voice*?

(Tyler picks up Village Voice *from coffee table.)*

STEPHEN: "HIV Babies."

TYLER: Rates are going up for people our age.

STEPHEN: God, that's unfathomable to me—that gay men are having unsafe / sex

(Tyler's cell phone rings. He checks it.)

TYLER: It's Billy. I'm not gonna answer it.

STEPHEN *(Laughing)*: Billy calling to tell you to fuck off again?

TYLER: He probably met some guy and wants to ask me if he should go home with him. "He's cute but he's not *hot, I* don't know, he has a nice *ass* . . ."

STEPHEN: Huh. Well—I'm sorry you got depressed.

TYLER: Yeah. *(Beat)* Did you read your horoscope?

STEPHEN: No. —Is it good?

TYLER *(Laughs)*: Taurus, for far too long now you've been / waiting for—

(Tyler's cell phone rings again. He answers. Stephen puts photo of Tyler in frame.)

Hello? Okay. Thank you. Okay. I have to go. I love you too. *(Hangs up)* Billy apologizes. He wanted to tell me he loves me.

STEPHEN: Uh-huh . . . so . . . Billy really hates me, doesn't he?

TYLER: No—why do you say that?

STEPHEN: He's never very polite to me. He didn't even look at me at the / club

TYLER: Part of that was the Ecstasy—we got our pills from different guys. I got mine from this guy Derek knew, but that guy didn't have that many, so Billy had to just sort of find his own and I don't think his were that good.

STEPHEN: He got the "fuck off" Ecstasy.

TYLER: Billy's Billy. I've known him for so long, I guess I'm just used to him. He didn't have the easiest life, so he's sort of abrasive. You either get his world or you don't, is how he looks at it.

(Pause.)

STEPHEN: "Billy's Billy."

TYLER: What?

STEPHEN: I don't know . . . I mean, someone says, "Fuck off" to you . . .

TYLER: It's hard for Billy—he doesn't have a boyfriend, his career isn't going well, sometimes people don't take him seriously because he's so campy . . .

STEPHEN: Well you have to take yourself seriously.

TYLER: Like you, you silly goose! Mr. Serious!

STEPHEN: Ha.

(A knock on the door. Pause.)

What time is it?

(Stephen gets up, goes to the door. Tyler rises.)

Hello?

TIMOTHY'S VOICE: Hey, I heard you were up, I'm sorry, do you have two cigarettes you could lend me?

(Pause.)

TYLER *(Muted)*: Tell him you quit.

(Pause. Stephen opens the door.)

TIMOTHY: Hi.

STEPHEN: Hey.

(Stephen gives him three cigarettes.)

Here you go.

TIMOTHY: Hey, you know, my check is late, you know? It was supposed to / come

STEPHEN: Uh-huh?

TIMOTHY: And I have to go to the hospital tomorrow, and the Medicaid is all—and my check is late—I'm trying to get, I'm trying to get this leg, keeps being delayed—if you got ten dollars, I pay you back when my check comes. Two days late now, nothing I can do . . .

STEPHEN: Sure.

(Stephen gives him ten dollars.)

TIMOTHY: God bless you.

(Timothy goes. Stephen locks the door. Pause.)

TYLER: Ten dollars?

STEPHEN: —What?

TYLER: I just—that makes me worried.

STEPHEN: Worried about what?

TYLER: Just—that he'll think—you're a pushover.

STEPHEN: Right. But—his check hasn't come.

TYLER: You believe that?

STEPHEN: Yeah—I think it's pretty common, actually. Social Security, Disability—I think the checks only come once a month. It's a disaster for people when they don't come on time.

TYLER: But if his son is dealing *drugs* . . . and *threatened* you tonight . . .

STEPHEN: He didn't *threaten* me.

TYLER: You said you were freaked-out.

STEPHEN: Yeah, but—I don't—think he would / actually

TYLER: Like, what if they're working as a team or something? Like, now they know you're scared, so they can ask you for money and you're scared so you give it to them.

STEPHEN: I don't—think he and his son get along. His son won't buy him cigarettes . . . I mean, if he comes tomorrow and asks for ten more dollars, I won't give it to him, but . . .

TYLER: But what if they're, like, working as a team?

(Pause. Stephen looks away.)

I don't know. —I just worry. I get scared for you. I love you and—a cigarette, okay. But ten dollars—and taking him to the deli—you can't help everyone, people have to take care of themselves.

STEPHEN: Well you—you know, I mean—like—your trust fund helps you, right?

TYLER: What—do you mean?

STEPHEN: You don't have to worry the way most people do.

TYLER: But—I *do* stuff. My acting class, going to the gym, preparing for auditions.

STEPHEN: I'm just saying—you know, he doesn't have any protection. He's black, he's—

TYLER: But what I'm saying is, what if he just takes that money and buys alcohol?

STEPHEN: I'm sure he's not going to buy alcohol.

TYLER: You don't know that.

STEPHEN: Well, I mean, even if—I drink—we all—you're on drugs now.

TYLER: What does that have to do with anything?

(Pause.)

STEPHEN: Nothing, just . . . *(Beat)* Like—talking to that kid in the club—made you sad. He—makes me sad. That he's in trouble the way he is, that makes me sad. So—I feel better helping him.

TYLER: Yeah, but I was in a club, I didn't—try to help him. I'm never going to see him again.

STEPHEN: Exactly. I—he's right across the hall. I see him every day.

TYLER: But you don't *know.*

STEPHEN: Know what?

TYLER: You have no idea what his life is really like, and I don't see how you / think you

STEPHEN: There *are* facts.

TYLER: You don't know—

STEPHEN: —He has no leg.

(Pause.)

TYLER: —I'm sorry. I just—I had a bad night. And I don't—want you to get taken advantage of. That's all. People with good hearts, they get hurt in this world. They do . . .

STEPHEN: I understand your concern . . . but—I think I'm okay here . . .

(Pause. Tyler moves to Stephen. He begins to nuzzle him.)

TYLER: Anyway, you should quit smoking . . . it's not good for you . . .

(Stephen smiles. They start kissing rather madly, and undress each other.)

STEPHEN: I love you.

TYLER: I love you so much, Stephen.

STEPHEN: Oh Tyler . . .

Scene 6

Timothy struggles into his apartment, carrying a large brown paper bag in his mouth. Lily watches TV. Shed is asleep on the couch. Timothy shuts door, leans against wall, takes bag with hand, goes over to chair, sits.

TIMOTHY: He sleeping?

LILY: Yeah.

(Timothy takes a forty ounce of beer out of the bag, along with a pack of Newports and a candy bar.)

TIMOTHY: Can I ask you, are you with Shed?

LILY: No. I was with Dave.

TIMOTHY: Dave. You here, though, a lot.

LILY: Me and Shed are pals.

TIMOTHY: Oh.

LILY: We're buddies! We're buds! I was with Dave.

TIMOTHY: I don't know about Shed. Things getting quiet around here.

LILY: He's a big boy now.

TIMOTHY: Yeah?

(They laugh. Timothy lights a cigarette, laughs.)

Where are the boys?

LILY: He doesn't want the boys here anymore.

TIMOTHY: Why not?

LILY: He's a big boy, I'm telling you. No boys, no drugs.

TIMOTHY: No weed?

LILY: No—weed. But no drugs. Can I have a cigarette?

TIMOTHY: You don't got any?

LILY: Smoked them all.

(Timothy gives her a cigarette.)

TIMOTHY: I used to drive trucks. Now I can't drive. I had a good / career.

LILY: I met Dave my first week here. We were together three months.

TIMOTHY: Three months . . . I loved driving, get out of the / city

LILY: Are you with anyone?

TIMOTHY: —I don't know, that might be over, all that. I got a photo album of me from before? Every time I would look at the pictures, I couldn't even / look at them

LILY: Mm, I love menthols.

TIMOTHY: Yeah. —Did Shed tell you / about what

LILY: Dave has this ex-girlfriend Maryanne who keeps manipulating him, ugh . . . So you're not with anyone?

TIMOTHY: No—nobody wants to sleep with someone who has no leg.

LILY: Awww. Maybe there's a woman with no leg, too.

TIMOTHY: I never seen a woman with one leg. Well, that's not true. But I wouldn't want a woman with one leg! Two things make people sleep with you is, you have a job, or you're young. I'm old with no job. I can't even look at the pictures of me / from before

LILY: Do you jerk off at least?

TIMOTHY: —I used to be a janitor before I was a truck driver. I can't do that either. Where are you from?

LILY: Chorleywood. Probably never heard of it. Fucking crap.

TIMOTHY: Chorleywood?

LILY: Everyone knows everyone's business there, fucking crap. New York's different, has a different energy, do you know what I mean?

TIMOTHY: Is he trying to get me out of here?

(Pause.)

LILY: I dunno. That's sad.

TIMOTHY: I just can't—the Social Security went down, after a certain time, after I got out of the hospital, I get less now. But it's my name on the lease, he can't / do anything

LILY: That's sad no one wants to sleep with you.

TIMOTHY: Oh.

LILY: Does your dick work?

TIMOTHY: Wh? —Yeah—it works, it wasn't damaged.

LILY: When's the last time a lady touched it?

TIMOTHY: My wife.

(Lily goes over to Timothy and touches his crotch.)

What are you? . . .

(She unzips him, puts her hand inside, fondles him for some time.)

Stop.

LILY: It's okay, you're getting hard.

TIMOTHY: No.

LILY: There. That's nice. Is that nice?

TIMOTHY: Y—yeah.

LILY *(Still masturbating him)*: Yeah . . . that's nice . . . Does Shed have any other girls over?

TIMOTHY: Used to . . .

LILY: Used to?

TIMOTHY: Not so much now . . .

(Lily continues to masturbate him. He closes his eyes and begins to moan quietly. Lily's cell phone rings. She stops, looks at the number, answers it.)

LILY: Hello? Hi Dave. Nowhere, just hanging. Nothing. Where you at? *(Beat)* Fuck her, she's a stupid cunt anyway. Okay! *(She hangs up and gathers her things)*

TIMOTHY: You're going?

(Lily goes back to Timothy, puts her hand in his pants again.)

LILY: I bet you could come really fast for me.

(She masturbates him for a while. He orgasms, stifling sound. She takes her hand out of his pants, wipes it on his pants, giggles.)

I gotta go. See you later, sexy man!

TIMOTHY: Bye . . .

(Lily exits. Door slams. Shed stirs a little. Timothy starts to cry. He zips up his pants, tucks in his shirt. Shed awakens. Timothy stops crying. He quickly lights a cigarette. Shed looks at Timothy.)

SHED: . . . You stealin' from me when I sleep?

TIMOTHY: No, these aren't Camels. These are Newports. These are mine.

SHED: The faggot give 'em to you?

TIMOTHY: I bought them.

SHED: Why you crying?

TIMOTHY: I'm not. I was just thinking.

SHED: Where's Lily?

TIMOTHY: She left.

SHED: She left? What, you scare her off?

TIMOTHY: No.

SHED: When you gettin' your leg? Sick of this shit already.

TIMOTHY: They keep saying next week! Then they say, there's some reason—you need to wait till the leg, you need to wait a certain time till it heals—they need me to practice, they have a leg there for me to practice but they say maybe next week—I can't tell—I think that it's not ready, the leg, but they don't say it's not ready, they say it needs / to heal before

SHED: —Talking her ear off. You annoy people, you talk too much, you don't do anything, sit here, do nothing, fucking useless—

TIMOTHY: What am I gonna do?

(Pause.)

SHED: Something besides annoy people make them leave / 'cuz you annoy them
TIMOTHY: No, Dave called. She went to Dave.

(Pause. Shed looks for a cigarette, his pack is empty.)

I don't know why she likes Dave so much. But you don't know / with girls
SHED: Fucking cigarettes, where's my pack?
TIMOTHY: You all out? Want one?

(Shed keeps looking in empty packs, lifting things. He gets angry.)

You want one? Here.

(Shed goes over to Timothy, takes his pack away from him. He goes to the couch. He lights a cigarette. Pause.)

Come on. Gimmie back.

(Shed goes to the stereo, puts in a CD.)

Shed. Gimmie one, just to wake up to. One to go to sleep and one to / wake up to—

(Over the stereo an Eminem-like rapper blasts. Shed sits down on the couch.)

EMINEM-LIKE RAPPER:
>   Don't give me no fag on the corner in the park
>   walking like a girl looking like a shark
>   trying to get at my balls
>   bitch get ready to fall
>   make a pass?
>   fag, I'll take that ass
>   empty it of gas

and put it in a cast—
Shit, what time is it?
eleven o'clock
here, suck on this
no not my cock
boy, this a Glock

(Timothy rises. He exits, with his forty and his candy bar. Shed moves to the song.)

all the faggots in the world today make me sick
it's a mystery to me why a man would like dick
'cuz I don't take that
no I don't take that
all the faggots in the world today make me mad
wanna make me happy? die and I'll be glad
'cuz I don't take that
no I don't take that
boy I ain't take that
who gon' take that . . .

(Lights rise on Stephen and Tyler. They are making out, naked. They can clearly hear the song. Stephen stops.)

TYLER: What?
STEPHEN: This song.
TYLER: I know. —Don't worry about it.

(The song continues. Tyler kisses Stephen, they continue to make out. Shed rises, acting out the song, as if performing it.)

EMINEM-LIKE RAPPER:
Damn, when I was six
growin' up in the proj-ix
with my bitch mom
every night she was gone
so my Uncle Rick'd baby sit
and try to get in my shit
"Wanna play hide and seek?"
Uncle Rick, Uncle Rick, peeking at my little dick
man that's motherfucking sick

So suck
suck
No not on me
man, suck this blade
swallow your tongue
watch your faggot life fade
next I'm a puncture your lung . . .

(Stephen pulls away from Tyler.)

STEPHEN: I can't.
TYLER: Just block it out. I'm here. Think about me.
STEPHEN: I—I / just

(Tyler leans in, kisses Stephen. He fellates Stephen.)

EMINEM-LIKE RAPPER:
all the faggots in the world today love my shit
wanna get in my pants and suck on it
for real, gays love me and my song's number one
and if you don't believe me just ask Elton John!

(Song continues. Stephen orgasms.)

STEPHEN: Ohh!—

Scene 7

Slide: August 14, 2001

Stephen and Patricia in a museum. In one corner, a black Security Guard crosses on and off. In another, a Violinist plays. Stephen and Patricia speak quietly, moving slowly across the stage. A white Young Art Student, sloppily dressed, sketches, looking in Patricia's direction. He wears headphones and moves somewhat to their music.

PATRICIA: It's good you're having a party. —That's beautiful.
STEPHEN: It'll be a little hot, but I guess that's okay.
PATRICIA: Frank's gonna come, which is a miracle. —Isn't that
   beautiful?

STEPHEN: It's so chaotic. All that color.

PATRICIA: I don't understand this violinist—since when does art need music to go along / with it

STEPHEN: I read about this, museum attendance is down, they did focus groups, people think museums are dull, so they're trying new things to attract more visitors.

PATRICIA: Great, next it'll be strippers holding up the paintings.

STEPHEN: That'll make Giuliani happy.

(Beat.)

Do you think people—do you think—how do you think people change?

PATRICIA: What's this about?

STEPHEN: Just a question.

PATRICIA: It's about Tyler.

STEPHEN: Well—yeah, but—generally, I mean . . .

PATRICIA: But there's a specific . . . ?

STEPHEN: We just—the other / night

PATRICIA: Is that kid drawing us?

STEPHEN: What?

PATRICIA: That kid behind us.

(Stephen looks briefly at the Art Student, who stops sketching when he does, then resumes sketching when Stephen turns away.)

STEPHEN: I think he is. —Yeah, it was just—Tyler and I got into it about my neighbor again the other night, he was upset that I gave him ten dollars.

PATRICIA: We should probably keep our voices down a little.

STEPHEN: Oh—yeah, I'm sorry.

PATRICIA *(Moving to next painting)*: Mm-hmm? —What year is this?

STEPHEN: —I just, I wondered what I could have said to him to make him see my point more . . .

PATRICIA: Well—you know, you have to be gentle because—and patient. Think of where Tyler's coming from. You know, you dealt with your trauma by identifying with the pain of others, trying to understand it, in order to solve it. So maybe you're empathetic, but his history hasn't allowed him to develop— *(Looks back at Art Student)* He is, he's drawing us.

STEPHEN *(Derisively)*: I think I saw a Ralph Nader sticker on his bookbag.

PATRICIA: How rude is that. Who goes to a museum to draw people? Look at the paintings.

STEPHEN: Maybe you're inspiring him.

PATRICIA: Great, I'm glad I can be of service.

(Patricia moves to next painting. Violinist begins new song. Stephen follows, looking briefly at Art Student.)

STEPHEN: —But maybe I *should* have better tried to explain to Tyler why he thinks the way he does.

PATRICIA: Well—people have a lot to think about on their own without thinking about how they think.

STEPHEN: What do you mean?

PATRICIA: Maybe you have to learn to tolerate a certain amount of narcissism, you know? It's not easy to be alive and—all this, all these right and wrong ways to think—I think you should make room for just—who people are.

STEPHEN: But that's really scary, to think that way, it's so defeated. That's like / saying—

PATRICIA: —I need to sit, I have a headache.

STEPHEN: Art gives you headaches.

PATRICIA: It's not—talking and looking at paintings, it's a little / much

STEPHEN: I'm sorry, I know I'm / babbling

PATRICIA: No, it's—you're asking valid questions, it's just . . .

(They go to a bench. Art Student gets up, moves behind them, continues sketching.)

I don't know. When I listen to you, I hear this—you're always looking for something that isn't there—something better—as opposed to reality. Who someone might be instead of who they are.

STEPHEN: Uh-huh? . . .

PATRICIA: I think you're setting yourself up when you look at things like that. —Okay, this has to stop.

STEPHEN: What?

(Patricia turns to the Art Student and stares at him directly. Stephen follows. The Art Student exits. The Security Guard laughs, then exits as well.)

PATRICIA: How rude is that? Visual artists, my God. Voyeurs.

STEPHEN: Maybe he'll go home and create a masterpiece.

PATRICIA: Sometimes, this city, I wish I could be invisible.

(Pause. The Violinist begins a new song.)

STEPHEN: *I* see what you're saying. Like—his history—like, Tyler's dad was an alcoholic. So I guess you're right—it makes sense that he's so passive. When he was growing up, you know, nothing he did ever altered his dad's behavior. So he learned to protect himself by just cutting off . . . Did you know Tyler tried to kill himself? —Almost every gay man I know my age either tried to kill himself or fantasized about it.

PATRICIA: He tried to kill himself? Oh, that's awful.

STEPHEN: He drove his father's truck to a cliff, and he sat there, the engine idling, trying to get up the courage to drive over. When he was sixteen. He says he came so close . . . And I put myself there. I'm beside him. I'm with him at the edge of the cliff, passenger side.

PATRICIA: Empathy.

STEPHEN: Love.

PATRICIA: Mm. What's the difference, I wonder.

(Pause.)

STEPHEN: I hope people have fun at my party.

PATRICIA: I hope *you* have fun at your party.

(They laugh.)

Scene 8

Slide: August 14, 2001

Timothy's apartment. Shed and Lily cuddle on the couch. The TV is on. Timothy enters. He sits down on the couch next to Shed and Lily.

TIMOTHY: What's this? *(Neither answers)* Ha! Oh, this show is a funny one.

(Neither says anything. Timothy looks briefly over at Lily, who does not return the look. He gets up, then exits. Shed's cell phone rings. He picks it up, looks at it. A little alarmed.)

SHED: Dave.
LILY: Dave?

(Shed answers the phone.)

SHED: Hello? Yeah. Come up. *(Hangs up)*
LILY: Where is he?
SHED: He outside.
LILY: What should I do, stay here or go?
SHED: Up to you.
LILY: He won't go in back, will he?
SHED: No. He probably be here just a minute. He not gonna care— he gonna be like, "Okay, you don't wanna deal, okay." I'll give him his money and that's it. It'll be cool.
LILY: Is Maryanne with him?
SHED: I dunno. He gonna be up here, so go back.

(Lily gets up and goes in back. An insistent, manic knock on the door. Shed answers it. Dave enters. He speaks in an affected manner, often using black rhythm and emphasis without mimicking black pronunciation—his accent is that of a white upper-class person.)

DAVE: What's up, dog!
SHED: What's up.

(Dave looks around. Shed shuts the door.)

DAVE: Looking nice in here, looking neat! Where your boys at?
SHED: I told them, find some other place to party. Too crazy 'round here.
DAVE: Lily said, Lily said. What's up, man!
SHED: Not much, not much, you.
DAVE: Other than the bitches, everything is sweet. —I'm rolling right now.

268

SHED: Yeah?

DAVE: Three pills. *Good* Ecstasy, very clean, I met this guy, European motherfucker, shit's hot!

(Dave flips through channels on TV.)

Yeah, man, my mom wanted to have a *talk* tonight. Where can I *go*, like—the *re*hab talk. I couldn't deal, so I took three pills. Told her I had a headache, told her they were aspirin! She believed me!

SHED *(Laughs)*: Aw.

DAVE: She's like, "You're twenty." She's like, "I re*mem*ber you. You were a *sweet* boy. You were *sensitive*. What *happened*." Truth, though—I was fucked-*up*, dog! I was never *sweet*. One thing I did, I never told anyone this—I started rolling, and I remembered—I remembered I used to be able—I could hear my parents *fucking*, and I was four*teen* maybe, and I would go to the bedroom *door*, and I would—when they were fucking, I would jack *off*—I would hear them—I would hear my stepfather slap my mother's ass, or else it was her slapping *his* ass—and I would jack off picturing it and listening to it!

SHED: Damn.

DAVE: "Sensitive." I would *come* on the *carpet* and I would rub it into the carpet with my *foot*.

SHED: Damn, why you do that?

DAVE: She's like, "You were a good child." She's like, "Why are all your friends *black*?"

SHED: How she know that?

DAVE: Fuck, I have people *over* now. You gotta come over and see this shit. *(Dave sniffs cocaine)* "You've changed." But nothing changed—that's what I'm realizing, sitting there rolling.

SHED: What you mean?

DAVE: I was *always* like this, I just didn't know what to *do*. Like, why you do jack off when you hear your parents fucking? —I tried to fuck the au *pair* when I was fifteen!

SHED: What's that?

DAVE: Like, the *maid*—the black *maid*, I tried to *fuck* her.

SHED: Oh.

DAVE: I didn't know what I was doing but. It was funny, I tried to *hug* her. I didn't know how to do it so I *hugged* her. Bitch hugged me back! I think I came right then!

SHED: Damn.

(Dave hits a music video channel; we hear the Eminem-like song from earlier; it plays quietly throughout scene. Dave moves to the music, as does Shed. Then:)

DAVE: He's so over, don't you think?

SHED: Oh yeah—he done.

DAVE: —Old Timmy here? Old man beating off back there?

SHED: He here, he here.

DAVE: He's eating pepperoni?

SHED: I don't know.

DAVE: Every time I see him, he's eating. I think, like, what, is he trying to grow a new leg? A new leg made of fat, like if he keeps eating he'll grow a new leg made of fat?

SHED: Shit's fucked-up, Medicaid, I don't know, keeps getting delayed, his new leg. He supposed to be getting it. —On my fucking tit all the time, you know?

DAVE: —Things don't change, I'm telling you. Nothing changes, man. Nothing changes! —So I told my mom, listen, fuck rehab, I don't need rehab, give me the money you'd spend on rehab for me to make a movie and I'll stop doing drugs. Make a movie, right! Digital video—you can be in it! So she said if I write a script she'd do it. I'm like, You don't make movies with a script. You make it up as you go along. She didn't understand, though, she was all like, "You need a script," and I was like, "No, you need a *concept.*"

SHED: Yeah. What—what would it be about?

DAVE: Me. Not *me*-me, but me, like, my life, you know?

SHED: Yeah. That's cool. Hey—um—remember we went to that hotel couple weeks ago?

DAVE: Yeah.

SHED: Remember, you said—you knew that guy? That guy, he was like a manager in the bar?

DAVE: Right.

SHED: I was wondering, like—maybe he could like, like if you could call him, like maybe they're / hiring people or

DAVE: Who are you sleeping with now?

SHED: Sleeping with? I don't know.

DAVE: I'm manic, man, I apologize. Bump?

SHED: Naw, I'm okay. But / if

DAVE: I'm fucking manic. Have a bump, come on.

(Dave smiles. Pause. Shed does a bump of cocaine.)

There we go. —Damn it's good to see you. I wish I had some E's to throw you so you could be up with me. How long is it since we met, six months?

SHED: Yeah—since I met you in the club? —But that guy, like, remember / you said

DAVE: You see Lily lately?

(Pause.)

SHED: You know, here and there, that girl all over the place.

DAVE: Jesus. Other night, I was fucking her and I was, like, Can I smack you a little? She was like, Yeah—and then she was like, You can smack me harder—Goddamn, British girls, right? —So I started smacking her—she's grooving on that—she's saying it's turning her on more—so she's like, she tells me to smack her hard when I start to come. I was like, *hard*? She was like, Yeah! She said it was the best she came in a long time!

SHED: Damn.

DAVE: Unbelievable. And then she wanted me to fuck her in the ass—and the bitch wasn't clean! I was like, you want people to fuck you in the ass you best be clean, doll! —You have the cash?

SHED: —Yeah.

(Shed reaches into his pocket, takes out a wad of bills. Dave takes a long knife out of his backpack.)

DAVE: Look at this, beautiful, right?

SHED: Wow.

DAVE: I decided to start collecting knives. *(He laughs, shrugs, and hands Shed the knife)* Antique, ivory handle, fucking gorgeous, right?

SHED: Wow.

(Pause. Dave takes the knife back from Shed, puts the knife in his bag. Shed holds out the cash to him.)

DAVE: You know what? I had a good day.

(Dave nods for Shed to keep the money, rises.)

My mom went to the Hamptons, I'm gonna go home and party.

SHED *(Still holding out money)*: What are you? —No man, take / it

DAVE: Keep it, dog.

(Dave takes package of cocaine from the bag, gives it to Shed, who now has money in one hand, cocaine in the other. Dave slings his backpack over his shoulder. Shed rises.)

SHED: Yeah, I—I got some stuff coming up, I got to ask you about something.

DAVE: —Damn, you got that hungry look in your eyes.

SHED: I do?

DAVE: We need to find you some pussy, I think.

SHED: Ha, no, I'm all right.

DAVE: Let's get you some pussy. When's the last time you fucked the shit out of a girl, for real?

SHED: I'm okay, take care of myself.

DAVE: Dude—come to my house with me.

SHED: That's all right. But if we could / talk

DAVE: Timmy can take care of himself for a night! *(Yelling)* Right, Timmy?

SHED: No, I should / stay

DAVE: You know I love you? *(Pause. Dave wipes a tear from his eye. Shed laughs it off)* No—I don't just say that 'cuz I'm rolling. But, like, that we can be friends, from such different worlds. That's amazing. That didn't used to be the way it was. But it's that way now. People from different groups. People from different worlds. That's so beautiful—you know how special that is?

SHED: Yeah—I just. I—I never meant to get so deep in dealing.

(Pause.)

DAVE: Oh. You want to *talk*. You're, like—taking stock of your / life

SHED: Yeah, if we could / talk

DAVE: Bottle of wine, blow, talk all night—if you want to roll, call my European boy—we can sit out on the terrace. You can see the whole city, look out, king of the world, for real!

SHED: I'd like to, but I / have to

DAVE: Let's call some girls and start putting an / itinerary together

(Dave dials his cell phone.)

SHED: No, I really can't, / man

DAVE: Fuck, let's call Lily! *(Hits button on phone)*

SHED: I would / but

(We hear a cell phone ring loudly. Short pause.)

DAVE: Shit, did I call you by mistake?

(Shed looks at the ringing cell phone. Dave looks at his.)

No, I called Lily—

SHED: —She's—she left her—

DAVE: —Is she here?—

SHED: She—she's / napping or something

(Lily enters.)

LILY: Hi Dave.

DAVE: What are you doing here?

SHED: No, yeah—Lily just hangin' . . .

(Dave looks at Shed. Pause. Shed braces himself. Then Dave laughs.)

DAVE: Whatever. Lily, we're going up to my mom's, you gotta come. Who else can I call. Or should it just be us three?

SHED: I don't / think

LILY: Where's Maryanne?

DAVE: I don't know and I don't *wanna* know.

LILY: —You're rolling.

DAVE: How'd you know?

LILY: You're so nice when you're rolling. Your face looks so sweet.

DAVE: Let's move everybody! Move move!

(Dave starts to go; Lily hangs back a second.)

SHED: —Naw, I gotta—I don't know, I gotta—I gotta make sure— *(Lily takes her cell phone and bag)* I gotta—I gotta—hang out, I can't—maybe later, when he goes to sleep, but . . .

(Pause.)

DAVE: Okay, call me later. Peace, brother.
SHED: Yeah, peace.
LILY: Bye!

(Lily and Dave exit. Shed still holds the coke and cash.)

Scene 9

Stephen's bedroom. Party in progress outside the bedroom; each time the door opens, loud music and party sounds increase. Billy and Patricia are talking, both with drinks in their hands.

BILLY: But I have to admit, the rhymes are great, the music is really interesting—he's really hot—I don't agree with what he's saying, but he definitely represents what's already out there, he didn't cause it.
PATRICIA: Yeah. That's an interesting point. *(Pause. Off, music is changed)* . . . So—how long have you been friends with Tyler?
BILLY: Since college.
PATRICIA: Oh. Stephen and I met at college, too. Where are you from?
BILLY: Long Island.
PATRICIA: Oh. I'm from Queens.
BILLY: Okay, can I confide in you? Can I make you my little confidante?
PATRICIA: What—what do you want to / tell me?
BILLY *(Hearing new music)*: —Oh God, this—who is putting this awful solemn music on?
PATRICIA: It's probably Frank, my boyfriend—he doesn't like parties, this is what he does, he fiddles with music. It's like he wants to make everyone as miserable as he is.

BILLY: Well *we* have the majority here. It's not 1993 and we are *not* in Seattle!

PATRICIA: I'll tell him to change it.

BILLY: I want to *dance.* Do you dance, Patricia?

PATRICIA: I do.

BILLY: Okay, go yell at your boyfriend and come back and I'll tell you my secret.

(Patricia laughs, then exits. Stephen enters.)

STEPHEN: Oh. Was Patricia in here?

BILLY: She just went out to change the music. Can I ask you a question?

STEPHEN: Sure.

BILLY: Is there any cocaine here?

STEPHEN: Um—I haven't seen any.

BILLY *(Faux-sheepishly)*: Do you hate cocaine?

STEPHEN: Um—I don't make a point of it but—occasionally I do / like it

BILLY: I think this party could use some cocaine.

STEPHEN: Um. Let me look around.

(Stephen exits. Music off goes from rock to dance mix.)

BILLY: Yes!

(Billy starts to dance. Tyler enters, dancing.)

There you are!

TYLER: Hi!

(Patricia enters.)

BILLY: Patricia, I love this song!

PATRICIA: My boyfriend hates me now.

(Billy starts dancing with Patricia. The three dance. Stephen enters.)

BILLY: Anything?

STEPHEN: What's Adderall? There are boys in there who say they have Adderall.

275

PATRICIA: Adderall? My eight-year-old niece is / on Adderall.

BILLY: It's a prescription drug for attention deficit disorder, it's of the Ritalin family. Patricia, let's dance this song out there, and I'll tell you my secret.

PATRICIA: Oh, right.

TYLER: Billy has a secret?

BILLY: Not for long, of *course*!

(Giggling, Billy pulls Patricia off into the other room. Stephen looks at Tyler.)

STEPHEN: Hey you.

TYLER: "What's up, man."

STEPHEN: "Not much, dude."

TYLER: "Cool party."

STEPHEN: "Thanks."

TYLER: "What's your name?"

STEPHEN: "I'm Stephen."

TYLER: "Hey, what's up, I'm Tyler."

STEPHEN: "Would you like to dance, Tyler."

TYLER: "Umm . . . I actually have to go home right now and wash my hair."

STEPHEN: "Oh, right. Okay."

(Stephen gets up and mock-walks away. Tyler mock-rises.)

TYLER: "But . . . I have time for one dance."

(Stephen turns. They break the joke. They begin dancing.)

So when everyone leaves tonight . . . can we take a bath together?

STEPHEN: Yes.

TYLER: Yay!

STEPHEN: I don't know how clean the tub / is.

(Billy enters.)

BILLY: Patricia's boyfriend is *hot*!

(Stephen and Tyler turn and stop dancing.)

STEPHEN: Yeah, he's really / beautiful.

TYLER: Does anybody need a drink?

STEPHEN: I'm / fine.

BILLY: No.

(Tyler goes. Pause.)

STEPHEN: So—um—I know, Tyler, you know, tells me you're a musical theater actor—what is it like for musical theater actors? It must be tough, there aren't that many roles for younger people, right?

BILLY: Well, there's chorus.

STEPHEN: Right.

BILLY: So . . . there's someone here that I've *slept* with—I think. Except I'm not sure he remembers me—also, *I* have a *wee* bit memory problem?

STEPHEN: Yeah?

BILLY: It was a few years ago, I'm pretty sure it's him. He had, like— *(Billy measures out his hands)* —and I was like, um, hel-lo. Would you like me to *wrap* that for you? I think his name's Donald—such a bad name—but anyway, I sent Patricia on a mission to talk to him and find out his name.

STEPHEN: Wow.

BILLY: So . . . I'd love to read your work.

STEPHEN: Really? Oh, sure.

BILLY: Yeah, Tyler says it's so beautiful.

STEPHEN: Wow. Yeah, I'd be more / than happy

(Tyler and Patricia enter, Tyler with drink.)

BILLY: Patricia! Did you find out?

PATRICIA: His name is Philip.

BILLY: Philip? Oh. —Does anyone want, I really want cocaine. Why does nobody have any here? It doesn't make / sense

STEPHEN: I guess my friends / aren't

PATRICIA: There's a lot of people I don't know / here

STEPHEN: I / know.

BILLY: Oh—what about that guy? Tyler, you were / telling me about some guy.

PATRICIA *(To Stephen)*: Do you have that book you mentioned?

STEPHEN: Oh, the / Hobsbawm? Yeah.

TYLER: What guy?

PATRICIA: I don't want to / forget it.

BILLY: The guy in / the building, on the floor.

STEPHEN: Right, / yeah.

TYLER: Oh.

BILLY *(To Stephen)*: Stephen, there's some guy in your building who sells cocaine. On your floor.

STEPHEN: Oh.

(Pause.)

TYLER: I never said it was / cocaine

STEPHEN: Yeah, I don't know / what he

BILLY: Well what else would it be?

(Pause.)

Why don't we do that?

STEPHEN: Um—I don't know if that's . . .

BILLY: What apartment is he in?

STEPHEN: I think—I assume there's some system—I don't think you can just knock on the door.

BILLY *(Laughing)*: He knocks on your door all the time. What apartment is it?

STEPHEN: I don't—I think—I don't really feel comfortable, um— with his knowing that someone had come from this apartment . . .

BILLY: But Tyler said you were, like, friends with him.

TYLER: I didn't say they were / friends

STEPHEN: I basically have interactions with the father, / not

PATRICIA: Maybe someone will show up with cocaine.

(Pause.)

BILLY: What's amazing to me / is

TYLER: I'm gonna pee.

(Tyler exits.)

BILLY: What's amazing to me is that Tyler said they're also on *welfare*? That makes me, like, so angry. I had this actor friend whose father is a millionaire and who gave him money, but this kid, when his acting job ended, he went on unemployment, even though his father was sending him cash—I mean, how much money, if he's dealing drugs, / how much

STEPHEN: No—I don't think the kid—the one's who's dealing / drugs

(Tyler returns.)

TYLER: People are having sex in your bathroom. They forgot to lock the door, I just / walked

BILLY: I'm sure they didn't forget, everyone in this city is an / exhibitionist

STEPHEN: Who here would be having—I don't / like that

BILLY: Were they hot?

TYLER: I shut the door really quickly.

STEPHEN: Let me—knock on the door and hurry them up.

(Stephen exits. Pause.)

PATRICIA: I'm gonna check in with Frank.

BILLY: He is *hot*, Patricia!

(Patricia smiles politely, then exits. Billy dances. Tyler doesn't.)

What?

TYLER: Billy—now he knows I was talking about him.

BILLY: Who?

TYLER: Stephen—that I was talking to you about his neighbor.

BILLY: That you told me about his little project? His help the poor by handing out cigarettes project?

TYLER: Can we just not bring it up again?

BILLY: I'm sorry, I didn't mean to screw anything up. I just wanted some / blow.

(Stephen enters.)

STEPHEN: "The bathroom has been liberated by the forces of good."

TYLER: Yay!

(Tyler exits. Pause.)

STEPHEN: So . . . the guy turned out to be not the guy, huh?

BILLY: That's the thing—"Donald," "Philip." That's sort of the same name, in a way, it might be him. I guess there's only one way to find out.

(Billy and Stephen laugh.)

So . . . you've had a lot of contact with the drug dealer?

(Beat.)

STEPHEN: No—no, mostly with his father.

BILLY: The crippled guy.

STEPHEN: Yeah, the—disabled guy, right. Yeah, and—it's not— I'm not sure how much Tyler told you but—it's not the kid who's on welfare. He's not collecting money—it's / the father

(Tyler enters.)

TYLER: Now someone else is in there and I knocked and they were like, "It's gonna take a while."

BILLY: But that's so sick, though.

STEPHEN: What is?

BILLY: That on top of the drug money they're collecting / welfare

STEPHEN: No—I don't think the son gives the father any money— is what I'm saying.

(Tyler looks away.)

BILLY *(To Tyler)*: Stephen was just telling me some more about the neighbors.

TYLER: Oh.

STEPHEN: Just—I think it's / complicated

(Patricia enters.)

BILLY: Well thank God that welfare bill passed so that kind of stuff can't happen as much anymore, thank God.

PATRICIA: —Those boys doing Adderall are nuts, they asked me if I wanted to play strip poker.

TYLER: Really? Oh God—

STEPHEN *(To Billy)*: —No. No actually. The welfare bill—in this—in this building alone—in apartments no bigger than this one, there are people—families of *ten* living together, three generations.

(Stephen looks to Patricia.)

BILLY: Well, that's what they get, though. They had five years to get off welfare and find / jobs

STEPHEN: Are you—do you actually know about the welfare / bill?

TYLER: —Stephen

BILLY: Actually, I / do

TYLER: Stephen

STEPHEN: What?

BILLY: I grew up poor.

(Stephen looks back at Billy.)

STEPHEN: Right. But—the welfare / bill

BILLY: And we never went on welfare. My father worked two jobs.

STEPHEN: I hear that, definitely. And I'm speaking from an upper-middle-class perspective, / but

BILLY: I mean, my father and my mother—that was all they did—was work. No / one

STEPHEN: Right. —Okay. But—the welfare bill is actually—a really terrible—you know, the effects are not always visible, they're never immediately apparent, and it's coincided with a bright time for what's really a very fragile / economy

BILLY: But it made the poor take responsibility for themselves.

STEPHEN: Well—it terrorized them—I don't know how you can say / it

TYLER: Stephen

BILLY: You have to admit how much better this city is now.

STEPHEN: But—what do you mean "better," I / don't

BILLY *(To Tyler and Patricia)*: This city is *so* much better than it was even five years ago.

STEPHEN: Okay—do you really want to have a conversation about this?

BILLY *(To Stephen)*: There's less homeless, / there's

STEPHEN: You *see* them less—where *you* live—

BILLY: —it put a stop to all those welfare mothers who kept having / babies—

STEPHEN: Welfare—do you—*welfare* / mothers?

TYLER: Stephen

STEPHEN *(To Tyler)*: —Why do you keep saying my name?

TYLER: Just . . .

(Stephen turns to Billy.)

STEPHEN: I'd like to talk to you about this but—we're sort of talking around each other.

(Pause.)

BILLY: I guess it's that—you know, my mother and father worked so hard for me. They gave up their lives for me. No one handed them anything.

STEPHEN: Right.

BILLY: You know?

STEPHEN: Sure. But—did you ever think that it was easier for them because they're white?

BILLY: Well—they faced anti-Semitism all their lives . . .

STEPHEN: Right. But—being Jewish is very different from being black.

BILLY: Whoa.

(Pause.)

STEPHEN: What?

BILLY: You don't know my life.

STEPHEN: I didn't say I did.

BILLY: Yes, you're talking about my life—"it was easier for them because they were white"—

STEPHEN: Well—I'm—talking about facts of history, facts of race, facts / of

BILLY: You don't know my life or their / lives

STEPHEN: I didn't say / I knew

BILLY: My mother is dead.

(Pause. Patricia takes her drink glass and exits.)

STEPHEN: We're not talking about that. (*Pause. Billy moves to leave the room*) No—I mean—of course—I'm sure your parents did work hard, I'm sure they encountered anti-Semitism. But—there are not jobs for everyone, particularly not for people who don't speak English well, who weren't given access to a good education, or, I mean—in terms of comparing—you can't really argue that Jews have had anywhere *near* the experience that blacks have had / in America

BILLY: You don't know their / lives, Jesus

STEPHEN: I'm—no, listen—just—stop being so defensive and listen a / second

BILLY: I / am

STEPHEN: A culture of poverty and racism breeds a—I mean, can't you, as a gay man, I mean, can't you identify with other / groups

BILLY: You just can't expect the world to give you things, that's all I'm saying. No one ever gave me anything. And say what you will about Giuliani, fuck him for shutting down the clubs and all that, and fuck him for trying to censor art, but he cleaned this city up.

(Pause.)

STEPHEN: It's apartment 6C.

BILLY: What is?

TYLER: Stephen

STEPHEN: If you want to buy drugs. Apartment 6C.

(Pause. Billy looks at Tyler. Billy exits. Pause. Stephen looks at Tyler, who looks at the floor.)

What? Let him go—let him get punched in the face—fucking privilege, fucking—I'm sorry, Tyler, if someone is going to stand in my apartment and say / racist

(Patricia enters.)

PATRICIA: Hey.

STEPHEN: Hey.

PATRICIA: So, Frank wants to go home, I have a lot of work to catch up on, so . . .

STEPHEN: Oh.

PATRICIA: I'll talk to you tomorrow. Bye, Tyler.

TYLER: Bye, Patricia.

(Patricia exits. Pause.)

(Quietly) You should let people have their opinions, Stephen.

STEPHEN: Not—not when they're racist and / wrong

TYLER: It's not racist to think welfare is bad, or, or, that all the problems of the world won't be solved if the government gives poor people more money.

STEPHEN: Tyler, people are / dying

TYLER: I just want you two to get / along

STEPHEN: People are dying in this building. They are dying of poverty, of drugs, I see them every day, there are no jobs, I see their children, they go to schools that are falling apart.

TYLER: Not all of them.

STEPHEN: Well—some of them.

(Tyler goes to Stephen and puts his hand on his shoulder.)

TYLER: Fine, but why does it upset you so much?

STEPHEN: —I *live* here!

TYLER: Whoa! Calm down.

(Tyler hugs Stephen.)

Shhhh.

(They begin dancing slowly.

Lights rise on Timothy's apartment. Shed stands, holding the cocaine and the cash. Billy knocks on his door. Pause. Shed goes to the door, looks in the peephole. He puts the money and the cocaine in his pockets and opens the door.)

BILLY: Hey . . . I'm from across the hall? At the party? *(Takes out forty dollars)* I have forty dollars. Do you have any coke?

(Pause. Shed looks at him. He lets go of the door. Billy holds the door open, steps inside. Shed turns around. He takes the forty dollars from Billy, gets cocaine, gives it to Billy.)

Thanks.

(Billy exits. Timothy enters.)

TIMOTHY: Who was that.

(Shed doesn't answer.)

Where's Lily? She go?
SHED: Yeah.
TIMOTHY: She go with Dave?
SHED: You a fucking eavesdropper now?
TIMOTHY: Don't worry about that—she's crazy, Shed—
SHED: —I don't care about that—
TIMOTHY: —Don't pay her no mind—
SHED: —Leave me alone—
TIMOTHY: —I'm just saying—she tried to grab my dick once—
she's crazy, she / just

*(Shed rushes Timothy and throws him against the wall. He
punches him in the shoulder. Timothy falls and cries out:)*

Ahhh! My leg!

*(Shed sits down on the couch and turns on the TV. Timothy
whimpers in pain.
    Billy enters the bedroom, where Stephen and Tyler dance.)*

BILLY: Can we make up, Stephen? *(Stephen looks at Billy)*

(In Shed's apartment:)

SHED: Here all the time—in people's shit all the time—can't do
nothing yourself—

*(Timothy just lies there.
    In Stephen's/Shed's apartments:)*

STEPHEN: Yeah, I don't—I didn't want to fight.
SHED: —You gonna just lay there now?
BILLY: Me, too. I'm sorry if what I said offended you.
SHED: —Get up!
STEPHEN: Don't worry about it.

SHED: Get up!
BILLY: Okay.

(Shed begins playing video game. Timothy reaches out for crutches. He can't reach.)

Could you apologize to me, too?
STEPHEN: —Excuse me?

(Tyler turns away.)

BILLY: For assuming you knew about my life.

(Shed kicks crutch over to Timothy, who can now reach it. Shed returns to couch and plays game.)

STEPHEN: Okay, I just. I think it's important that people—think about—other people, you know. Think about / what they

(Billy's cell phone rings. He checks it but does not answer. Pause. Stephen looks at Tyler.)

(Flippantly) I apologize.
BILLY: I accept. Now we can party? Tyler loves you, I want us to get along. He loves both of us so we should try to at least like each other.
STEPHEN: —Right.

(Pause.)

BILLY (Sing-songy): I got blo-ow!

(Billy takes out cocaine. He scoops some onto a key and sniffs it. He offers it to Tyler.)

TYLER: A little . . .

(Tyler sniffs cocaine. Billy offers it to Stephen. Pause.)

STEPHEN: I'm okay.
BILLY: You sure?

STEPHEN: Yeah, I'm fine.
BILLY: It's good, I think.

(Billy puts away the cocaine. Pause.)

TYLER: I'm gonna see if I can pee again.

(Tyler exits.
In Shed's apartment, Timothy finally rises, in pain. Shed
continues to play video game.)

BILLY: So . . . what are you writing these days?

(Timothy begins to exit.
Stephen doesn't respond, as if lost in thought.)

Oh, don't worry—that's just Tyler being Tyler. He'll be fine,
he doesn't like conflict.
STEPHEN: Why did you do that?
BILLY: Do what?

(A new song comes on from off. A sound of cheering from the
party.)

STEPHEN: You—you brought up—you created / a
BILLY *(Starting to dance)*: —I love this song—
STEPHEN: —Fuck off.
BILLY: What? —What is wrong with you?

(Pause. Billy exits.
In Shed's apartment, Timothy exits. Shed looks back, then
turns back to video game.
In Stephen's apartment, Tyler bounces into the bedroom,
dancing.)

STEPHEN: Hey.
TYLER: "What's up, man." The tub is clean . . . *(Stephen smiles)*
Let's dance.

(Tyler grabs Stephen, tries to dance. Stephen doesn't dance.)

Or not.

STEPHEN: I'm—just . . .
TYLER: Billy's fine, don't worry about it. Come on, dance.

(Stephen dances with Tyler tentatively, then stops again.)

STEPHEN: I don't—it's—*I'm* upset.
TYLER: You're upset.
STEPHEN: Yeah, I—I'm really sad now.

(Pause. They sit on the bed. Tyler places his hands on Stephen's head, and begins making a strange humming sound. Stephen laughs a little.)

What are you? . . .
TYLER: "I'm using my special powers to take away your pain." Hmmmmmmmmzzz.
STEPHEN: Oh.
TYLER: I have a call-back!
STEPHEN: For the TV show?
TYLER: Hmmmmmmzzz.

(Stephen pushes Tyler's hands off him.)

What.
STEPHEN: I'm—really sad, Tyler.
TYLER: It's a *party*, Stephen.
STEPHEN: I know it's—
TYLER *(Taking Stephen's hand)*: Let's go out to the party, come / on
STEPHEN: In—a minute.

(Long pause. Stephen and Tyler look at each other.)

TYLER: Fine.

*(Tyler exits. Stephen stays on his bed.
     Shed continues to play the video game, with growing intensity.)*

Scene 10

Slide: August 15, 2001

Stephen and Patricia sit in Stephen's living room.

PATRICIA: I always wondered why gay men had all these friends in the way they do. It's so clear. It's so they can separate their sexual and emotional needs, because they're frightened to combine them. Boyfriends who don't have sex, sex without having to have a boyfriend.

STEPHEN: Yeah . . . I dunno. Maybe he'll—maybe he'll change his mind. Just—like that. I just . . .

PATRICIA: I'm really sorry.

(Pause.)

I should get to work. Did you have that book? . . .

STEPHEN: Oh, right.

(Stephen gets book, gives it to Patricia. She looks at it.)

PATRICIA: *On the Edge of the New Century*. There's a title for you.

STEPHEN: It's really great.

(Patricia rises; Stephen follows. She moves to the door.)

PATRICIA: You know, anyone who's friends with that guy— "Billy"—all he would talk to me about was how attractive Frank was. And about—whoever this guy was he thought he had had sex with. He was actually why we left.

STEPHEN: Billy?

PATRICIA: Yeah.

STEPHEN: But you said you left because Frank wanted to go. Because you had work to do.

(Pause.)

PATRICIA: Yeah—I mean—we were just being polite. *(Laughs)* I felt like I was at work—except instead of a straight guy telling

289

me how attractive I am, it was a gay man telling me how attractive my boyfriend is.

STEPHEN: Why were you being polite? You weren't at work.

(Pause.)

PATRICIA: What do you mean?

STEPHEN: I thought you left because of Frank—but you're saying you were offended by Billy.

PATRICIA: Yeah.

STEPHEN: But you didn't say anything.

PATRICIA: About what?

(Pause.)

STEPHEN: I'm sorry, I'm just . . . I'm really angry.

PATRICIA: Well—of course you're angry. Tyler said he loved you. He was supposed to love you. He didn't love / you

STEPHEN: No. Not that.

PATRICIA: What?

STEPHEN: You know—You're talking about how you left and. You know, I—I had no support. No one . . .

(Pause.)

PATRICIA: I see. I think—you're talking about the discussion about / welfare

STEPHEN: Yes, when you left. Because I was thinking—I knew that you agreed with me. I knew that, and now you're saying on top of that you were offended by Billy but you just—

PATRICIA: Right. Okay. What I was thinking was, was that nobody's mind was going to be changed. Clearly. And it was a ridiculous conversation to be having.

STEPHEN: It wasn't a ridiculous conversation to be having.

PATRICIA: No—but at a party. And that guy wasn't going to budge an / inch

STEPHEN: But—you know, maybe if you had spoken up—maybe he could have been made to listen.

PATRICIA: That never would have happened. *(Beat)* Billy—what I was thinking, was—when you grow up poor, it's very painful to think of yourself as being like other poor people. I know what it's like to be / defensive about

STEPHEN: But you're not seeing how—how I was made to look like a jerk, while Billy gets to—and in front of Tyler, you know, I seem like the asshole.

(Pause.)

PATRICIA: I see now. You're feeling that maybe Tyler left you because of this conversation about welfare?

STEPHEN: Where I looked like an / asshole

PATRICIA: Right, but—I think the timing's fortuitous. I don't think it makes sense to say that this one moment—what did he say? "Different places"—"need to be alone"—clichés, they mean nothing. So of course you're searching for why, and it was at that moment that you felt Tyler pull away, but . . . But it's not just—it's not— Here's what I think happened in that moment—because it was more than just that moment, I mean: You were angry at Tyler for validating Billy because you found Billy offensive, because of how he looked at the world. And you wanted Tyler to look at the world like you do. You could sense that Billy was engaging you in a way meant to humiliate you and test loyalties and yet you couldn't censor / yourself

STEPHEN: But now you are implying a psychodrama. You are implying that politics isn't real, that a political discussion is merely a psychodrama. As if what we were talking about isn't valid—as if it's something / else

PATRICIA: That's not, / no

STEPHEN: Which allows you to leave. To pretend it's something else and to leave, so I'm left there. The way I look at the world, alone, unsupported, ridiculous, when I know / you

PATRICIA: You're making this too easy, Stephen.

STEPHEN: No. That's what you did. You made it easy for yourself and easy for Billy, you left. You were invisible. You made yourself invisible.

PATRICIA: Okay . . . you're—very angry at me.

STEPHEN: I—am. Yeah. Yeah, if you had supported me, Tyler might have seen that I wasn't—Billy might have listened and Tyler would have—fuck it, whatever. You can go.

PATRICIA: Well—now I don't want to go.

STEPHEN: Well I want you to.

(Pause. Patricia moves to the door.)

No one's mind can be changed. This is the world.

(Patricia stops, turns.)

PATRICIA: Would you like me to go?
STEPHEN: Let everyone have their own opinions, everyone's opinion is equal, everyone / is valid
PATRICIA: Maybe you need to change the way you talk to people who don't agree with you. Maybe that's what Tyler saw— that you / weren't
STEPHEN: Oh?
PATRICIA: Yeah. Maybe you need to change the way you talk to people you feel superior / to.
STEPHEN: Blah blah blah. Just go.

(Pause. Patricia goes to the table, places the book down, then leaves. Pause. Stephen lights a cigarette.
A knock on the door. Stephen calls:)

Hello?
TIMOTHY'S VOICE: Hey, sorry to bother you, you got a cigarette?

(Pause.)

STEPHEN: I quit.
TIMOTHY'S VOICE: What's that?
STEPHEN: I QUIT.

Scene 11

Slide: September 27, 2001

Shed's apartment. Lily sits alone, flipping through a photo album. Timothy, with prosthetic leg, enters from back, walking slowly.

TIMOTHY: He not back yet?
LILY: No.

TIMOTHY: Usually back by now.

(Timothy starts to walk off.)

LILY: How long have you lived here?

(Timothy turns. He sees she is looking at the photo album.)

TIMOTHY: Oh, you looking at the pictures? *(She nods)* Ten years.
    Yeah. Moved in when we got married.
LILY: Ten years. Wow. That's true love.
TIMOTHY: True love, I don't know about that . . .
LILY *(Regarding picture)*: Look at you. I've never known true love.
TIMOTHY: I don't know if you would call it true love.
LILY: I've only known passion.

(Pause. Timothy starts to walk off.)

No, look how much you loved each other, look at this.

(He turns. She holds up the album, shows him a picture.)

TIMOTHY: Yeah . . . But you wouldn't say we got along usually.
    (She keeps looking through the album) There was a time we
    partied a lot and that wasn't good. There's nothing you can
    do when certain things happen. You can wait for them to be
    over. Looking back. You wouldn't say we had a good mar-
    riage. Things just happen. But you look back. It's strange.
    I do wonder why God let me live. I did lots of things there
    was no need to do. We wasted a lot of years. I drove trucks.
    I was gone a lot . . .
LILY: How'd it happen? Shed never said.

(Pause.)

TIMOTHY: We went out to dinner. I was driving back. We had
    wine. I just drove wrong. *(Pause)* I was trying to pass a car
    that was going so slow. I was tired. —I wasn't working, we
    were talking about that. I was telling her we had to figure
    something out. We had debt. I pay child support. Shed's
    been paying the rent. She was just working part-time and

I wasn't, I wasn't working, we were trying to figure something out. It was an old lady—she was driving so slow. I misjudged it. I drove my whole life. You get cocky . . .

(Pause. Lily holds open the album, angles it toward Timothy. He does not look at the pictures.)

There's probably nothing in my future. Stupid leg.
LILY: But you have your leg now.
TIMOTHY: You can tell. I still limp. The color is wrong.
LILY: I've never had true love. At least you've had that.
TIMOTHY: I don't know . . .
LILY: It was true love.

(Pause. Timothy moves to the album, focuses on one photo, just stares at it.)

TIMOTHY: True love . . .

(Door opens. Shed enters, wearing a face mask. Timothy looks up.)

Home from work!
LILY: Hey!

(Shed takes off his face mask. Timothy exits.)

Smell getting to you?

(Shed crosses to the couch, puts down his backpack.)

SHED: Bad tonight.
LILY: Been a while.
SHED: What's up.
LILY: You doing good?

(Shed shrugs. Pause.)

You got a job!

(Shed nods.)

I'm—going home, I'm going back, so . . . I'm leaving tomorrow . . . Dave says hi.

SHED: Dave says hi.

LILY: He says you don't answer the phone anymore.

SHED: Got rid of it.

(Pause.)

LILY: He says he came here, he says you don't answer the door
either.

SHED: Don't answer the door, no.

LILY: You sent him his money in the mail?

SHED: Yup.

(Pause.)

LILY: You didn't miss much. Dave's back with Maryanne. He stays
in his room, doesn't leave the apartment, he bought all these
gas masks and night-vision goggles. Tell me about your job,
it sounds brilliant.

SHED: It's good.

LILY: It's at the hotel?

SHED: Yeah.

LILY: How'd you get it?

SHED: Just went there. Looked right, I guess. Knew how to act.

LILY: When did you start?

SHED: End of August.

LILY: What's it like, you like it?

SHED: Beautiful. It's this guy, Ian Schrager. He has a shitload of
hotels. This one, you go in there, it's like the world don't
exist. It's like, you got a escalator. Lime green light. You go
up, it's all dark, there's big plants everywhere, like growing
out the walls. Huge chandeliers, like. It's so cool, it's got,
like, special effects—like those 3-D things, holograms and
shit. Everybody wear a uniform, like. Beautiful women wait-
resses. Outdoor courtyard, trees, big chairs. Matt Damon's
having his birthday party there in a couple weeks, they got
famous people all the time in there, go there.

LILY: Wow. I love Matt Damon.

(Pause.)

Yeah. I got you—I wanted to give you something to remind you of me.

(Lily reaches into her pocket and pulls out a photo-booth photograph. She hands it to him.)

Three pictures of me. The first one is the crazy me, see. The second one is the sad me. The third one is the real me, no expression. *(Shed looks at the photograph)* I was thinking of lifting my top for the last one, but, you know, it was in the arcade, I felt weird.

SHED: Thanks.

(Pause.)

LILY: Plus, you don't know where those pictures end up, if they stay in the computer or whatever. Don't want my tits all over the place, even if I do have nice tits. —I think I might miss you the most, you know.

SHED: Yeah?

(Pause.)

LILY: Anyway. —You gotta give me something before I go.

SHED: What?

LILY: Something to remember you by. I gave you my picture now you gotta give me something.

(Pause. Shed looks around.)

SHED: Don't know what I got.

(Pause. Shed looks at her. She moves to him and hugs him hard. Pause. She reaches down to his crotch.)

LILY: I knew it!

(She laughs. Pause. She moves her hand on his crotch. Shed removes her shirt. They look at each other a beat, then embrace.)

Scene 12

A bar. Loud music. Stephen stands alone. Leo approaches. Pause.

LEO: YOU LOOK FAMILIAR.

STEPHEN: I DO?

LEO: HAVEN'T WE MET?

STEPHEN: I DON'T THINK SO.

LEO: I DON'T KNOW WHY I THINK SO. ARE YOU HERE ALONE?

STEPHEN: YEAH.

LEO: WHY DO I THINK I KNOW YOU. DO YOU COME HERE A LOT?

STEPHEN: NO.

LEO: WHY NOT?

STEPHEN: WHEN I HAD A BOYFRIEND, I DIDN'T GO OUT.

LEO: WHEN DID YOU BREAK UP?

STEPHEN: A WHILE AGO.

LEO: WHAT HAPPENED?

STEPHEN: I DON'T KNOW. HE BROKE UP WITH ME.

LEO: WHY?

STEPHEN: WHY DO PEOPLE BREAK UP WITH PEOPLE?

LEO: YOU MISS HIM?

(Stephen doesn't answer, swigs on his beer.)

YOU DON'T WANT TO TALK ABOUT IT?

STEPHEN: NOT PARTICULARLY.

(Pause.)

LEO: WHERE DO YOU LIVE?

STEPHEN: NEAR HERE.

(Pause.)

LEO: DO YOU WANT TO GO THERE?

Scene 13

Stephen's bedroom. Stephen and Leo enter.

LEO: I'm serious, it makes perfect sense. This was Giuliani's greatest fantasy and his greatest fear. He's always had a fascist impulse, which this fits perfectly. But, remember last summer, he had prostate cancer, and there was all that media coverage about how he might be impotent. Months later the two tallest most phallic buildings in New York City go down. What was happening in his body, happening in his city.

STEPHEN: Huh. That's really interesting.

(Leo takes out cocaine, does a bump. Leo gives Stephen cocaine. Stephen sniffs cocaine.)

LEO: What's funniest is he's just *like* the Taliban—obsessed with forcing his rules, his ideology, violently upon the people: close down the clubs where gays congregate, shut down the strip clubs where women reveal their bodies, cancel funding for art museums who show art that subverts his religious beliefs: he probably *deeply* identifies with the Taliban.

STEPHEN: Right . . .

LEO: —Is this the window?

STEPHEN: That's the window.

(Leo looks out the window. Long pause. The sound of a fighter jet passing.)

LEO: The F-14s are flying low tonight. *(Leo turns to Stephen. Brightly)* So. What are we going to do now that we've moved out of a public space and into a private one?

STEPHEN *(Smiling)*: Have sex.

(Leo laughs. He looks around and finds a photograph.)

LEO: Is this your boyfriend?

STEPHEN: Ex. Yeah.

LEO: What was his name?

STEPHEN: Why do you want to know?

LEO: I dunno.

STEPHEN: Tyler. —I'm gonna brush my teeth.

LEO: Okay.

(Stephen exits. Leo stares at the photograph. Then he puts it down and takes off his shoes. Stephen enters.)

STEPHEN: Hey.

LEO: Hey. Have you heard from him since the eleventh?

STEPHEN: Who?

LEO: Tyler.

STEPHEN: No . . .

LEO: No?

STEPHEN: Nope.

LEO: I don't believe in love.

STEPHEN: You don't?

LEO: No, I think it's a vague word that is applied indiscriminately.

STEPHEN *(Laughs)*: Oh.

LEO: To me, a more interesting question is what people are doing to each other in each other's company under the guise of "love."

STEPHEN: What do you mean?

LEO: Like—what is love. What *is* it. I mean, you can say, okay—okay, this person fucks me, he calls me, he eats meals with me, he tells me about his day, I am in his thoughts and fantasies, I do things and he has feelings about them—you can make a list of facts. But what makes those facts love. What. And—I couldn't figure it out. So I decided there was no such thing. And that I was fine with that.

STEPHEN: Uh-huh.

(Leo begins removing his clothes.)

LEO: The idea of love is so hetero-normative, and it's perfect for capitalism: it prevents people from thinking about real problems in their lives, it makes them think, when they feel bad, that something is wrong with them and not the world, it makes people form families and buy things for those families . . . *(Leo's in his boxers)* You're so adorable.

STEPHEN: You too.

(Stephen turns out the light. We can barely see them. They undress.)

LEO: Put on some music.

(Leo gets in bed. Stephen puts music on—R & B. He goes into bed. Leo begins to fellate Stephen, then kisses him. Leo gets on top of Stephen and begins moving.)

Mmm.

STEPHEN: That feels good.

LEO: You like that?

STEPHEN: Yeah.

(Leo continues. Stephen turns him over and gets on top of him and kisses him.)

LEO: You can kiss.

STEPHEN *(Laughs)*: I can?

LEO: Mm-hmm.

(They kiss. Leo wraps his legs around Stephen. Then Leo takes his own hands and puts them behind his head. He takes Stephen's right hand and clasps it to his two hands, as if to restrain them.)

Harder.

(Stephen thrusts against Leo harder. Then Leo eases Stephen off him. Leo gets on his hands and knees.)

(Sweetly) Rub against me like you're fucking me. *(Stephen does)* That's good. Mm.

(Leo masturbates himself as Stephen rubs against him from behind.)

Mmmm.

STEPHEN: Uh. Uh. Uhmm.

(Stephen moves more roughly. Leo takes Stephen's hand from his breast, puts it on top of his head.)

LEO: Pull on my hair a little.

(Stephen does. He arches his neck, kisses Leo.)

Mmmm.
STEPHEN: Uhhhh. Uhhhhh.
LEO: Mm. You're fine, right?
STEPHEN: What?
LEO: I'm fine—we're both fine—you don't have—you don't have
/ HIV
STEPHEN: No.
LEO: *More.* Oh God.

(Stephen continues, getting rougher.)

STEPHEN: You like that?
LEO: *Yes.*
STEPHEN: Yeah? You like that?
LEO: —Fuck me.
STEPHEN: Yeah, you want me to fuck you?
LEO: Yes please.
STEPHEN: Yeah?
LEO: I like it.
STEPHEN: I like it too. Uh. Uh.
LEO: Go inside me.
STEPHEN: Yeah?
LEO: You can go inside me.
STEPHEN *(Stopping for a moment)*: Wait—go?—literally?
LEO: Please fuck me.
STEPHEN: I / don't
LEO: Please.

(Pause. Then Stephen enters him, somewhat awkwardly. Leo grimaces a little. Stephen fucks him, slow at first, then faster.)

Oh my *God* . . . Oh *God* . . . Oh *God* . . .
STEPHEN: Uhhhhh. Uhhhh, uhhh uhhh
LEO: Mmmm mm mmm
STEPHEN: Uhh / uhh uhh
LEO: Mmm mmm mmm mmm / mmm mmm mmm
STEPHEN: Uhhhm uuhmm uhuuhmm—

(Stephen stops suddenly.)

LEO: What? Did you come?

(Pause. Stephen releases, lies back on the bed.)

STEPHEN: No . . .
LEO: Why did you stop?
STEPHEN: I'm sorry.

(Pause. Leo grabs Stephen's penis and begins to masturbate him.)

I'm sorry, I have to stop.

(Pause. Leo lies back, masturbates himself. Sound of a fighter jet cutting across the sky. Finally Leo orgasms.)

LEO: Uhhhhh—

(Pause.)

STEPHEN: Let me get you a towel.

(Stephen gets Leo a towel and gives it to him. Leo cleans himself. Stephen turns off music and dresses. Leo puts the towel on the floor and dresses. As they do this:)

That was interesting, the comparisons you were making before with the Taliban and Giuliani.
LEO: Uh-huh?
STEPHEN: I've been reading about Afghanistan—the chaos of the region. So many tribes—so many different groups—disconnected, historically, from their / central government
LEO: Right.
STEPHEN: Disconnected from their leaders—and disconnected from each other—all these various groups occupying the same space without being able to / find a common
LEO: Uh-huh.
STEPHEN: Just—how fractured and isolated they are—like New York, too, in some ways . . .

(Pause. Leo and Stephen are dressed. Leo looks at Stephen.)

LEO: Nice to meet you.

STEPHEN: You're gonna go? *(Leo smiles)* Are you sure? I could make some tea . . .
LEO: I'm fine. Bye.

*(Leo exits. Stephen sits down on his bed. He looks out the window.
Lights rise on Shed's apartment. Lily is finishing dressing.
Shed has his boxers on. Pause.)*

LILY: —Say a prayer the plane doesn't fly into the Empire State Building.
SHED: Ha. I will.
LILY: Yeah. So . . . *(Laughs)* Nice knowing you.
SHED: You too.
LILY: —Congrats again on your job, that's really great.
SHED: Yeah . . .
LILY: Yeah . . . we're friends, yeah?
SHED: What you mean?
LILY: We're buddies. We're pals.

(Pause.)

SHED: —Yeah . . .
LILY: Yeah. Anyway . . .

(She starts to go.)

SHED: Hold on.

(She stops.)

—It's bad out there—take this. *(Hands her his face mask)*
LILY: Oh.

(She looks at it. Beat.)

SHED: Here, I do it.

*(He stands behind her, puts it over her mouth and nose. She
stands, still for a moment, then begins to cry.)*

What's wrong, now?
LILY: Dunno . . .
SHED: It's okay . . .

LILY: Yeah . . . Okay. Bye.

(*She exits. Shed puts on his pants. Turns on video game, sits down. Timothy enters.*)

TIMOTHY: Lily go?
SHED: Yeah.

(*Pause. Shed plays video game.*)

TIMOTHY: Working late tonight?
SHED: Walked home.
TIMOTHY: Oh, you walked home?
SHED: I got laid off.
TIMOTHY: —What?
SHED (*Still playing game*): Nobody in the hotel. Nobody there, tourists not coming, so, they letting the most recent people go.
TIMOTHY: Oh Christ. You got fired? No!
SHED: And it's like—it's like, I don't understand—what's—wrong with—me—

(*Shed starts to cry, puts down video game controller.*)

TIMOTHY: Oh God.
SHED: It's like—I know what not to do, in my life, but I don't—know—what—*to* do, you know?
TIMOTHY: No—that's not—people get / fired
SHED (*Fighting tears with anger*): I don't know what to DO.
TIMOTHY: You be okay, you'll figure it out.
SHED: Figure out what. What. (*Pause*) What are we gonna figure out. (*Pause*) What are we gonna do. (*Pause*)
TIMOTHY: You can't blame yourself. It's just how things—it's not your fault—it's just the world . . .

(*Shed looks at Timothy. Pause. He opens his backpack, takes out a carton of cigarettes.*)

SHED: Fucking, you believe people pay ten dollars a pack? In the hotel, if you go on the street, five dollars, ten dollars inside. They fired me, I took some.

(*Timothy smiles.*)

TIMOTHY: Thank you.
SHED: Not a problem.

(Pause.)

TIMOTHY: Maybe . . . I can get a job when I'm done with rehab.
   I don't—they say I can't drive a truck, but. It might—maybe
   I can drive a van. I might, they / don't know
SHED: All right.
TIMOTHY: Something, there'll be something—we—we'll be able
   to—
SHED: All right, I hear you. Just go—go to sleep.

*(Pause. Timothy exits. Shed reaches for his backpack, looks in,
takes out two cartons of cigarettes. Puts them on the coffee table.
Goes to stereo. Turns on hip-hop. Picks up game controller again,
begins playing. Pause. Shed pauses the game. He takes one carton
from the table. He exits the apartment, goes to Stephen's door,
knocks. Stephen hears. He exits his bedroom and goes to the door.)*

STEPHEN: Hello?
SHED'S VOICE: Hey, it's your neighbor.
STEPHEN: Yes?
SHED'S VOICE: Got—something for you, wanna open up.
STEPHEN: What?
SHED'S VOICE: I got something for you.

(Pause. Stephen opens the door.)

STEPHEN: Hey, what's up.

(Shed holds out the carton.)

SHED: Hey—just—got these for you, you know . . .
STEPHEN: Oh. —Thank you . . .

(Stephen takes the cigarettes. Pause.)

   You guys—you guys okay?
SHED: Yeah, we fine.
STEPHEN: Your—dad's okay?
SHED: My dad. Oh. That's not my dad. That's my uncle. But yeah,
   he's okay.
STEPHEN: Oh—good.

SHED: He got his leg finally. They finally gave him his leg, so.

STEPHEN: That's great.

SHED: That's my uncle. He lived there, I lived there with him and my aunt, but she died in the car accident, where he lost his leg. So it's good he got his leg, so

STEPHEN: Oh—oh God.

(Pause.)

SHED: You see it happen?

STEPHEN: I—I saw it from my bedroom window. I saw the whole thing.

SHED: Yeah. I went up on the roof . . . saw that . . .

STEPHEN: Terrible.

SHED: Yeah. *(Pause)* Anyway. That's it.

STEPHEN: Thank you.

SHED: You welcome.

(Shed goes. Stephen shuts the door.)

Scene 14

Slide: October 9, 2001

The bar. Patricia stands behind the bar. It's empty. Stephen sits with a soda. An American flag draped, behind the bar.

PATRICIA: And then he says, "So I was thinking you and I would have an affair."

STEPHEN: Oh God.

PATRICIA: Sixty-two years old, this man. I'm telling you—visual artists.

STEPHEN: Painters are so weird . . .

PATRICIA: What's wrong with them?

STEPHEN: Aren't they stuck at the anal stage? Isn't paint—isn't it something to do with the child playing with feces? I think I read that in Freud.

(Young Businessman 1 enters, sits at the end of the bar.)

PATRICIA: Hey there Howard.

HOWARD *(Young Businessman 1)*: Hey, Patricia. *(Looks up at the TV)*

STEPHEN *(Quietly)*: How's he doing?

PATRICIA: I haven't seen him in a week.

(Patricia goes over to him.)

You want a Stella?

HOWARD: Thank you. *(She gets him a beer)* How's business?

PATRICIA: It's picking up. People still aren't eating out, but they're drinking.

HOWARD: That's good. I need this beer, Jesus.

PATRICIA: Yeah? What's going on, is there any news about Ron? Have they found his / body yet?

HOWARD: They're not gonna find him, it's all just ash, they should give / up

(The bar phone rings. Pause. Howard motions for her to answer.)

PATRICIA *(Picks up)*: Hello?

HOWARD *(Turning to Stephen)*: It's weird. I was at the subway, just now . . . The train was late, like five minutes. That happens all the time. But I started getting pissed-off. And more and more people started coming down, into the station. And the train kept not coming. Kept looking down the tunnel. Nothing. No announcement. Must have been two, maybe three hundred people on the platform. And I thought—I started getting, like, claustrophobic. *(Patricia hangs up the phone, listens)* And I knew—I knew the train would come. Rationally—I knew—trains are late all the time. But I had this feeling—like something was gonna happen. Even though I knew, I knew the train would come, nothing was wrong, there was just some delay. But it was like—like if I didn't get out of there, something bad was gonna happen. And I left—left the station, walked here.

STEPHEN: Wow.

HOWARD: I'm a rational guy. I knew the train was coming but— blah blah blah.

(Howard sips beer. Pause.)

PATRICIA: Market's doing better.

HOWARD: Market's fine. —It just doesn't make sense . . . how something that was there goes away . . .

(Howard looks up at the stock ticker on the TV. Patricia moves to Stephen.)

PATRICIA: What are you doing tonight?

STEPHEN: I was actually thinking of taking a walk down there. Be a witness. Say that I saw it. I was there. This is what it was like.

(On the TV, footage of George Bush, stock ticker running below.)

HOWARD: That's right. Bomb the shit out of them. Go over there and bomb them to the fucking Dark Ages. *(Chanting)* U-S-A! U-S-A! U-S-A! *(Laughing)* Come on, Patricia. Show a little patriotism.

PATRICIA: That's okay, you got enough for both of us.

HOWARD *(Smiling)*: Yeah, I do, don't I?

(He sips his beer. Patricia turns to Stephen. She smiles at him.)

STEPHEN: You're so good with these guys, you know that.

PATRICIA: What else are you gonna be?

HOWARD: U-S-A! U-S-A! *(Howard raises his beer)* A toast, what do you say?

(Beat. Stephen smiles, raises his soda. Patricia raises a bottle of water.)

To the USA!

STEPHEN: —To where we live.

PATRICIA: Cheers.

(They toast. Howard turns back to TV. Patricia starts wiping down the bar. Stephen watches her.)

END OF PLAY

Christopher Shinn was born in Hartford and lives in New York. His plays have been produced at Playwrights Horizons, Vineyard Theatre, Royal Court Theatre, Manhattan Theatre Club, South Coast Repertory and Soho Theatre. His most recent plays are *On the Mountain* (Playwrights Horizons) and *Dying City* (Royal Court).

He is a winner of an OBIE Award in Playwriting and a Guggenheim Fellowship in Playwriting. He has received grants from the NEA/TCG Theatre Residency Program, the Ovid Foundation and the Peter S. Reed Foundation, and he is a recipient of the Robert Chesley Award.

He teaches playwriting at the New School Drama School.